Hamlyn
All Colour
Cook Book

HAMLYN

Hamlyn
All Colour
Cook Book

over 300 quick
and easy recipes
all illustrated in
full colour

First published in Great Britain in 1970 by Hamlyn,
an imprint of Reed Consumer Books Limited
Michelin House, 81 Fulham Road, London SW3 6RB
and Auckland, Melbourne, Singapore and Toronto

29th, revised impression 1992
Reprinted 1993 (twice)

A CIP catalogue record for this book is available
from the British Library.

ISBN 0 600 575 292

Produced by Mandarin Offset
Printed and bound in Hong Kong

Contents

Introduction

I have particularly enjoyed contributing to this big, exciting, cookery book because I know how much housewives will appreciate the beautiful illustrations of every recipe in full colour. It is most helpful and encouraging to see just how the finished dish should look in a colour photograph immediately above the recipe itself. Then it is so easy to refer to the photograph as one prepares the dish, and use it as a guide to the garnishing and presentation. Readers have often expressed a wish to me in their letters that every recipe should be illustrated and that the photograph could appear on the same page. I feel that this book is the answer.

Not only are these dishes attractive, they really are simple and speedy to make. In every one of the 336 recipes, special thought has been given to the speed and ease of preparation. I, and the other contributors, busy housewives ourselves, realise how important it is to streamline cooking chores whenever possible to the minimum. Yet, as you turn the pages, you will see how tempting and appetising each dish looks, every single one followed by a useful tip with a clearly detailed drawing to help you give a professional touch to the appearance of even the simplest dish. These tips provide an invaluable store of information to draw on – the kind of information that distinguishes an accomplished cook, and wins compliments on her cooking from both family and guests!

In preparing the various sections under which the recipes appear, we have tried to include a really varied selection of dishes. Any cook who could include in her repertoire all the recipes given here would be able to make up an almost endless selection of menus for every meal and occasion, from family tea to a formal dinner party.

Some of the dishes are plain, some traditional, all of proved excellence. But there are also a good number of more unusual and imaginative ones, many of foreign origin, conjuring up the flavour of far away countries or perhaps bringing back memories of a holiday in the sun.

It may surprise you to find that you will have no difficulty in preparing dishes that seem elaborate, in your own kitchen, following our carefully tested recipes. Especially surprising, perhaps, to those who, up to now, have thought of themselves as average rather than adventurous cooks.

However, test and try out any of these dishes and you will agree that as well as being entirely successful, they all live up to our claim that they are not only delicious but quick and easy to prepare.

Mary Berry

Useful facts and figures

Notes on metrication

In this book quantities are given in metric and Imperial measures. Exact conversion from Imperial to metric measures does not usually give very convenient working quantities and so the metric measures have been rounded off into units of 25 grams. The table below shows the recommended equivalents.

Ounces	Approx g to nearest whole figure	Recommended conversion to nearest unit of 25	Ounces	Approx g to nearest whole figure	Recommended conversion to nearest unit of 25
1	28	25	9	255	250
2	57	50	10	283	275
3	85	75	11	312	300
4	113	100	12	340	350
5	142	150	13	368	375
6	170	175	14	396	400
7	198	200	15	425	425
8	227	225	16 (1 lb)	454	450

Note: When converting quantities over 16 oz first add the appropriate figures in the centre column, then adjust to the nearest unit of 25. As a general guide, 1 kg (1000 g) equals 2.2 lb or about 2 lb 3 oz. This method of conversion gives good results in nearly all cases, although in certain pastry and cake recipes a more accurate conversion is necessary to produce a balanced recipe.

Liquid measures The millilitre has been used in this book and the following table gives a few examples.

Imperial	Approx ml to nearest whole figure	Recommended ml	Imperial	Approx ml to nearest whole figure	Recommended ml
¼	142	150 ml	1 pint	567	600 ml
½	283	300 ml	1½ pints	851	900 ml
¾	425	450 ml	1¾ pints	992	1000 ml (1 litre)

Spoon measures All spoon measures given in this book are level unless otherwise stated.

Can sizes At present, cans are marked with the exact (usually to the nearest whole number) metric equivalent of the Imperial weight of the contents, so we have followed this practice when giving can sizes.

Oven temperatures The table below gives recommended equivalents.

	°C	°F	Gas Mark		°C	°F	Gas Mark
Very cool	110	225	¼	Moderately hot	190	375	5
	120	250	½		200	400	6
Cool	140	275	1	Hot	220	425	7
	150	300	2		230	450	8
Moderate	160	325	3	Very Hot	240	475	9
	180	350	4				

Notes for American and Australian users

In America the 8-fl oz measuring cup is used. In Australia metric measures are now used in conjunction with the standard 250-ml measuring cup. The Imperial pint, used in Britain and Australia, is 20 fl oz, while the American pint is 16 fl oz. It is important to remember that the Australian tablespoon differs from both the British and American tablespoons; the table below gives a comparison. The British standard tablespoon, which has been used throughout this book, holds 17.7 ml, the American 14.2 ml, and the Australian 20 ml. A teaspoon holds approximately 5 ml in all three countries.

British	American	Australian
1 teaspoon	1 teaspoon	1 teaspoon
1 tablespoon	1 tablespoon	1 tablespoon
2 tablespoons	3 tablespoons	2 tablespoons
3½ tablespoons	4 tablespoons	3 tablespoons
4 tablespoons	5 tablespoons	3½ tablespoons

An Imperial/American guide to solid and liquid measures

Imperial	American	Imperial	American
Solid measures		**Liquid measures**	
1 lb butter or margarine	2 cups	¼ pint liquid	⅔ cup liquid
1 lb flour	4 cups	½ pint	1¼ cups
1 lb granulated or castor sugar	2 cups	¾ pint	2 cups
1 lb icing sugar	3 cups	1 pint	2½ cups
8 oz rice	1 cup	1½ pints	3¾ cups
		2 pints	5 cups (2½ pints)

Note: When making any of the recipes in this book, only follow one set of measures as they are not interchangeable.

Main meals to cook ahead

This particularly useful chapter will enable a busy housewife to prepare a meal in advance, at a time she is unlikely to be disturbed. All that is needed when the time comes, is to reheat and decorate. Some of these dishes can be eaten either hot or cold, so they could be served at very short notice.

Casserole cooking provides many opportunities to be adventurous and try new, exciting recipes: the flavour of herbs with lamb, or wine with chicken or beef, gives casserole dishes a special appeal. Homely stews and the familiar steak and kidney pudding are represented for those with more conventional tastes.

1 Breton quiche

(illustrated on front cover)

You will need . . .

Preparation time
10 minutes

Cooking time
50 minutes

Oven setting
190°C; 375°F; Gas Mark 5
180°C; 350°F; Gas Mark 4

For the pastry:
175g/6 oz plain flour
pinch salt
50g/2 oz butter
40g/1½ oz lard
about 6 teaspoons water
For the filling:
100g/4 oz Emmenthal or Gruyère cheese
4 rashers streaky bacon, de-rinded
150ml/¼ pint single cream
2 large eggs
1 tablespoon chopped parsley
2 teaspoons chopped chives
salt and pepper

Make short crust pastry in usual way with flour, salt, butter, lard and water. Roll it out on a lightly floured table and use to line a shallow 23-cm/9-inch fluted flan tin or ring, placed on a baking tray. Prick pastry well, line with greaseproof paper and fill with baking beans, or fill with crumpled foil. Bake for 20 minutes in a moderately hot oven, then remove from the oven. Remove the paper and beans, or foil, and reduce the oven temperature to moderate.

Slice the cheese and arrange in base of flan case, fry bacon very lightly for 1 to 2 minutes. Cut each rasher in half and arrange on top of cheese.

Mix together the cream, eggs, parsley, chives and seasoning. Pour in to the flan case and bake for 30 minutes or until the filling is pale golden and just set. Serve hot or cold. *Serves 4-6.*

QUICK TIP

The two main causes for tough short crust pastry are: using too much liquid, about 1 teaspoon to 25g/1 oz flour is usual, and overhandling. For success, roll out lightly and quickly and rest the pastry before baking.

Lamb chops 2 with ratatouille

You will need . . .

Preparation time
15 minutes

Cooking time
15 minutes

Oven setting
200°C; 400°F; Gas Mark 6

50g/2 oz butter
1 tablespoon salad oil
4 loin chops
½ level teaspoon mixed herbs
For the ratatouille:
2 large green peppers
2 medium onions, quartered
50g/2 oz butter
2 small aubergines
225g/8 oz tomatoes
salt and pepper
mustard and cress

Melt 50g/2 oz butter with oil in a meat tin. Add chops, sprinkle with dried herbs and cook in a hot oven for 15 minutes or until tender.

Meanwhile prepare ratatouille. Cut peppers in half, remove seeds and cut in 1-cm/½-inch wide strips. Shred onions coarsely. Melt butter in a pan and fry peppers and onions for about 5 minutes or until they are soft and onion is pale golden brown. Remove stalks from aubergines and cut them in 5-mm/¼-in thick slices. Plunge tomatoes in boiling water for 10 seconds then drain and remove skins. Quarter them and remove seeds. Add aubergines and tomatoes to pan and cook for a further 5-10 minutes.

Season the ratatouille with salt and pepper. Turn it on to a serving dish and arrange chops on top. Decorate with mustard and cress. *Serves 4.*

QUICK TIP

Using herbs: dried herbs are invaluable; buy small quantities at a time and renew supplies each year as they lose their potency and some flavour on storage. They are cheap to buy.

3 Lasagne in a hurry

You will need . . .

Preparation time
15 minutes

Cooking time
1 hour

Oven setting
180°C; 350°F; Gas Mark 4

For the Bolognese sauce:
1 × 425g/15 oz can minced steak with onion
1 × 225g/8 oz can tomatoes
3 level teaspoons tomato purée
¼ level teaspoon mixed herbs
1 heaped teaspoon sugar
salt and pepper
For the cheese sauce:
25g/1 oz butter
25g/1 oz flour
450ml/¾ pint milk
½ level teaspoon made mustard
¼ level teaspoon nutmeg
175g/6 oz Gruyère cheese, grated
225g/8 oz lasagne
1 tablespoon salad oil

Put minced steak in a pan with tomatoes and juice, tomato purée, herbs, sugar and, if liked, a good shake of garlic powder, salt and pepper to taste. Bring to boiling point, simmer for 5 minutes then put on one side.

Make cheese sauce. Melt butter in a pan, blend in flour, then milk and bring to boil, stirring constantly. Simmer for 3 minutes until thick. Stir in 150g/5 oz cheese, mustard, nutmeg, seasoning. When cheese has melted remove pan from heat.

Bring a large pan of salted water to boiling point. Put in lasagne a piece at a time, add oil and simmer for about 12 minutes or until lasagne is tender. Rinse with cold water and drain on a clean tea towel. Layer up lasagne, cheese sauce and bolognese sauce in a shallow, ovenproof casserole, finishing with a layer of cheese sauce. Sprinkle with remaining cheese. Bake in a moderate oven for 40 minutes until top is pale golden. *Serves 4-6.*

QUICK TIP

Lasagne is a ribbon type pasta usually available in sheets measuring 15 × 10 cm (6 × 4 inches). The green lasagne is flavoured with spinach.

4 Orange tarragon chicken

You will need . . .

Preparation time
30 minutes

Cooking time
1 hour 30 minutes

Oven setting
180°C; 350°F; Gas Mark 4

40g/1½ oz butter
2 tablespoons oil
4 chicken quarters
1 large onion
1 × 185g/6¼ oz can frozen orange juice
150ml/¼ pint water
1 chicken stock cube
4 sprigs fresh tarragon, chopped *or* 1 tablespoon dried tarragon
15g/½ oz cornflour
150g/5 oz carton soured cream

Melt butter and oil in a flameproof casserole dish and brown chicken quarters thoroughly on all sides. Remove from dish and, if desired, skin chicken; keep on one side.

Chop onion finely and cook gently for 2-3 minutes in butter and oil. Stir in concentrated orange juice, water, stock cube and tarragon. Bring to boil and add chicken. Cover with lid or foil and bake in a moderate oven for 1½ hours until chicken is tender. Baste occasionally with orange sauce.

Remove chicken and place down the centre of an oval serving dish. Skim off any excess fat from the sauce. Blend the cornflour with 2 tablespoons water and add to the sauce. Return to the boil and cook for 2-3 minutes stirring continuously. Cool slightly and stir in the soured cream. Pour over chicken and decorate with fresh tarragon or parsley. *Serves 4.*

QUICK TIP

Soured cream is not dairy cream which is off; it is carefully soured commercially giving a fresh delicate flavour. Fresh cream can be soured successfully by adding a little lemon juice.

5 Bœuf bourguignonne

6 Blanquette de veau

You will need . . .	750g/1½ lb chuck steak *or* top leg of beef
	25g/1 oz bacon fat *or* dripping
	175g/6 oz streaky bacon
	1 level tablespoon flour
	300ml/½ pint water
Preparation time	1 beef stock cube
20 minutes	150ml/¼ pint cheap red wine
	bay leaf
Cooking time	½ level teaspoon dried mixed herbs
2 hours 30 minutes	sprig parsley
	about ½ level teaspoon salt
Oven setting	dash of pepper
160°C; 325°F; Gas Mark 3	12 baby onions, peeled

Cut the steak in 4-cm/1½-inch cubes. De-rind and chop bacon. Melt fat or dripping in a fairly large pan and crisp the bacon in it. Remove bacon and place in a 1.75-litre/3-pint ovenproof casserole. Fry steak in fat remaining in pan until it is golden brown. Add to bacon in casserole.

Pour away most of fat in pan, leaving about 2 tablespoons. Blend in flour and cook until browned. Stir in stock and wine. Bring to boiling point and simmer until thickened then stir in bay leaf, herbs, parsley and seasoning. Pour this liquor over meat, cover and cook for 1½ hours in a very moderate oven.

Add onions to casserole and cook for a further hour or until meat is really tender. Add more seasoning if necessary. Skim off any excess fat. *Serves 4.*

You will need . . .	750g/1½ lb boned shoulder *or* knuckle of veal
	2 onions, peeled and quartered
	2 large carrots, sliced
	3 bay leaves
Preparation time	1 tablespoon lemon juice
15 minutes	salt and pepper
	175g/6 oz button mushrooms
Cooking time	40g/1½ oz butter
1 hour 45 minutes	40g/1½ oz flour
	1 egg yolk
	150g/5 oz carton single cream
	sprig parsley

Cut veal in 4-cm/1½-inch pieces. Put in a pan, cover with cold water, bring to boiling point then strain veal into colander and rinse off scum. Replace veal pieces in pan with onions, carrots, bay leaves, lemon juice and plenty of salt and pepper. Add 1.2 litres/2 pints water, bring to boiling point then cover and simmer for 1½ hours or until tender. Half an hour before end of cooking time, add button mushrooms.

Melt butter in a small pan, blend in flour and cook over a low heat for 1 minute without letting it brown. Arrange the cooked veal and vegetables in a serving dish. Reduce the cooking liquor to 600ml/1 pint by boiling rapidly.

Strain liquor into pan containing butter and flour. Stir sauce until it is smooth then bring to boiling point and simmer for 5 minutes. Add more seasoning if necessary. Blend egg yolk and cream together, remove sauce from heat and stir in the egg mixture. Return the pan to heat and reheat mixture, but do not allow it even to simmer. Pour the sauce over the veal. Decorate with parsley. *Serves 4.*

QUICK TIP

Using red wine for cooking: if you have wine left after a meal keep it for stews, casseroles and sauces. It will keep best in a small corked bottle, or screwtop jar, in a cool place.

QUICK TIP

Add the blended egg yolk and cream carefully seeing that the sauce does not boil. If it becomes too hot it will curdle.

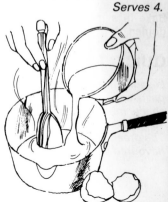

7 Chicken in wine

You will need . . .

Preparation time
20 minutes

Cooking time
1½-4 hours

Oven setting
160°C; 325°F; Gas Mark 3

1.5-1.75kg/3-4 lb boiling or roasting chicken
40g/1½ oz butter
1 tablespoon salad oil
100g/4 oz piece smoked streaky bacon, cubed
225g/8 oz pickling onions, peeled
2 sticks celery, finely chopped
175g/6 oz button mushrooms
1 clove garlic, crushed
25g/1 oz flour
450ml/¾ pint cheap Burgundy
150ml/¼ pint water
bay leaf
sprig fresh thyme or ½ level teaspoon dried thyme
salt and pepper
chicken giblets, washed

Cut chicken into 6 joints, remove skin. Melt 25g/1 oz butter in pan with oil, fry bacon cubes until golden. Remove and drain. Fry chicken joints on both sides, then put them with bacon, in a 1.75-litre/3-pint ovenproof casserole. Fry onion and celery until soft and add to casserole. Melt remaining butter in a pan and cook mushrooms for about 2 minutes. Remove mushrooms from pan and put aside.

Blend garlic and flour with fat remaining in the pan. Cook until brown, blend in wine, water, bay leaf, thyme, salt and pepper. Bring to boil, simmer until thick. Pour over chicken, add giblets. Cover the casserole and cook in a very moderate oven for 1½ to 4 hours, depending on size of bird and whether it is a boiling or roasting chicken.

When chicken joints are almost tender remove giblets and bay leaf. Stir in mushrooms and cook for a further 10 minutes. Skim off any excess fat and add more seasoning if necessary.
Serves 6.

QUICK TIP

When browning meat in fat choose a large, deep pan. This will enable you to fry quickly, without splashing the stove with fat and meat juices.

8 Porc à la crème

You will need . . .

Preparation time
15 minutes

Cooking time
30-40 minutes

750g/1½ lb pork fillet or boned loin of pork
2 tablespoons salad oil
25g/1 oz butter
1 onion, peeled and chopped
1 level tablespoon paprika pepper
1 level tablespoon flour
300ml/½ pint water
1 beef stock cube
5 tablespoons sherry
1 level teaspoon tomato purée
salt and pepper
175g/6 oz small button mushrooms
1 level tablespoon cornflour
150g/5 oz carton double cream

Cut pork in 4-cm/1½-inch pieces. Heat oil in a pan, add butter, then fry pork pieces quickly until they are just beginning to turn brown. Remove from pan and drain on kitchen paper.

Fry onion and paprika for 2 minutes. Blend in flour and cook for a further minute. Remove from heat and blend in stock. Add sherry and tomato purée, return to heat and simmer until thick. Season with salt and pepper, then add the meat. Cover and simmer for 30 to 40 minutes or until the pork is tender.

At the end of cooking time add mushrooms to pan. Blend cornflour to a smooth paste with 2 tablespoons cold water and add to pan. Reboil and, just before serving, blend in cream. This can be decorated with triangles of fried bread and sprigs of parsley.
Serves 4.

QUICK TIP

If you find that chopping several onions makes you cry, keep the cut side of the onion towards the board. Do not lean unnecessarily over the board and chop in short bouts.

9 Italian veal

You will need . . .

750g/1½ lb boneless shin *or* pie veal
3 carrots, peeled and thinly sliced
2 sticks celery, sliced
1 onion, chopped
1 clove garlic, crushed

Preparation time
15 minutes

1 tablespoon salad oil
25g/½ oz butter
25g/½ oz flour

Cooking time
2 hours 30 minutes

150ml/¼ pint dry white wine (optional)
300ml/½ pint white stock *or*
300ml/½ pint water and 1 chicken stock cube

Oven setting
160°C; 325°F; Gas Mark 3

1 × 397g/14 oz can tomatoes
sprig parsley
bay leaf
salt and pepper

Cut meat in 4-cm/1½-inch thick pieces. Prepare vegetables and garlic and put on one side. Heat oil in a heavy frying pan, add butter and fry half the meat at a time over a moderate heat, turning it once, until it is golden brown. Drain the meat on kitchen paper, then put in a 1.75-litre/3-pint ovenproof casserole.

Fry vegetables lightly in a frying pan for 5 minutes. Add flour and continue to cook until it has browned, stirring constantly. Blend in wine, stock, tomatoes, parsley, bay leaf, salt and pepper. Bring the mixture to boiling point.

Pour the sauce on to the meat. Cover casserole with a lid and cook in a very moderate oven for about 2½ hours or until veal is tender. *Serves 4.*

QUICK TIP

Always place oven shelves in position before lighting the oven as they expand when hot and are then often difficult to move.

10 Roast lamb lyonnaise

You will need . . .

750g/1½ lb potatoes, peeled
225g/8 oz onions, sliced
50g/2 oz dripping
1.5kg/3 lb leg of lamb
salt and pepper

Preparation time
10 minutes

1 or 2 cloves garlic

Cooking time
2 hours

Oven setting
180°C; 350°F; Gas Mark 4

Cut potatoes into 1-cm/½-inch thick slices. Arrange onions in a heavy ovenproof dish. Put potato slices, overlapping slightly, on top.

Spread dripping over lamb and season with salt and pepper. Cut garlic in small pieces and insert pieces in fat of lamb. Place joint on top of potatoes in dish.

Roast in a moderate oven, allowing 30 minutes to the pound plus 30 minutes over. Baste from time to time. Remove the joint and place on a serving dish. Surround with potatoes and onions. *Serves 4-6.*

QUICK TIP

If preparing this dish well beforehand keep potato slices covered with cold water until the joint is about to go in the oven. Use a heavy ovenproof dish otherwise the potato slices will brown too quickly.

11 Irish stew

You will need . . .

1.25kg/2½ lb middle neck of lamb
2 large onions, sliced
225g/8 oz carrots, sliced
450g/1 lb potatoes, peeled and sliced
salt and pepper
few sprigs parsley

Preparation time
20 minutes

Cooking time
2 hours 30 minutes

Oven setting
160°C; 325°F; Gas Mark 3
180°C; 350°F; Gas Mark 4

Cut lamb in neat pieces and remove the spinal cord. Put layers of meat, onion, carrot and potato into a 1.75-litre/3-pint oven-proof casserole, seasoning each layer with salt and pepper and finishing with a layer of potato.

Pour in just enough water to come half way up the casserole. Cover with a lid and cook in a very moderate oven for 2 hours or until the meat is nearly tender.

Remove lid, increase the oven to moderately hot and cook for a further half hour or until the top layer of potato is golden brown. Place in a serving dish and decorate with parsley.

Serves 4.

QUICK TIP

If you prefer no bones in stew use lamb fillets cut from scrag ends of neck instead of middle neck. The remaining bones can then be used for Scotch broth.

12 Steak and kidney pudding

You will need . . .

For the filling:
450g/1 lb skirt beef stewing steak
100g/4 oz ox kidney
25g/1 oz seasoned flour
1 onion, peeled and chopped
For the pastry:
225g/8 oz self-raising flour
½ level teaspoon salt
100g/4 oz shredded suet
8 tablespoons cold water

Preparation time
20 minutes

Cooking time
4 hours 30 minutes

Cut steak in 2.5-cm/1-inch cubes. Remove skin, core and fat from kidney then cut into 1-cm/½-inch pieces. Coat the steak with seasoned flour.

Sieve flour and salt for pastry into a bowl. Stir in suet, then add enough water to make a fairly soft dough. Roll out two-thirds of pastry to a circle large enough to line a greased 1.2-litre/2-pint pudding basin. Roll out the remaining pastry to a circle the size of the top of the basin.

Put steak, kidney, and onion in alternate layers in basin, then add sufficient water to come within 2.5cm/1 inch of the top of the basin. Moisten edges of pastry 'lid' and press firmly on top. Cover with lid of greaseproof paper, then cover with a lid of foil; both pleated to allow for expansion. Steam or boil the pudding for 4½ hours, topping up with boiling water as necessary.

Serves 4.

QUICK TIP

Add a teaspoon of vinegar to the water in an aluminium saucepan when steaming to prevent discolouration of the pan.

13 Pork tandoori

You will need . . .

4 pork chops
225g/8 oz Patna rice
¼ teaspoon powdered saffron
For the marinade:
2 × 150g/5 oz cartons natural yogurt
½ teaspoon ground ginger
¾ teaspoon paprika pepper
¼ teaspoon garlic powder *or*
1 clove garlic, finely crushed
4 bay leaves
6 peppercorns
1 tablespoon tomato purée
grated zest of 1 lemon
1 tablespoon salt

Preparation time
15 minutes *plus*
6-8 hours to marinate

Cooking time
1 hour 15 minutes

Oven setting
190°C; 375°F; Gas Mark 5

Prick pork chops well with a fork or skewer and place in a casserole dish. Place ingredients for marinade in a bowl or jug and mix well. Pour over pork chops making sure that they are all covered with the marinade.

Cover dish with foil or lid and leave for 6-8 hours. At the end of this time remove bay leaves and peppercorns. Remove lid from casserole dish and baste pork. Re-cover and bake in a moderate oven for about 1¼ hours, basting occasionally until all the marinade is used. 15-20 minutes before the end of cooking time, cook rice in boiling salted water with the saffron.

Drain rice and place on a round serving dish. Top with the chops and serve. Peas can be added to the rice if liked.
Serves 4.

QUICK TIP

When peeling and chopping vegetables prepare sufficient for at least two meals. Keep part in a sealed polythene bag in a cool place, preferably a refrigerator. This will help to save time.

14 Carbonnade of beef

You will need . . .

750g/1½ lb chuck steak
25g/1 oz butter
2 tablespoons salad oil
2 medium onions, chopped
1 level tablespoon flour
300ml/½ pint light ale
150ml/¼ pint water
pinch dried thyme
bay leaf
1 level teaspoon sugar
salt and pepper

Preparation time
15 minutes

Cooking time
2 hours

Cut beef into strips 2.5 cm/1 inch wide, 5cm/2 inches long and about 1 cm/½ inch thick. Melt butter in a pan with oil and brown meat quickly on all sides.

Remove meat from pan, add onions to fat and fry until golden brown. Blend in flour and cook for 1 minute. Blend in light ale and water, then bring to boiling point and simmer until thickened.

Add meat, thyme, bay leaf, sugar and seasoning. Cover pan and simmer over a very low heat for 2 hours or until meat is tender.
Serves 4.

QUICK TIP

If you are having a big cooking session keep a jug of hot water handy for rinsing knives, forks and spoons so that they are ready to use again immediately

15 Chicken pilaff

You will need . . .

Preparation time
20 minutes

Cooking time
1 hour

4 chicken joints
3 tablespoons salad oil
1 onion
1 green or red pepper
2 sticks celery
225g/8 oz long-grain rice
1 chicken stock cube
1 clove garlic, crushed
¾ level teaspoon curry powder
¼ level teaspoon dried mixed herbs
¼ level teaspoon chilli powder
1 × 227g/8 oz can tomatoes
50g/2 oz mushrooms, sliced
100g/4 oz frozen peas
salt and pepper

Heat 2 tablespoons oil in a pan and fry chicken joints fairly quickly until golden brown on both sides, then reduce heat, cover and continue to cook until joints are tender, about 20 minutes in all. Remove joints from pan and leave to drain on absorbent kitchen paper.

Chop onion and celery, de-seed and slice pepper. Fry in fat remaining in pan for a few minutes until they are soft. Add rice and fry for a further few minutes. Add 750ml/1¼ pints water, tomatoes, stock cube, garlic, curry powder, mixed herbs and chilli powder. Bring mixture to boiling point, stir with a fork, then cover and simmer for about 25 minutes, or until all liquid has been absorbed and the rice is cooked.

Fry mushrooms, with the remaining oil for a few minutes in a small pan. When rice mixture is ready stir in chicken, and peas. Reheat mixture, stirring frequently, and add salt and pepper to season it well. *Serves 4.*

QUICK TIP

Left-over cooked chicken may also be used for this recipe. It should be removed from the bone, added at the end and be reheated with the rice.

16 Cidered glazed gammon

You will need . . .

Preparation time
20 minutes

Cooking time
1 hour 40 minutes

Oven setting
220°C; 425°F; Gas Mark 7

1.75kg/4 lb piece boned and rolled gammon
1.2 litres/2 pints dry cider
For the topping:
100g/4 oz demerara sugar
1 level tablespoon dry mustard
For the spiced peaches:
1 × 411g/14 oz can peach halves
25g/1 oz demerara sugar
¼ level teaspoon cinnamon
2 tablespoons peach juice
4 tablespoons cider vinegar
mustard and cress

The day before cooking soak bacon joint in cold water overnight. Next day, take out of water and put in a large pan. Add cider and enough fresh cold water to cover. Bring to boil, cover and simmer very gently, allowing 20 minutes per pound. When cooked, remove from pan, cool slightly and peel off skin.

Mix together sugar and mustard. Pat mixture on fat surface of bacon and score surface in diamond shapes. Put joint in a meat tin, cover lean meat with foil. Brown joint in hot oven for about 15 minutes. Brush with a little melted butter during browning to give a rich golden colour.

Drain peaches. In a large, shallow pan dissolve sugar with cinnamon, peach juice and vinegar. Add peach halves, cut side downwards, cover and poach gently for 15 minutes. Arrange peaches and mustard and cress round bacon. Serve hot or cold. *Serves 6.*

QUICK TIP

Take care to simmer bacon joints slowly. Rapid boiling causes shrinkage and toughens the meat fibres. The last cutting from the bacon joint gives excellent flavour to chicken and meat dishes.

17 Trawlers' pie

You will need . . .

25g/1 oz butter
750g/1½ lb cod fillets
salt and pepper
For the sauce:
40g/1½ oz butter
40g/1½ oz flour
about 300ml/½ pint milk
2 teaspoons anchovy essence
3 hard-boiled eggs, roughly chopped
salt and pepper
For the topping:
450g/1 lb potatoes, cooked and mashed
with little butter and milk, seasoned

Preparation time
20 minutes

Cooking time
40 minutes

Oven setting
160°C; 325°F; Gas Mark 3
200°C; 400°F; Gas Mark 6

Spread a 1.5-litre/2½-pint ovenproof serving dish with 15g/½ oz butter, put cod in the dish and season. Put the rest of butter, cut in very small pieces, on top. Cover and cook in a very moderate oven for 20 to 30 minutes, until fish flakes easily. Strain liquor from dish into a measuring jug. Remove skin and any small bones from fish.

Melt butter for sauce in a pan, blend in flour and cook for 1 minute to make a *roux*. Add enough milk to liquor to make up to 450ml/¾-pint, blend with the roux to make a smooth sauce. Bring to boil and simmer for 2 minutes, stirring. Blend in anchovy essence and chopped egg. Season the sauce well. Add flaked fish to the sauce, turn into ovenproof dish.

Spread prepared potato over the fish. Mark with a fork making a pattern. Increase oven temperature to hot and reheat the pie for about 20 minutes, until it is piping hot and the top is golden brown. *Serves 4.*

QUICK TIP

If a white sauce lacks gloss it is because of lack of cooking after the liquid has been added. Return to the heat, bring to the boil and simmer for 2 minutes, beating well all the time.

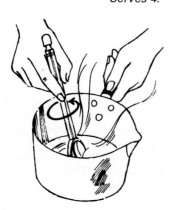

18 Hungarian lamb

You will need . . .

25g/1 oz lard
1kg/2 lb middle neck of lamb cut into joints
1 onion, chopped
1 clove garlic, crushed
2 level tablespoons paprika pepper
1 × 397g/14 oz can tomatoes
bay leaf
salt and pepper
½ level teaspoon sugar
450g/1 lb potatoes
1 tablespoon chopped parsley

Preparation time
20 minutes

Cooking time
2 hours 10 minutes

Oven setting
160°C; 325°F; Gas Mark 3

Melt the lard in a pan and brown pieces of lamb on both sides for about 5 minutes. Remove meat from the pan and put in an ovenproof casserole. Fry onion in fat remaining in the pan until soft, add garlic, paprika and continue to cook for a further minute. Add tomatoes and juice, bay leaf, salt, pepper and sugar. Bring the mixture to the boil, and pour over the meat.

Cover casserole and cook for 1 hour in a very moderate oven, then remove from the oven. Allow the fat to settle, then skim it off.

Peel the potatoes and cut in 2cm/¾-inch cubes; place on top of contents of the casserole, put on the lid and cook for a further hour, removing lid for the last half hour. Scatter chopped parsley over potatoes. *Serves 4.*

QUICK TIP

Adding sugar to tomatoes when cooking takes away that slightly bitter taste. This also applies when using tomato purée.

19 Swiss steak

You will need . . .

4 slices topside of beef, each weighing about 175g/6 oz
40g/1½ oz flour
1 level teaspoon salt
¼ level teaspoon pepper
40g/1½ oz lard
2 onions, finely sliced
2 sticks celery, chopped
1 × 227g/8 oz can tomatoes
2 level teaspoons tomato purée
½ teaspoon Worcestershire sauce
150ml/¼ pint water

Preparation time
10 minutes

Cooking time
2 hours 30 minutes

Oven setting
150°C; 300°F; Gas Mark 2

Cut steak in 8 pieces. Mix together flour, salt and pepper. Toss meat in flour mixture, pressing it in so that all flour is used. Melt lard in a pan and fry meat quickly on all sides until it is brown. Transfer meat to an ovenproof casserole.

Add onion and celery to fat remaining in pan. Fry until pale golden brown, then add to meat with the tomatoes, tomato purée, Worcestershire sauce and water.

Cover casserole and cook in a very moderate oven for 2½ hours or until meat is tender. *Serves 4.*

20 Sherried kidneys

You will need . . .

12 lambs' kidneys
50g/2 oz butter
1 large onion, finely chopped
20g/¾ oz flour
1 clove garlic, peeled
150ml/¼ pint plus 5 tablespoons water
1 beef stock cube
9 tablespoons dry sherry
bay leaf
salt and pepper
1 tablespoon chopped parsley

Preparation time
15 minutes

Cooking time
15 minutes

Remove fat and skin from kidneys, then cut in half lengthwise and remove cores. Melt 25g/1 oz of the butter in pan and fry onion slowly until pale brown and soft. Add halved kidneys and cook for about 2 minutes on each side until they have become firm and are just turning brown. Remove onion and kidneys from pan and keep hot.

Melt remaining butter in pan, blend in flour. Add clove of garlic, water, stock cube and sherry, blending until smooth. Add bay leaf, salt and pepper to taste. Bring to the boil, stirring, and simmer until sauce has thickened.

Return onion and kidneys to pan, cover and simmer for 5 minutes or until kidneys are just cooked. Remove bay leaf and add more seasoning if necessary. Arrange on a serving dish, pour sauce over and sprinkle with parsley. *Serves 4.*

QUICK TIP

When reheating casseroles and stews reheat them quickly at a fairly high temperature. Make sure that they simmer for at least 10 minutes before serving.

QUICK TIP

Boiled rice goes well with this dish. For ease, use refined long grain rice and boil in plenty of salted water until just tender – about 12 minutes. Allow 50g/2 oz for each person.

21 Chilli con carne

You will need . . .

1 tablespoon salad oil
25g/1 oz butter
2 medium onions, finely chopped
2 cloves garlic, crushed
100g/4 oz bacon trimmings
750g/1½ lb stewing steak
1 × 65g/2¼ oz can tomato purée
450ml/¾ pint water
salt and pepper
½ to 1 level teaspoon chilli powder
1 × 439g/16 oz can red kidney beans, drained

Preparation time
15 minutes

Cooking time
3 hours

Heat oil in a pan, add butter and fry onion and garlic until soft and pale golden brown. Remove from pan and put to one side. Cut bacon trimmings into 1-cm/½-inch pieces and steak into 2-cm/¾-inch cubes. Add to pan and fry until pale golden brown.

Replace onion and garlic in the pan, add tomato purée, water, salt, pepper and chilli powder. Bring to the boil, cover and let it simmer for 3 hours.

Add the kidney beans and simmer for a further 10 minutes. Adjust seasoning. *Serves 4.*

QUICK TIP

As a substitute for red kidney beans use baked beans in tomato sauce. The sweet flavour is more popular with children.

22 Chicken curry

You will need . . .

40g/1½ oz lard
4 frying chicken joints
2 onions, peeled and chopped
25g/1 oz flour
1 tablespoon curry powder
300ml/½ pint water
1 chicken stock cube
1 tablespoon mango chutney
1 tablespoon blackcurrant jelly
salt and pepper
25g/1 oz sultanas
1 dessert apple

Preparation time
20 minutes

Cooking time
40 minutes

Melt 25g/1 oz of lard in a fairly large pan and fry chicken joints on both sides until golden brown. Take them from pan, remove skin and bones carefully.

Melt remaining fat in pan and fry onions until they are soft. Blend in flour and curry powder (more if desired) and fry mixture for 1 minute. Add stock a little at a time, then bring to boiling point and simmer until sauce has thickened. Stir in chutney and blackcurrant jelly. Season with salt and pepper.

Replace chicken joints in the pan, cover and simmer gently for 30 minutes or until tender. Meanwhile, peel, core and chop apple; stir in sultanas and apple and cook for further 5 minutes. Serve with boiled rice and side dishes (*see Quick Tip below*) *Serves 4.*

QUICK TIP

The side dishes can also be prepared ahead.
A couple of bananas sliced and sprinkled with lemon juice and coated in desiccated coconut. Fried poppadums, sliced tomatoes or peppers, mango chutney and peanuts.

23 Chicken and mushroom pie

24 Pork barbecue-style

Chicken and mushroom pie

You will need . . .

Preparation time
25 minutes

Cooking time
40 minutes

Oven setting
220°C; 425°F; Gas Mark 7
190°C; 375°F; Gas Mark 5

225g/8 oz cooked chicken
225g/8 oz cooked boiled bacon
25g/1 oz butter
50g/2 oz mushrooms, sliced
25g/1 oz flour
150ml/¼ pint water
½ chicken stock cube
150ml/¼ pint milk
2 tablespoons cooked peas
For the pastry:
225g/8 oz plain flour
¼ level teaspoon salt
50g/2 oz butter
50g/2 oz lard
a little milk

Cut the chicken and bacon in chunks of about 2-cm/¾-inch. Melt butter in a pan, add mushrooms and cook gently for 2 minutes. Stir in flour and cook for another minute. Slowly blend in water, crumbled stock cube and milk, stirring until smooth. Bring the sauce to boiling point and stir until it thickens. Turn into a bowl. Add peas, chicken and bacon, leave to cool.

Make short crust pastry and divide in two. Roll each piece into a 23-cm/9-inch circle. Lift one of these on to a 20-cm/8-inch ovenproof plate and spread meat mixture in centre. Moisten edge of pastry with water, place second circle on top of first and gently press the edges of both circles to seal together. Trim edges and press with a fork. Decorate with a plait made from pastry trimmings.

Brush pie with milk, make two slits in the top and bake in a very hot oven for 25 minutes, then in a moderately hot oven for 15 minutes. *Serves 4.*

Pork barbecue-style

You will need . . .

Preparation time
15 minutes

Cooking time
30 minutes

Oven setting
190°C; 375°F; Gas Mark 5

4 pork chops
½ level teaspoon each salt and pepper
½ level teaspoon castor sugar
½ level teaspoon ground ginger
25g/1 oz butter
For the barbecue sauce:
½-1 tablespoon chilli sauce *
1 tablespoon mushroom ketchup
1 tablespoon Worcestershire sauce
2 level teaspoons castor sugar
2 tablespoons vinegar
2 tablespoons tomato ketchup
1 teaspoon soy sauce
2 cloves garlic, crushed
2 bay leaves

Trim pork chops carefully. Mix together salt, pepper, sugar and ginger and rub over chops. Heat the butter in a heavy meat tin and add the chops. Brown in a moderately hot oven, turning chops once to brown on both sides.

Meanwhile, mix together thoroughly all the ingredients for the barbecue sauce.

When chops are brown pour off all the fat from baking tin, pour sauce over and cover with a lid of foil. Bake for 20 to 30 minutes, basting occasionally, until tender. Then arrange on a serving dish and spoon sauce over. Decorate with parsley. *Serves 4.*

* The strength of chilli sauce varies, therefore use according to taste.

QUICK TIP

To glaze savoury pies: brush with milk or blended milk or water with egg. For sweet pies use the same or brush with blended egg white and sprinkle with castor sugar.

QUICK TIP

Due to modern refrigeration pork has no specific season, so forget the old story of eating pork only when there is an R in the month.

Cold sweets and desserts

There are desserts suitable for the every-day family meal, and there are those that are meant to provide an impressive finish to a small dinner party. This selection caters for each of these categories. The ever popular trifle and the delicious gâteaux, to name but a few, are sure to find favour with every member of the family, and no hostess needs to be at a loss as to how to end a festive meal: what could be more suitable than a truly spectacular crème brûlée or the delicate chocolate dessert cups!

Nearly all these recipes can be prepared in advance, the finishing touch to be added just before serving.

25 Strawberry meringue

(illustrated on front cover)

You will need . . .

For the meringue case:
4 egg whites
225g/8 oz castor sugar
few drops vanilla essence
½ teaspoon lemon juice
100g/4 oz blanched almonds, toasted and ground
For the filling:
450ml/¾ pint double cream, whipped
225g/8 oz strawberries, halved

Preparation time
25 minutes

Cooking time
40-45 minutes

Oven setting
180°C; 350°F; Gas Mark 4

Line 2 large baking trays with well-greased silicone paper, greaseproof paper or foil. Mark a 23-cm/9-inch wide heart on each.

Whisk whites until stiff. Add sugar a teaspoon at a time, whisking well after each addition. Gently fold in vanilla essence, lemon juice and nuts. Spoon into a piping bag fitted with a large star nozzle. Pipe a heart shape on 1 tray following the mark as a guide. Working inwards, pipe smaller and smaller hearts until you have a solid base of concentric hearts; repeat for the other heart. Bake in a medium oven for 40 to 45 minutes or until crisp and lightly coloured. Leave to cool.

Reserve about ⅓ of the cream and 13-15 strawberry halves for decoration. Sandwich the 2 hearts together with the remaining cream and strawberries. Pipe cream rosettes around the edge of the top heart and decorate with the reserved strawberry halves. *Serves 6.*

QUICK TIP

Storing meringues – when meringues are cooked, and thoroughly cooled, whether small or large, wrap in foil or arrange in an airtight tin, putting greaseproof paper between each layer. They will still be beautifully fresh in two months' time.

26 Lemon soufflé

You will need . . .

3 lemons, grated rind and juice
3 large eggs, separated
150g/5 oz castor sugar
3 tablespoons cold water
4 level teaspoons powdered gelatine (15g/½ oz)
150ml/¼ pint double cream
For the decoration:
pistachio nuts, chopped (optional)
whipped cream

Preparation time
25 minutes

Cut a piece of greaseproof paper long enough to go round the outside of a 750-ml/1¼-pint soufflé dish and about 5 cm/2 inches deeper than dish. Tie this round outside to form a collar.

Put finely grated lemon rind, juice, egg yolks and sugar in a basin over a pan of hot water. Whisk until just beginning to thicken. Dissolve gelatine with water in a small bowl over a pan of simmering water (*see Quick Tip below*). When it has dissolved stir into lemon mixture. Leave mixture in a cold place until just beginning to set.

Whisk cream until it forms soft peaks. Fold into mixture. Whisk egg whites stiffly and fold into mixture. Turn soufflé into the prepared dish and leave in a cold place to set. Just before serving remove paper carefully. Pipe a little cream round the edge and, if liked, decorate the side with pistachio nuts. *Serves 5-6.*

QUICK TIP

Using gelatine – always soak powdered gelatine in a little cold water for a few minutes to allow the gelatine to swell, before dissolving over a pan of simmering water in a small bowl.

27 Crème brûlée

28 Pineapple salad

You will need . . .

For the cream custard:
4 egg yolks
50g/2 oz castor sugar
300ml/½ pint double cream
300ml/½ pint single cream
few drops vanilla essence
For the caramel topping:
75g/3 oz granulated sugar
3 tablespoons water

Preparation time
20 minutes

Cooking time
1½ hours

Oven setting
140°C; 275°F; Gas Mark 1

Blend together egg yolks and sugar. Pour cream on to egg mixture, stir in a few drops of vanilla essence. Strain custard into a 900-ml/1½-pint serving dish.

Stand dish in a meat tin containing 2.5cm/1-inch of hot water. Bake custard for 45 minutes or until just firm in a very cool oven. Leave in a refrigerator or other cold place overnight.

Next day make caramel. Put sugar and water in a heavy pan, dissolve over a low heat then boil rapidly until a pale caramel colour. Quickly pour three-quarters of caramel over top of the custard and pour the remainder on to a well oiled tray. When set crush and arrange round edge of dish. *Serves 4.*

You will need . . .

2 small pineapples
1 apple
3 pears
225g/8 oz white grapes
castor sugar
1 tablespoon Grand Marnier *or* Cointreau (optional)

Preparation time
15 minutes

Cut pineapples in half lengthwise. Scoop out the flesh and remove the core. Cut the flesh in small pieces and place in a bowl.

Peel the fruit if desired and seed the grapes. Core and slice the apple and pears and add to the pineapple with the grapes. Sprinkle with castor sugar to taste and add the liqueur, if used. Leave the bowl covered, in a cool place until the sugar has dissolved.

Just before serving pile the fruit back in the pineapple shells. The remaining fruit may be offered separately. *Serves 4.*

QUICK TIP

To keep spare egg whites, put in a lidded jar in the refrigerator and use for meringues within two weeks. If you lose count of how many egg whites are in the jar, four egg whites are about 150ml/¼ pint and to this, for meringues, add 225g/8 oz castor sugar.

QUICK TIP

To skin grapes – plunge into boiling water for two minutes, then into cold water. The skins will come off without any difficulty.

29 Chilled cheesecake

You will need . . .

350g/12 oz carton cottage cheese, sieved
150ml/¼ pint single cream
4 level teaspoons powdered gelatine
(15g/½ oz)
4 tablespoons cold water
2 large lemons
3 eggs, separated
100g/4 oz castor sugar
150ml/¼ pint double cream, lightly
whipped
10 digestive biscuits, crushed
25g/1 oz demerara sugar
50g/2 oz butter, melted
For the decoration:
100g/4 oz redcurrants

Preparation time
35 minutes

Butter a 20-cm/8-inch deep cake tin. Line first the sides, then the base with greaseproof paper. Mix cottage cheese with single cream. Dissolve gelatine with water in a small bowl placed over a pan of simmering water. Place lemon juice and rind, egg yolks and sugar in a large bowl over a pan of simmering water. Whisk until thick and foamy, then remove from heat and whisk until cool.

Blend together egg yolk mixture, gelatine and cottage cheese mixture. Leave until thick but not set. Fold in whisked egg whites and double cream. Turn into prepared tin. Chill until set.

Blend together biscuits, demerara sugar and butter. Sprinkle over cheesecake. Press down lightly. Chill until firm. Turn cheesecake out on to a 25-cm/10-inch plate. Remove paper. Top with bunches of redcurrants. *Serves 6-8.*

QUICK TIP

Using up egg yolks: if they are not needed at once cover with a layer of water. Use to enrich a white sauce or soup, for home-made mayonnaise or custard, or to add to scrambled egg.

30 Orange sorbet

You will need . . .

75g/3 oz castor sugar
300ml/½ pint water
2 level teaspoons powdered gelatine
1 × 175g/6 oz can frozen concentrated
orange juice
1 egg white

Preparation time
15 minutes

Put the sugar and water into a pan and heat slowly until the sugar has dissolved. Allow this syrup to cool.

Dissolve the gelatine in a little water and add with the undiluted orange juice to the sugar syrup. Blend them together, then pour the liquid into a 600-ml/1-pint shallow, plastic lidded container. Put the sorbet in the freezing compartment of the refrigerator for half an hour or until barely firm.

Turn into a bowl and mash down until there are no large pieces. Then fold in the stiffly whisked egg white. Return to the container, cover and return to the freezing compartment until required. Thaw the sorbet in the refrigerator for 30 minutes before serving in individual glasses. *Serves 4.*

QUICK TIP

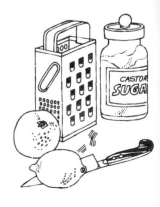

Lemon and orange sugar – when using only the juice of either lemons or oranges finely grate off the rinds first and blend with castor sugar. Store in separate jars and use the flavoured sugar for lemon or orange Victoria sandwiches.

31 Chilled lemon flan

32 Chocolate dessert cups

You will need . . .

For the flan case:
100g/4 oz digestive biscuits
50g/2 oz butter
1 level tablespoon castor sugar
For the filling:

Preparation time
15 minutes

150ml/¼ pint double cream
175g/6 oz can condensed milk
2 large lemons

Cooking time
8 minutes

For the topping:
lightly whipped double cream
fresh or crystallised lemon slices

Oven setting
150°C; 300°F; Gas Mark 2

Crush digestive biscuits with a rolling pin. Melt butter in a pan, add sugar then blend in biscuit crumbs. Mix well. Turn mixture into an 18-cm/7-inch pie plate or flan dish and press into shape round base and sides of plate, with the back of a spoon. Bake in a slow oven for 8 minutes. Remove from the oven and leave to cool. Do not turn the flan case out of dish as it will crumble.

Mix together cream, condensed milk and finely grated lemon rind. Slowly beat in lemon juice. Pour mixture into the flan case and chill for several hours until firm.

Just before serving decorate the flan with a whirl of lightly whipped cream and the lemon slices. *Serves 4.*

You will need . . .

175g/6 oz plain chocolate
15g/½ oz butter
3 eggs
1 tablespoon rum (optional)
1 tablespoon coffee essence
chocolate curls to decorate

Preparation time
15 minutes

Cooking time
5 minutes

Put the chocolate and butter in a bowl placed over a pan of hot, not boiling water. Leave to dissolve, stirring constantly.

When the chocolate is completely melted remove it from the heat and beat in the egg yolks, rum if used, and coffee essence. Whisk the egg whites stiffly then fold them into the mixture. Pour into 4 small cups or glasses and leave in a cool place until set.

Just before serving top each with a few chocolate curls.
Serves 4.

QUICK TIP

When crushing biscuits with a rolling pin, lie a clean tea towel on the table and put the biscuits between greaseproof paper on the tea towel and fold over. Apply pressure with the rolling pin. The tea towel will remain clean.

QUICK TIP

Coffee cups for mousses and creams – choose small demi-tasse size cups for serving chocolate, coffee or caramel flavours. They look smart and are indeed different. Biscuits to go with these are ideally served alongside in the saucer.

33 Coffee ice cream

You will need . . .
2 eggs, separated
50g/2 oz icing sugar, sieved
2 tablespoons coffee essence
150ml/¼ pint double cream

Preparation time
15 minutes

Whisk egg whites until very stiff, then gradually whisk in icing sugar. Whisk egg yolks and coffee essence together and whisk gradually into egg whites. Lightly whip cream and fold into coffee mixture.

Pour into 900-ml/1½-pint ice cube tray or shallow tin and freeze. This ice cream does not need any further beating.

To vary, fold in with the cream 50g/2 oz finely chopped walnuts, or 50g/2 oz lightly crushed meringue, or 50g/2 oz crushed macaroons.   *Serves 6.*

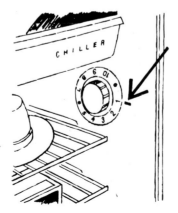

QUICK TIP

It is best to turn the refrigerator to coldest setting one hour before freezing ice cream. Turn back to normal setting once ice cream has frozen.

34 Traditional English trifle

You will need . . .
6 small sponge cakes
strawberry jam
50g/2 oz ratafia biscuits
5 tablespoons sherry *or* sherry and fruit juice
8 maraschino cherries
1 tablespoon juice from cherry bottle
For the custard:
2 eggs
25g/1 oz castor sugar
300ml/½ pint milk
For the topping:
300ml/½ pint double cram
15g/½ oz almonds, split

Preparation time
20 minutes

Cooking time
10 minutes

Split the sponge cakes in half and sandwich them together with jam. Arrange in the base of a 1.2-litre/2-pint serving dish and sprinkle the ratafia biscuits in between. Sprinkle the sherry, chopped cherries and maraschino juice over sponge cakes.

Blend together egg yolks and sugar in a bowl. Warm the milk then pour it on to egg mixture. Stir well, return the custard to pan and cook over a low heat. Do not allow it to simmer or it will curdle. When it is thick enough to coat back of a wooden spoon remove from heat. Strain custard over sponge cakes and leave to set.

Just before serving whip cream with egg whites until it forms soft peaks, then spread it over trifle. Lightly toast almonds under the grill and sprinkle on top of the trifle.

QUICK TIP

Shred almonds lengthways using a sharp knife. If the almonds are inclined to break through being too dry, soak in hot water for half an hour.

35 Ginger biscuit roll

36 Chestnut cream vacherin

You will need . . .
300ml/½ pint double cream
225g/8 oz ginger biscuits
For the decoration:
crystallised or stem ginger

Preparation time
10 minutes

Put half the cream in a bowl and whisk until it forms fairly stiff peaks. Use it to sandwich the ginger biscuits together in a long roll.

Arrange the roll on a serving dish and leave in the refrigerator or some other cool place overnight.

Next day whip the remaining cream and use it to cover the ginger biscuit roll completely. Decorate the roll with small pieces or slices of crystallised or stem ginger. Cut diagonal pieces from the loaf shape or cut into slices.   *Serves 4.*

You will need . . .
For the meringue:
3 egg whites
175g/6 oz castor sugar
For the chestnut filling:
1 × 250g/8¾ oz can sweetened chestnut purée
150ml/¼ pint double cream
1-2 tablespoons sherry (optional)
marrons glacé (optional)

Preparation time
15 minutes

Cooking time
2 hours

Oven setting
110°C; 225°F; Gas Mark ¼

Line a baking tray with silicone paper. Whisk the egg whites very stiffly. Add sugar a teaspoon at a time, whisking well after each addition.

Draw a 20-cm/8-inch circle on silicone paper. Use half the meringue to fill circle and smooth it with a knife. Put spoonfuls of remaining mixture on to rest of paper in seven heaps, drawing them up to a peak with the handle of a teaspoon. Bake meringues in a very cool oven for 2 hours or until crisp. Remove from oven and leave to cool on a wire tray.

Put chestnut purée in a bowl. In another bowl whip cream until it forms soft peaks. Fold cream into purée with sherry if used. Spread filling on to meringue base. Arrange small meringues on the top. Use the marrons glacé to decorate.   *Serves 4-6.*

QUICK TIP

Another simple yet special recipe on the same lines – soak Marie biscuits in rum and coffee essence then sandwich together with cream. Leave overnight then cover with cream. Decorate with halved walnuts.

QUICK TIP

Cooking meringues – it is far better to cook meringues on the slow side, just gently drying them out. (Use the coolest oven in a solid fuel cooker). Too hot an oven causes the sugar to weep out as a syrup, and also makes the meringues over-coloured.

37 Coffee cream cake

38 Apricot mousse

37 Coffee cream cake

You will need . . .

175g/6 oz butter
175g/6 oz castor sugar
3 eggs, lightly beaten
175g/6 oz self-raising flour
For the coffee syrup:

Preparation time
25 minutes

225g/8 oz sugar
450ml/¾ pint water
1-2 tablespoons brandy *or* rum (optional)
3 tablespoons coffee essence

Cooking time
45-50 minutes

For the decoration:
300ml/½ pint double cream

Oven setting
190°C; 375°F; Gas Mark 5

few drops vanilla essence
walnut halves

Grease a 20-cm/8-inch cake tin and line base with a circle of greased greaseproof paper. Cream butter and sugar together until light and creamy. Gradually beat in eggs, adding one tablespoon of flour with the last addition of egg. Fold in remaining flour. Turn into prepared tin and bake in a fairly hot oven for 45-50 minutes.

Make the coffee syrup by dissolving sugar in water over a low heat. Boil until syrupy. Remove from heat, add brandy and coffee essence. Stand cake on a deep serving plate, pierce all over with a skewer and pour over coffee mixture (*see Quick Tip below*). Leave to soak for at least 12 hours.

Whip cream and a few drops of vanilla essence until just stiff. Cover top and sides with cream and decorate with walnut halves. *Serves 10.*

38 Apricot mousse

You will need . . .

450g/1 lb fresh apricots
4 tablespoons cold water
thinly peeled rind and juice of ½ lemon
150g/5 oz castor sugar
15g/½ oz powdered gelatine (1 packet)

Preparation time
20 minutes

3 large eggs, separated
1 tablespoon apricot brandy *or* brandy (optional)

Cooking time
10 minutes

150ml/¼ pint double cream
150ml/¼ pint single cream
few flaked almonds

Wash apricots. Put in a pan with 1 tablespoon of the water, lemon peel and 50g/2 oz of the sugar. Cover and simmer until tender. Discard lemon peel and apricot stones. Sieve apricot pulp to make about 300ml/½ pint purée. Dissolve gelatine with remaining water in a small bowl over a pan of hot water.

Put egg yolks, remaining castor sugar and lemon juice in a large bowl over a pan of hot water. Whisk until thick and pale. Remove from heat and blend in apricot purée, dissolved gelatine and apricot brandy if used. Leave in a cold place until just beginning to set.

Whisk cream until it forms soft peaks. Whisk egg whites until stiff. Fold most of cream and all of egg whites into apricot mixture. Pour into a 1.2-litre/2-pint glass dish and leave in a cool place until set. Just before serving pipe a small whirl of remaining cream on top of each; decorate with flaked almonds. *Serves 6.*

QUICK TIP

It is essential to pour the hot coffee syrup over the cake whilst it is still warm otherwise the syrup is not easily absorbed.

QUICK TIP

If fresh apricots are not in season use 175g/6 oz of dried apricots soaked overnight, and cooked in a little of the soaking liquid. Continue as recipe adding a little water if necessary to make juice up to 300ml/½ pint.

39 Chocolate rum torte

You will need . . .

3 eggs
75g/3 oz castor sugar
50g/2 oz self-raising flour
25g/1 oz cocoa
2 tablespoons corn oil
150ml/¼ pint double cream
3 tablespoons rum
For the decoration:
2-4 tablespoons evaporated milk
100g/4 oz plain chocolate
chocolate curls

Preparation time
25 minutes

Cooking time
40-45 minutes

Oven setting
180°C; 350°F; Gas Mark 4

Line and grease an 18-cm/7-inch deep cake tin. Whisk eggs and sugar together until mixture is pale and thick. Sift flour and cocoa together. Fold into egg mixture with corn oil. Turn into prepared tin and bake in a moderate oven for about 40 minutes. Remove from tin and leave to cool before cutting in half.

Whip cream until it forms soft peaks. Fold in 2 tablespoons rum. Use to sandwich cake together.

Heat evaporated milk and remaining rum slowly together until hot. Remove from heat and add chocolate, broken in pieces, all at once. Stir until chocolate has dissolved. Cool until just warm, and of a coating consistency. Thin down with a little more evaporated milk if necessay. Pour icing over top of cake. Decorate with chocolate curls. *Serves 4-6.*

QUICK TIP

Fresh cream goes off quickly so if you want to make this dessert well ahead, fill with a rum flavoured buttercream instead of fresh cream. It will then keep for 10 days.

40 French apricot tart

You will need . . .

175g/6 oz rich shortcrust pastry
2 eggs
40g/1½ oz castor sugar
20g/¾ oz flour
150ml/¼ pint plus 5 tablespoons milk
few drops vanilla essence
For the topping:
1 × 425g/15 oz can and 1 × 227g/8 oz
can apricot halves
For the glaze:
1½ level teaspoons arrowroot
150ml/¼ pint fruit juice
1 tablespoon apricot brandy (optional)

Preparation time
35 minutes

Cooking time
35 minutes

Oven setting
200°C; 400°F; Gas Mark 6

Line a 20-cm/8-inch shallow fluted flan tin with pastry. Fill with a piece of crumpled foil, or greaseproof paper, and baking beans and bake in a hot oven for 25 minutes. Remove paper, or foil, and baking beans and bake for a further 5 minutes to dry base of flan case. Leave to cool.

Mix eggs and sugar together for confectioner's custard. Add flour and sufficient milk to make a smooth paste. Boil rest of milk. Add to eggs, stirring. Return to pan. Simmer 2 to 3 minutes until thick. Remove from heat. Stir frequently while cooling so a skin does not form. Stir in vanilla essence. Spread custard in base of flan case.

Drain fruit. Arrange on top of custard. Put arrowroot in a pan. Blend in fruit juice. Bring to boil and simmer until thick. Stir in apricot brandy if used. Spoon glaze over fruit. Leave to set. *Serves 6.*

QUICK TIP

For a quicker glaze use 4 tablespoons apricot jam warmed with a tablespoon water. Sieve well and spoon or brush over the tart whilst still warm.

41 Loganberry mousse

You will need . . .

1 × 385g/14 oz can loganberries
1 packet raspberry jelly
1 × 170g/6 oz can evaporated milk
1 teaspoon lemon juice
2 tablespoons double cream, whipped

Preparation time
20 minutes

Strain juice from loganberries into a measuring jug and make up to 300ml/½ pint with water. Put juice in a pan and bring to boiling point. Add jelly in small pieces and stir until dissolved. Leave in a cold place until just beginning to set.

Sieve loganberries. Put evaporated milk and lemon juice in a bowl and whisk until it will form soft peaks. Fold loganberry purée and evaporated milk into half-set jelly. Mix well, then spoon into a serving dish.

Leave in a cool place. Just before serving decorate mousse with whipped cream and, if desired, fresh loganberries.

Serves 4.

42 Lemon meringue pie

You will need . . .

175g/6 oz plain flour
100g/4 oz butter
1 egg yolk
20g/¾ oz castor sugar
2 teaspoons water

Preparation time
30 minutes

For the lemon filling:
2 large lemons
40g/1½ oz cornflour
300ml/½ pint water
2 egg yolks
75g/3 oz castor sugar

Cooking time
35 minutes

Oven setting
200°C; 400°F; Gas Mark 6
180°C; 350°F; Gas Mark 4

For the meringue topping:
3 egg whites
150g/5 oz castor sugar

Make shortcrust pastry in usual way. Use to line a 20-cm/8-inch flan ring, placed on a baking sheet. Prick base with a fork and leave in cold place for 20 minutes. Fill with a piece of crumpled foil or greaseproof paper and baking beans. Bake in a hot oven for about 15 minutes. Remove paper and baking beans.

Put grated lemon rind and juice in a bowl with cornflour. Add 2 tablespoons of the water and blend until smooth. Boil remaining water and pour it on to cornflour mixture. Return mixture to pan, bring to boil and simmer for 3 minutes until thick. Remove from heat and add egg yolks and sugar. Cool slightly then spoon into flan case.

Whisk egg whites until they form soft peaks. Add sugar a teaspoon at a time, whisking well after each addition. Pipe or spoon meringue over lemon filling. Bake in a moderate oven for 15 minutes.

Serves 4-6.

QUICK TIP

Before whisking evaporated milk for cold desserts chill first. This not only means that you get more volume, but helps to set the jelly more rapidly.

QUICK TIP

Fabulous lemon filling for a sponge flan – lightly whip 200ml/⅓ pint double cream, fold in 2 tablespoons home-made lemon curd. Turn into flan case. Chill overnight then decorate with fresh lemon slices.

43 Oranges in liqueur

You will need . . .

6 large seedless oranges
175g/6 oz castor sugar
2-3 tablespoons Cointreau, Grand
Marnier *or* Curaçao

Preparation time
10 minutes

Peel one orange thinly with a potato peeler. Cut peel in fine shreds. Put in a bowl and cover with boiling water. Leave for 10 minutes then drain and put on one side.

Cut peel and pith from all oranges. Cut oranges in thin slices. Arrange orange slices, overlapping, in a serving dish. Sprinkle with the sugar and liqueur. Cover and leave in a cold place to chill overnight.

Just before serving top with orange shreds. Serve with whipped cream. *Serves 6.*

44 Syllabub

You will need . . .

1 large lemon
150ml/¼ pint sweet sherry
2 tablespoons brandy
50g/2 oz castor sugar
300ml/½ pint double cream
lemon slices to decorate

Preparation time
15 minutes

Finely grate rind from the lemon and squeeze out juice. Put the rind and juice in a bowl with sherry, brandy and sugar. Stir until the sugar has dissolved.

Pour in the cream and whisk mixture until it will form soft peaks when whisk is lifted out. Spoon into individual glasses and leave in a cool place until required.

Top each glass with a slice of fresh lemon. This syllabub can be made a day in advance as it keeps very well. *Serves 4.*

QUICK TIP

To prepare orange segments instead of slices, peel orange and remove pith. Then hold orange in the left hand and, with a sharp knife, dissect out each segment, leaving the membrane and skin behind. This takes longer than slices but it is well worth it.

QUICK TIP

Lemon versus oranges – an average-sized lemon gives about 3 tablespoons of juice. A good-sized orange yields about 5 tablespoons juice.

45 German cheesecake

You will need . . .

225g/8 oz plain flour
¼ teaspoon salt
100g/4 oz butter
50g/2 oz castor sugar
2 tablespoons water
1 × 225g/8 oz carton cottage cheese
4 egg yolks
100g/4 oz sugar
25g/1 oz ground almonds
finely grated zest of 1 large lemon
1 × 150g/5 oz carton soured cream
50g/2 oz sultanas
50g/2 oz candied peel, finely chopped
2 egg whites
100g/4 oz castor sugar

Preparation time
25 minutes

Cooking time
1¼-1½ hours

Oven setting
200°C; 400°F; Gas Mark 6
160°C; 325°F; Gas Mark 3

Make up pastry and line a Swiss roll tin 18 × 28 × 2.5-cm/7 × 11 × 1-inch and crimp edges. Cover with foil, then baking beans and bake 'blind' in a hot oven, for 15 minutes. Remove beans and foil and continue baking for 7-10 minutes until pastry is completely cooked.

Sieve cottage cheese. Cream egg yolks and sugar. Stir almonds (or 25g/1 oz self-raising flour), egg mixture, lemon zest, soured cream, sultanas and candied peel into cottage cheese. Mix well. Remove pastry case from oven and turn oven to very moderate. Whisk egg whites for lattice topping until they are very stiff. Whisk in half the sugar. Fold in remaining sugar.

Fill pastry case with cottage cheese mixture. Pipe a fine lattice of meringue over the top, using a 5-mm/¼-inch plain tube. Return cheesecake to oven and bake for 50-60 minutes. At the end of this time turn off oven and leave cheesecake for further half an hour. Remove and chill.   *Serves 8.*

QUICK TIP

This cheesecake improves with keeping for 2-3 days before eating, it becomes more moist. If you have an electric blender use it instead of sieving for puréeing the cottage cheese.

46 Montelimar pudding

You will need . . .

1 × 175g/6 oz can evaporated milk
25g/1 oz glacé cherries
50g/2 oz marshmallows
½ lemon jelly tablet
150ml/¼ pint very hot water
juice of ½ lemon
25g/1 oz castor sugar

Preparation time
20 minutes

Chill the evaporated milk in the refrigerator. Chop the cherries and cut the marshmallow in small pieces using wet scissors.

Dissolve the jelly tablet in the hot water. Cool until it is thick but not set. Whip the evaporated milk until it is light and foamy. Add the cooled jelly, blending it in well.

Stir in the lemon juice, cherries, marshmallows and castor sugar. Turn into a serving dish or mould and chill until set. Just before serving, turn out and decorate with canned or maraschino cherries.

QUICK TIP

Marshmallows make a quick topping for a special dessert. Arrange sliced peaches in an ovenproof dish, sprinkle with icing sugar and brandy; cover with marshmallows then brown under the grill.

Scandinavian 47 apple charlotte

You will need . . .

75g/3 oz butter
225g/8 oz fresh white breadcrumbs
50g/2 oz demerara sugar
750g/1½ lb cooking apples
1 lemon
2 tablespoons water
50g/2 oz castor sugar
150ml/¼ pint double cream
coarsely grated chocolate

Preparation time
20 minutes

Melt butter in a frying pan. Add breadcrumbs and fry slowly until crisp and golden, stirring frequently. When they are ready, remove from heat and blend in the demerara sugar.

In another pan put peeled, cored and sliced apples, lemon juice, water and castor sugar. Cover and cook until the apples are soft, then mash to a smooth purée. Leave to cool.

Put half the cooled apple purée into a 900-ml-1.2 litre/1½-2 pint glass serving dish. Spread half the breadcrumbs on top. Repeat with a layer of apple and breadcrumbs. Leave to chill before serving. Just before serving spread or pipe lightly whipped cream on top of pudding and sprinkle with coarsely grated chocolate. *Serves 4.*

48 Caramel custard

You will need . . .

For the caramel:
75g/3 oz granulated sugar
3 tablespoons water
For the custard:
4 eggs
40g/1½ oz castor sugar
600ml/1 pint milk
few drops vanilla essence

Preparation time
15 minutes

Cooking time
1 hour 15 minutes

Oven setting
160°C; 325°F; Gas Mark 3

Put granulated sugar into a heavy pan with water and dissolve without boiling. When it has dissolved bring the syrup to boiling point and boil until it is golden brown. Pour the caramel into dariole moulds and make sure the bases are evenly covered. When cool, butter sides of moulds.

Blend together eggs and castor sugar. Warm milk, then pour it on to egg mixture. Mix well and add a few drops of vanilla essence. Strain the custard into the moulds. Place moulds in a meat tin half filled with hot water. Bake in a very moderate oven for about 1 hour or until a knife inserted in the centres comes out clean.

Leave the custards in a cold place overnight before turning them out on to a flat serving dish (*see Quick Tip below*). *Serves 4-6.*

QUICK TIP

When you have too much bread in the house make fresh breadcrumbs. These keep in a polythene bag in the refrigerator for a week or more. Use for Queen of Puddings, hot apple charlotte and not forgetting the old favourite, treacle tart.

QUICK TIP

When baking the custard do not cook too quickly or there will be bubbles in the mixture. Turn out just before serving, having left it in the refrigerator for at least 12 hours so that the moist custard has fully dissolved the caramel.

Traditional bread and scones

The tempting smell of freshly baked bread stealing from the kitchen is surely one of the things most certain to whet the appetite. And the sense of achievement when proudly presenting a home-baked loaf or a basket full of delicious looking scones is an experience which no housewife should deny herself.

It is often thought today that the baking of bread or buns involves lengthy preparation and that particular skill is needed to use yeast in the dough. The recipes in this chapter, which are easy to follow, and the quick tips providing invaluable information on how to treat yeast dough, will soon dispel such fears.

49 Harvest loaf

(illustrated on back cover)

You will need . . .

450g/1 lb plain flour
2 level teaspoons salt
15g/½ oz lard
beaten egg to glaze
For the yeast liquid:
1 teaspoon sugar
300ml/½ pint warm water less 2 tablespoons
2 level teaspoons dried yeast

Preparation time
25 minutes

Cooking time
30-40 minutes

Oven setting
230°C; 450°F; Gas Mark 8

Prepare yeast liquid (*see method, recipe 51*). Rub lard into flour and salt. Add yeast liquid, mix to firm dough until sides of bowl are clean. Turn onto floured table, knead for about 10 minutes until smooth. Leave to rise in greased polythene bag, loosely tied, until double in bulk.

Remove polythene bag, knock out air bubbles and knead dough well on a lightly floured table. Divide into 4 pieces. Roll 3 pieces into strands 50 cm/20-inches long, join together at one end. Place on a greased baking sheet, plait loosely together and tuck ends underneath. Brush with beaten egg and milk or water. Divide remaining dough in half and roll each into strands. Join at one end, twist strands loosely. Lay twist along centre of plait, tuck ends underneath. Brush with beaten egg or milk and water.

Cover, leave to rise at room temperature, about 30 minutes. Bake in hot oven, 30-40 minutes. Cool on a wire tray.

QUICK TIP

Strong plain flour is best for yeast recipes as it absorbs liquid easily and kneads quickly into a firm dough. Some plain flours are labelled strong. If not available, buy a top quality plain flour.

50 Glazed fruit bread

You will need . . .

350g/12 oz self-raising flour
½ level teaspoon salt
50g/2 oz castor sugar
50g/2 oz walnuts, chopped
50g/2 oz dates, stoned and chopped
2 rounded tablespoons malt extract
50g/2 oz butter
150ml/¼ pint milk
2 eggs, beaten
For the glaze and topping:
3 tablespoons apricot jam
50g/2 oz icing sugar
25g/1 oz walnuts
4 dates, stoned and halved
glacé cherries and apricots

Preparation time
10 minutes

Cooking time
1 hour

Oven setting
160°C; 325°F; Gas Mark 3

Well grease a 1-kg/2-lb loaf tin. Sift flour and salt into a bowl, add sugar, walnuts and dates. Gently heat malt and butter until butter has melted. Pour into centre of flour mixture with blended milk and eggs. Mix to smooth, soft dough.

Turn dough into tin. Bake in a very moderate oven for about 1 hour.

To make glaze, heat jam slowly with a little water and spread over top of loaf. Place glacé or dried apricots down the centre with a cherry in middle of each. Arrange walnuts and dates along either side. Mix icing sugar with 1 tablespoon water and trickle icing over top to give a criss-cross effect.

QUICK TIP

For a quicker finish, brush the top of the loaf with warmed honey or golden syrup and scatter with chopped walnuts.

51 Chelsea buns

You will need . . .

Preparation time
20-25 minutes

Cooking time
30-35 minutes

Oven setting
190°C; 375°F; Gas Mark 5

175g/6 oz plain flour
½ teaspoon salt
1 egg, beaten
15g/½ oz butter, melted
For the yeast liquid:
2 level teaspoons dried yeast
150ml/¼ pint warm milk less 3
tablespoons
½ teaspoon sugar
50g/2 oz plain flour
For the filling:
15g/½ oz butter, melted
50g/2 oz soft brown sugar
75g/3 oz currants
25g/1 oz mixed peel, chopped
honey for glazing

Blend yeast with warm milk (43°C/110°F), sugar and 50g/2 oz flour. Leave until frothy, about 20-30 minutes. Mix remaining flour and salt together. Add to yeast mixture with beaten egg and melted butter, mix well. Knead dough on a lightly floured table for about 10 minutes.

Put to rise in a large greased polythene bag, loosely tied, until double in size (*see Quick Tip, recipe 57*). Remove polythene; knead well on a lightly floured table and roll into a rectangle approximately 23 × 30cm/9 × 12 inches. Brush with remaining butter and sprinkle on sugar and fruit. Roll up as for a Swiss roll and seal edge. Cut into 9 slices. Place in a greased 18-cm/7-inch square cake tin, cut side down. Leave to rise inside a greased polythene bag until dough feels springy.

Remove polythene bag. Bake in a moderately hot oven for 30-35 minutes. Place on a wire tray and glaze hot buns with a wet brush dipped in honey.

QUICK TIP

Always cover dough well during rising to prevent a skin forming on the surface. Use a lightly greased polythene sheet or bag, a large saucepan or mixing bowl covered with a lid.

52 Hot cross buns

You will need . . .

Preparation time
25 minutes

Cooking time
15-20 minutes

Oven setting
220°C; 425°F; Gas Mark 7

350g/12 oz plain flour
1 level teaspoon salt
½ level teaspoon *each* mixed spice,
cinnamon and nutmeg
50g/2 oz sugar
50g/2 oz butter, melted
1 egg, beaten
100g/4 oz currants
25-50g/1-2 oz mixed peel
For the yeast liquid:
1 level tablespoon dried yeast
1 level teaspoon sugar
150ml/¼ pint warm milk (43°C/110°F)
150ml/¼ pint warm water less 3
tablespoons
100g/4 oz plain flour

Blend yeast with mixed warm milk and water, sugar and flour. Leave until frothy, about 20-30 minutes. Sift together remaining flour, salt, spices and sugar; add fruit. Stir butter and egg into yeast batter, add flour and fruit. Mix well. Knead dough on a floured table for approximately 10 minutes.

Divide dough into 12 pieces and shape into buns by using the palm of one hand, first pressing down hard and then easing up. Place on a floured baking sheet spaced well apart. Put inside a greased polythene bag and leave to rise at room temperature for about 45 minutes. Remove bag. Make a cross with a very sharp knife to just cut surface of dough. Bake in a hot oven for 15-20 minutes. Cool on a wire tray.

For the glaze, bring 2 tablespoons milk and 2 tablespoons water to the boil, stir in 40g/1½ oz sugar and boil for 2 minutes. Brush hot buns twice.

QUICK TIP

For a more definitely shaped cross place two strips of short crust pastry on to the buns before glazing and baking.

53 Orange raisin ring

You will need . . .

½ teaspoon salt
175g/6 oz plain flour
15g/½ oz butter, melted
1 egg, beaten
For the yeast liquid:
2 level teaspoons dried yeast
½ teaspoon sugar
150ml/¼ pint warm milk less 3
tablespoons
50g/2 oz plain flour
For the filling and decoration:
15g/½ oz butter, melted
50g/2 oz brown sugar
50g/2 oz raisins
grated rind of 1 orange
50g/2 oz icing sugar
25g/1 oz almonds, shredded

Preparation time
20-25 minutes

Cooking time
30-35 minutes

Oven setting
180°C; 350°F; Gas Mark 4

Blend yeast with warm milk (43°C/110°F), sugar and 50g/2 oz flour. Leave until frothy, about 20-30 minutes. Mix ½ teaspoon salt with remaining flour. Add to yeast mixture with beaten egg and melted butter, mix well. Knead dough on a floured table for about 10 minutes.

Put to rise in a large greased polythene bag, loosly tied, until double in size (*see Quick Tip, recipe 51*). Remove polythene bag and roll dough into a rectangle 30 × 23cm/12 × 9 inches, brush with remaining melted butter. Sprinkle sugar, raisins and orange rind on top. Roll as for a Swiss roll and seal edge. Bring roll ends together to form a ring, seal ends and put on a greased tray. With scissors make 2.5-cm/1-inch slashes to within 1cm/½ inch of centre and separate by turning each piece gently sideways. Rise inside a greased polythene bag for about 30 minutes. Remove polythene, bake in a moderate oven for 30-35 minutes. Cool on a wire tray. Ice with water icing (*see Quick Tip below*) and decorate with shredded almonds.

QUICK TIP

To make water icing: sieve the icing sugar twice. Beat in a teaspoonful of cold water at a time until the mixture coats the back of a wooden spoon. Use this icing for covering cakes as well as bread.

54 Rolls

You will need . . .

750g/1½ lb plain flour
1 level tablespoon salt (15g/½ oz)
15g/½ oz lard
For the yeast liquid:
1 teaspoon sugar
450ml/¾ pint warm water (43°C/110°F)
2 level teaspoons dried yeast

Preparation time
30 minutes

Cooking time
15-20 minutes

Oven setting
230°C; 450°F; Gas Mark 8

Prepare the dough and put to rise (*see method, recipe 57*).

Remove dough from polythene bag and divide into 18 equal pieces, shape each piece as desired:
Dinner rolls – on an unfloured table, roll each piece of dough into a ball, pressing down hard at first with floured palm of hand then easing up.
Finger rolls – prepare as for dinner rolls and then roll into a sausage-shape, about 10cm/4 inches long.
Knot – shape as for dinner rolls then roll into a 20-cm/8-in rope; tie rope into a simple knot.
Clover leaf – divide each piece of dough into 3 and shape as for dinner rolls. Place together to form a clover leaf.

Place all rolls on baking sheet about 2.5-cm/1-inch apart. Put to rise in a greased polythene bag for approximately 30 minutes at room temperature. Remove bag and bake in a hot oven for 15-20 minutes. Cool on a wire tray.

QUICK TIP

Flours vary in the quantity of liquid they absorb – 450g/1 lb flour usually takes approximately 300ml/½ pint liquid. Add extra flour if dough is too soft to make the correct consistency.

55 Baps

56 Welsh currant bread

You will need . . .

450g/1 lb plain flour
1 teaspoon salt
50g/2 oz lard
For the yeast liquid:
1 teaspoon sugar
300ml/½ pint warm milk and water
(43°C/110°F)
2 level teaspoons dried yeast

Preparation time
25 minutes

Cooking time
15-20 minutes

Oven setting
200°C; 400°F; Gas Mark 6

Prepare the yeast liquid by dissolving the sugar in the milk and water, sprinkle the yeast on top and leave until frothy, about 10 minutes. Rub the lard into the flour and salt. Add yeast liquid to flour and work to a soft dough. Turn on to a lightly floured table and knead until dough is smooth, about 10 minutes. Leave to rise in a lightly greased polythene bag, loosely tied, until double in size (*see Quick Tip, recipe 51*).

Remove polythene bag, knock out air bubbles and knead to make a firm dough. Divide dough into 10 equal pieces. Shape each into a ball, roll out to an oval about 1-cm/½-inch thick. Place on a floured baking sheet and dredge tops with flour.

Cover with greased polythene and leave to rise at room temperature for approximately 30 minutes. Remove polythene. Bake in a moderately hot oven for 15-20 minutes. Cool on a wire tray.

You will need . . .

75g/3 oz margarine
450g/1 lb plain flour
75g/3 oz demerara sugar
1 level teaspoon salt
1 level teaspoon mixed spice
350g/12 oz mixed raisins, currants, sultanas *and* peel
1 egg, beaten
For the yeast liquid:
1 teaspoon sugar
300ml/½ pint warm water (43°C/110°F) less 6 tablespoons
1½ level teaspoons dried yeast
honey for glazing

Preparation time
20 minutes

Cooking time
40 minutes

Oven setting
190°C; 375°F; Gas Mark 5

Prepare the yeast liquid by dissolving the sugar in the water. Sprinkle the yeast on top and set aside until frothy, about 20 minutes.

Rub margarine into the flour and mix in sugar, salt, spice and fruit. Add egg and yeast liquid to flour mixture and mix well. Knead dough thoroughly on a lightly floured table. Place in a greased polythene bag, loosely tied, and allow to rise until double in size.

Turn out dough and knock out air bubbles; knead well. Divide in half and shape to fit two greased 450-g/1-lb loaf tins. Place each tin in a greased polythene bag and allow dough to rise to 2.5-cm/1-inch above top of tins. Remove polythene bags. Bake in a moderately hot oven for about 40 minutes. Turn loaves out, place on a wire tray and, whilst still hot, glaze with a wet brush dipped in honey.

QUICK TIP

Add the liquid all at once before mixing in the flour to give an even mixture. Extra liquid cannot successfully be added once the dough is mixed.

QUICK TIP

To test if a loaf is cooked, tap underneath with knuckles; it should sound hollow; the loaf will also shrink slightly from sides of tin.

57 White bread

You will need . . .

750g/1½ lb plain flour
1 level tablespoon salt (15g/½ oz)
15g/½ oz lard
For the yeast liquid:
1 teaspoon sugar
450ml/¾ pint warm water
2 level teaspoons dried yeast

Preparation time
20 minutes

Cooking time
30-40 minutes

Oven setting
230°C; 450°F; Gas Mark 8

Prepare the yeast liquid by dissolving the sugar in the water (43°C/110°F) and sprinkling the yeast on top. Leave until frothy, about 10 minutes. Rub the lard into the flour and salt and mix in yeast liquid. Work to a firm dough, until sides of bowl are clean. Turn on to a lightly floured table and knead thoroughly, about 10 minutes.

Place in lightly greased large polythene bag, loosely tied, and leave to rise until double in size (*see Quick Tip, recipe 51*). Remove polythene and turn out on to a lightly floured table, flatten to knock out air bubbles, and knead to make dough firm. Grease two 450-g/1-lb loaf tins. Divide dough in half, stretch each piece into an oblong the same width as tin and fold over in three. With the seam underneath, smooth over top, tuck in ends and place in tin. Place in greased polythene bags and leave to rise until dough comes to top of tins.

Remove polythene bags and bake in a very hot oven for 30-40 minutes. Turn out and cool on a wire tray.

QUICK TIP

Pick a rising time to fit in with the day's plans:
Quick rise: 45-60 minutes in a warm place
Slower rise: 2 hours at average room temperature
Overnight rise: up to 12 hours in cold larder or up to 24 hours in a refrigerator.

58 Cheese scones

You will need . . .

225g/8 oz self-raising flour
¼ teaspoon salt
½ teaspoon dry mustard
25g/1 oz butter
100g/4 oz cheese
150ml/¼ pint milk

Preparation time
10-15 minutes

Cooking time
12 minutes

Oven setting
220°C; 425°F; Gas Mark 7

Sift together flour, salt and mustard. Rub in butter until mixture resembles fine breadcrumbs. Finely grate the cheese and add 85g/3½ oz to the flour mixture; bind together with milk to form a soft dough.

Roll out on a floured table to 1-cm/½-inch thickness and cut into 15 rounds with a 4-cm/1½-inch plain cutter. Place on greased baking sheet, brush with milk and sprinkle remaining cheese on top.

Bake in a hot oven for about 12 minutes. Cool on a wire tray. Serve with butter.

QUICK TIP

Store flour, in its bag, on a cool, airy shelf. If kitchen is damp, keep bag in a tin or storage jar with a lid. Plain flour will keep for 4-6 months, self-raising flour for 2-3 months. Store wheatmeal flour separately and it will keep for up to 2 months.

59 Apple scone

You will need . . .

1 medium cooking apple
225g/8 oz self-raising flour
½ teaspoon salt
1 level teaspoon baking powder
50g/2 oz butter

Preparation time
15 minutes

50g/2 oz castor sugar
scant 150ml/¼ pint milk
For the glaze:
little milk

Cooking time
20-25 minutes

25g/1 oz demerara sugar

Oven setting
200°C; 400°F; Gas Mark 6

Peel, core and finely chop apple. Sift together flour, salt and baking powder. Rub in butter, then add castor sugar and chopped apple. Mix to a soft, but not sticky dough with milk.

Roll out on a floured table a 5-mm/¼-inch thick, 20-cm/8-inches round. Mark into 8 wedges. Place on a greased baking sheet, brush top with milk and sprinkle with demerara sugar. Bake in a moderately hot oven for 20-25 minutes.

Serve warm with butter.

60 Gingerbread

You will need . . .

100g/4 oz margarine
175g/6 oz black treacle
50g/2 oz golden syrup
50g/2 oz brown sugar
150ml/¼ pint milk

Preparation time
10-15 minutes

2 eggs
225g/8 oz plain flour
1 rounded teaspoon mixed spice

Cooking time
1¼-1½ hours

1 level teaspoon bicarbonate of soda
2 level teaspoons ground ginger
100g/4 oz sultanas

Oven setting
150°C; 300°F; Gas Mark 2

Grease and line an 18-cm/7-inch square cake tin. Using a large saucepan, warm together margarine, treacle, syrup and sugar. Add milk and allow to cool. Beat eggs and blend with cooled mixture.

Sift dry ingredients together into a bowl, add the cooled mixture and sultanas folding in gently with a tablespoon.

Turn into the greased and lined tin. Bake in a slow oven for 1¼-1½ hours. Turn out and cool on a wire tray.

QUICK TIP

For a change, roll dough to 1-cm/½-inch thick and cut into 10-12 rounds with a 5-cm/ 2-inch plain cutter. Place on a greased baking sheet and brush tops with milk. Bake in a moderately hot oven for 15-20 minutes.

QUICK TIP

To vary the gingerbread: use equal quantities of white and wholemeal flour or add 100g/4 oz dried figs or chopped dates instead of sultanas or add 50g/2 oz each of crystallised ginger and shredded ginger.

61 Quick wheatmeal bread

62 Barm brack

You will need . . .

225g/8 oz plain white flour
225g/8 oz brown flour
2 level teaspoons salt
10g/¼ oz lard
1 level teaspoon sugar

Preparation time
15 minutes

For the yeast liquid:
1 level teaspoon sugar
2 level teaspoons dried yeast
300ml/½ pint warm water (43°C/110°F)

Cooking time
30-40 minutes

Oven setting
230°C; 450°F; Gas Mark 8

Mix flours, salt and 1 teaspoon of sugar together and rub in lard. Dissolve remaining sugar in half the water, sprinkle yeast on top and leave until frothy, about 10 minutes. Add, with rest of water to flour, and mix to a soft scone-like dough.

Turn on to a lightly floured table and knead well. Divide dough in half. Shape each half into a ball and place in two greased 12.5-cm/5-inch cake tins. Brush tops with salt and water and sprinkle with cracked wheat or oatmeal.

Put to rise inside a large greased polythene bag, loosely tied, until dough doubles in size and springs back when lightly pressed with a floured finger, about 1½ hours at average room temperature or half-an-hour in a warm place. Remove bag and bake in a hot oven for 30-40 minutes. Turn out and cool on a wire tray.

You will need . . .

350 ml/12 fl oz cold tea
200g/7 oz soft brown sugar
350g/12 oz mixed dried fruit
275g/10 oz self-raising flour
1 egg

Preparation time
10 minutes

Cooking time
1 hour 45 minutes

Oven setting
180°C; 350°F; Gas Mark 4

Put tea, sugar and dried fruit in a bowl, cover and leave to soak overnight. Tea that has been leftover during the day can be saved and used. Well grease a 20-cm/8-inch round cake tin, or a 1-kg/2-lb loaf tin.

Mix the soaked fruit and sugar plus the liquid into the flour. Add the beaten egg to make a smooth mixture. Turn into the tin and bake in a moderate oven for about 1 hour 45 minutes. Turn out and cool on a wire tray.

Serve sliced with butter.

QUICK TIP

To recrisp a crusty loaf, or refresh a stale one, wrap in foil and bake in a hot oven, 230°C 450°F Gas Mark 8, for 8-10 minutes. Cool in foil.

QUICK TIP

For electric mixer owners, use dough hook attachment for yeast doughs. Mix dough on lowest speed for 1 minute, then 2 minutes at a slightly higher speed to knead the dough. The manufacturer's instructions should be read carefully.

63 Cheese and celery loaf

You will need . . .

450g/1 lb self-raising flour
2 teaspoons salt
40g/1½ oz butter
3 large sticks celery
175g/6 oz mature Cheddar cheese
1 clove garlic *or* a few dehydrated flakes
1 egg
300ml/½ pint milk less 2 tablespoons

Preparation time
15 minutes

Cooking time
55 minutes

Oven setting
220°C; 425°F; Gas Mark 7

Grease a 1-kg/2-lb loaf tin. Sift flour and salt into a bowl and rub in fat until mixture resembles fine breadcrumbs.

Wash and chop celery finely. Crush garlic if a clove is used and grate cheese coarsely. Add celery, garlic and cheese to flour. Beat egg and milk together, add gradually to dry ingredients and mix to form a soft dough. Knead lightly and quickly on a floured table, then shape into an oblong. Place in the loaf tin and bake in a hot oven for about 55 minutes.

Turn out and cool on a wire tray. Serve fresh with butter.

64 Strawberry shortcakes

You will need . . .

225g/8 oz self-raising flour
½ teaspoon salt
75g/3 oz butter
25g/1 oz castor sugar
1 egg
4 tablespoons milk
milk to glaze
For the filling:
150ml/¼ pint double cream
1 rounded tablespoon icing sugar, sieved
225g/8 oz strawberries, hulled

Preparation time
15-20 minutes

Cooking time
10-12 minutes

Oven setting
220°C; 425°F; Gas Mark 7

Sift together flour and salt and rub in butter. Beat the egg with the milk. Add sugar and mix to a soft, but not sticky, dough with egg and milk.

Turn out on to a lightly floured table, knead quickly until smooth, then roll out to 1-cm/½-inch thickness. Cut into 6 rounds with an 8-cm/3½-inch plain cutter. Place on a greased baking tray and brush tops with milk. Bake in a hot oven for 10-12 minutes. Cool on a wire tray but, whilst still warm, split each shortcake in half by pulling carefully apart and not cutting with a knife.

To serve, slice strawberries keeping 6 whole for decoration. Whip the cream and sweeten with icing sugar. Sandwich shortcakes together with cream and sliced strawberries. Dust tops with icing sugar and decorate serving plate with whole strawberries.

QUICK TIP

When cooking with yeast, store fresh yeast in a loosely tied polythene bag. It will keep for 4-5 days in a cold place, up to 1 month in a refrigerator and up to 1 year in a deep freeze.

QUICK TIP

When strawberries are not available, make an apple cinnamon shortcake. Sift ½ teaspoon of powdered cinnamon with the flour and fill with stewed apple and sultanas, flavoured with cinnamon.

65 Doughnuts

You will need ...

	175g/6 oz plain flour
	½ teaspoon salt
	1 egg, beaten
	15g/½ oz butter, melted
	For the yeast liquid:
Preparation time	2 level teaspoons dried yeast
15-20 minutes	150ml/¼ pint warm milk less 3
	tablespoons
Cooking time	½ teaspoon castor sugar
4 minutes	50g/2 oz plain flour
	For the filling:
Fat temperature	3 tablespoons raspberry jam
177°C; 350°F	*For the coating:*
	50g/2 oz castor sugar
	½ teaspoon cinnamon

Blend yeast with warm milk (43°C/110°F), sugar and 50g/2 oz flour. Leave until frothy, about 20-30 minutes. Mix salt and remaining flour together. Add to yeast mixture with beaten egg and melted butter, mix well.

Knead dough well on a lightly floured table and divide into 8 equal pieces. Roll into rounds (*see method, recipe 54*), cover with a greased polythene sheet and leave to rise for about 30 minutes at room temperature. Remove polythene. Make a hole in the middle of each round with handle of a wooden spoon. Fill with ½ teaspoon of jam and pinch into shape.

Deep fry in hot fat, 177°C/350°F, for 4 minutes. Drain on crumpled absorbent paper and roll in mixed sugar and cinnamon.

QUICK TIP

Risen dough should double in size and spring back when lightly pressed with a floured finger. The time will vary according to the temperature; cold merely retards the growth of yeast and only extreme heat destroys it.

66 Lardy cake

You will need ...

	450g/1 lb plain flour
	2 level teaspoons salt
	115g/4½ oz lard
	For the yeast liquid:
	1 teaspoon sugar
Preparation time	300ml/½ pint warm water (43°C/110°F)
30 minutes	2 level teaspoons dried yeast
	For the glaze:
Cooking time	oil
30 minutes	50g/2 oz castor sugar

Oven setting
220°C; 425°F; Gas Mark 7

Prepare the yeast liquid and rub 15g/½ oz of the lard into the flour and make the dough (*see method, recipe 57*). Place in lightly greased large polythene bag, loosely tied and leave to rise until double in size.

Turn dough on to lightly floured table and roll into a rectangle approximately 37 × 15 cm/15 × 6 inches and 5-mm/¼-inch thick. Dot one-third of lard over top two-thirds of dough. Fold uncovered one-third upwards and top one-third over it. Seal edges, turn dough so folded edge is on the left and repeat rolling twice more. Roll dough out to fit a 20 × 25 cm/8 × 10 inch shallow baking tin, press down to fill corners. Place in a greased polythene bag and leave to rise until double in size. Remove bag. Brush with oil and sprinkle with sugar. Criss-cross top by lightly scoring with a very sharp kife. Bake on middle shelf of a hot oven for about 30 minutes. Turn out and cool on a wire tray.

Serve hot with jam as a pudding, or cold as cake for tea.

QUICK TIP

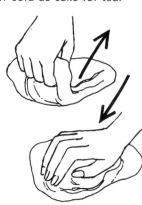

Knead dough thoroughly to get a good rise. Fold dough towards you; push down and away with palm of hand. Give dough a quarter turn, repeat developing a rocking rhythm for about 10 minutes until dough is firm and elastic.

67 Malt loaf

68 Savarin

You will need . . .

450g/1 lb plain flour
1 level teaspoon salt
3 tablespoons malt extract
2 tablespoons black treacle
25g/1 oz margarine

Preparation time
20 minutes

For the yeast liquid:
1 teaspoon sugar
150ml/¼ pint *plus* 3 tablespoons warm water
1 level tablespoon dried yeast
honey for glazing

Cooking time
40-45 minutes

Oven setting
200°C; 400°F; Gas Mark 6

Prepare the yeast liquid (*see method, recipe 57*). Sift flour and salt together. Warm together malt extract, black treacle and margarine. Cool. Add with yeast liquid to flour and work to a soft dough. Add a little extra flour if too soft. Turn on to a floured table and knead well until smooth and elastic.

Divide dough in half, flatten each piece and roll up as for a Swiss roll to fit two greased 450-g/1-lb loaf tins. Put to rise in large lightly greased polythene bags until dough rises to top of tins and springs back when lightly pressed.

Remove bags and bake in a hot oven for 40-45 minutes. Turn out and brush top of hot loaves with a wet brush dipped in honey; cool on a wire tray.

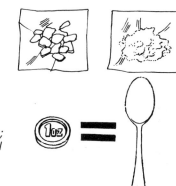

QUICK TIP

If fresh yeast is used instead of dried, double the quantity i.e. 15g/½ oz fresh yeast or 2 level teaspoons dried yeast; 25g/1 oz fresh yeast or 1 level tablespoon dried yeast.

You will need . . .

½ teaspoon salt
175g/6 oz plain flour
15g/½ oz sugar
4 eggs, beaten
100g/4 oz butter, soft not melted

Preparation time
10 minutes

For the yeast liquid:
1 tablespoon dried yeast
6 tablespoons warm milk (43°C/110°F)
15g/½ oz sugar
50g/2 oz plain flour

Cooking time
20 minutes

For the filling:
grapes and dessert apple

Oven setting
200°C; 400°F; Gas Mark 6

For the syrup:
6 tablespoons honey
6 tablespoons water
rum to taste

Blend yeast with warm milk, 50g/2 oz flour and sugar. Leave until frothy, about 20-30 minutes. Mix ½ teaspoon salt with remaining flour, sift well. Add flour and all remaining ingredients to yeast batter; beat well for 4 minutes.

Half fill a greased and floured 20-cm/8-inch fluted ring mould and cover with a greased polythene bag. Leave to rise until mould is two-thirds full. Bake in a hot oven for about 20 minutes. Turn on to a warm serving plate, and prick with a skewer.

Prepare syrup by warming honey and water together, add rum. Pour over two-thirds of the honey rum syrup whilst savarin is still warm and leave to soak. Pour remainder of the syrup over the grapes and apple, which has been sliced, and leave to soak. Fill centre of savarin and decorate serving dish with the fruit.

QUICK TIP

To make rum babas use the savarin recipe and add 100g/4 oz currants. Half fill greased dariole moulds and bake in a hot oven for 15-20 minutes. To serve, soak in syrup and sprinkle with rum.

69 Brioche

Orange
70 and cinnamon swirl

You will need . . .

225g/8 oz plain flour
½ teaspoon salt
15g/½ oz sugar
2 eggs
50g/2 oz butter
beaten egg for glazing
For the yeast liquid:
2 level teaspoons dried yeast
½ teaspoon sugar
1½ tablespoons warm water (43°C/110°F)

Preparation time
20-25 minutes

Cooking time
10 minutes

Oven setting
230°C; 450°F; Gas Mark 8

Prepare the yeast liquid (*see method, recipe 57*). Melt the butter and allow to cool; beat eggs. Add yeast liquid, eggs and butter to flour, salt and sugar. Work to a soft dough. Turn out on to a lightly floured table and knead well for 5 minutes. Place dough in lightly greased polythene bag and allow to rise in a cool place for 2-3 hours or in a refrigerator for up to 12 hours. A cool rising makes the dough easier to shape.

Grease 12 7.5-cm/3-inch brioche or deep bun tins. Turn out risen dough on to a lightly floured table and divide into quarters and each quarter into three. With each piece use ¾ to form a ball, place in tin and firmly press a hole in centre. Form remaining quarter into a knob and place in centre. Place tins on a baking sheet inside a greased polythene bag and rise in a warm place, about 1 hour, until light and puffy. Remove polythene bag.

Brush risen brioches with beaten egg or milk and water. Bake in a very hot oven for about 10 minutes. Serve warm.

You will need . . .

450g/1 lb plain flour
2 level teaspoons salt
2 tablespoons sugar
2 eggs, beaten
juice and grated rind of 1 orange
For the yeast liquid:
1 level teaspoon sugar
150ml/¼ pint warm water (43°C/110°F)
2 level teaspoons dried yeast
For the filling:
1 tablespoon powdered cinnamon
50g/2 oz soft brown sugar
4 tablespoons apricot jam

Preparation time
25 minutes

Cooking time
30-35 minutes

Oven setting
200°C; 400°F; Gas Mark 6

Prepare the yeast liquid by dissolving the sugar in the water, sprinkle the yeast on top and leave until frothy, about 10 minutes. Mix together flour, salt, sugar, egg, orange rind and add juice with yeast liquid. Work to a firm dough, adding 2-3 tablespoons extra water if required. Turn out and knead well on a floured table for about 10 minutes. Put to rise in a lightly greased polythene bag, loosely tied, until double in size.

Turn out and knead dough until firm. Roll into two 15 × 33cm/6 × 13-inch rectangles. Spread each rectangle with apricot jam and sprinkle on cinnamon and sugar. Roll up as for a Swiss roll and place in two greased 450-g/1-lb loaf tins. Put inside a greased polythene bag and rise again for about 30 minutes. Remove bag and bake in a moderately hot oven for 30-35 minutes. Turn out and cool on a wire tray.

Serve sliced with butter and apricot jam.

ICK TIP

or something different, scoop out centres of brioches, and fill with fir   chopped fruit
m, fruit
e mixture.

QUICK TIP

Do not use too much flour on the table for kneading and shaping. It spoils the colour and texture of the crust.

71 Devonshire scones

You will need . . .

450g/1 lb self-raising flour
1 teaspoon salt
100g/4 oz butter
50g/2 oz castor sugar
300ml/½ pint milk
beaten egg to glaze
For the filling:
strawberry or raspberry jam
150ml/¼ pint double cream, whipped

Preparation time
10-15 minutes

Cooking time
8-10 minutes

Oven setting
230°C; 450°F; Gas Mark 8

Sift flour and salt into a bowl. Rub in butter until mixture resembles fine breadcrumbs. Add castor sugar and mix to a soft dough with the milk.

Turn on to a lightly floured table, knead quickly, then roll out to 1-cm/½-inch thickness. Cut into 20 rounds with a 6-cm/2½-inch cutter. Place scones on greased baking trays and brush tops with beaten egg or milk. Bake in a very hot oven for 8-10 minutes. Cool on a wire tray.

When cold, split and serve with jam and whipped cream.

QUICK TIP

To save time and effort make up 1.5kg/3 lb of rubbed in scone mixture using 1.5kg/3 lb flour and 350g/12 oz butter. Store in polythene bags for up to 3 months in a refrigerator. To use, simply weigh out required quantity.

72 Honey loaf

You will need . . .

350g/12 oz self-raising flour
1 level teaspoon salt
3 level teaspoons mixed spice
50g/2 oz candied peel
100g/4 oz soft brown sugar
175g/6 oz clear honey
150ml/¼ pint milk
For the topping:
25g/1 oz lump sugar

Preparation time
10 minutes

Cooking time
1 hour 15 minutes

Oven setting
180°C; 350°F; Gas Mark 4

Line and grease a 1-kg/2-lb loaf tin. Chop the peel finely. Sift together flour, salt and spice, mix in peel and brown sugar. Add honey and milk, and blend together until a smooth, stiff dough is formed.

Place in loaf tin. Lightly crush the lump sugar and sprinkle over the top of the loaf. Bake for about 1¼ hours in a moderate oven.

Turn out and cool on a wire tray. A little more sugar can be sprinkled on top of the loaf if liked; serve sliced and spread with butter.

QUICK TIP

When cooking with yeast, store dried yeast in a tightly lidded tin in a cool place. It will keep for up to 6 months. Dried yeast can be bought from supermarkets, delicatessens or good grocers.

Favourite family cakes

74 Chocolate brownies

The recipes in this chapter are certain to prove a boon to any housewife wanting to provide attractive and filling cakes for a hungry family or who likes to give a homely touch to Christmas, with a home-baked Christmas cake, or to Easter with a traditional Easter cake.

It is surprising how little time it takes to prepare such satisfying favourites as flapjacks, Swiss roll or the delicate looking Viennese biscuits. And even the larger cakes and pastries need not be abandoned as too complicated in a busy household. It is precisely in busy families that a sustaining piece of cake at tea time will be particularly welcome!

73 Dundee cake

(illustrated on front cover)

You will need . . .

Preparation time
20 minutes

Cooking time
1½-2 hours

Oven setting
180°C; 350°F; Gas Mark 4
160°C; 325°F; Gas Mark 3

175g/6 oz currants
100g/4 oz dates, chopped
175g/6 oz seeded raisins, chopped
25g/1 oz glacé cherries, quartered
50g/2 oz mixed peel, chopped
225g/8 oz plain flour
1 level teaspoon baking powder
175g/6 oz butter
100g/4 oz castor sugar
1 tablespoon clear honey
3 large eggs
3 tablespoons milk
rind of 1 lemon, finely grated
25g/1 oz almonds, blanched and split

Grease and line an 18-cm/7-inch round cake tin with greased greaseproof paper. Clean fruit. Sift together flour and baking powder.

Cream fat, sugar and honey until pale and creamy. Add eggs one at a time, beating well after each addition. Lightly fold in the flour, milk, prepared fruit and lemon rind. Turn the mixture into the tin and arrange a ring of almonds around the edge.

Bake in a moderate oven for half-an-hour, then in a very moderate oven for a further 1 to 1½ hours, covering the top of the cake with greaseproof paper if necessary, to prevent it going too brown. Cool in tin for 10 minutes before turning out on to a wire tray.

You will need . . .

Preparation time
15 minutes

Cooking time
35 minutes

Oven setting
190°C; 375°F; Gas Mark 5

100g/4 oz self-raising flour
¼ level teaspoon salt
40g/1½ oz cocoa
100g/4 oz butter
100g/4 oz soft brown sugar
2 eggs, blended
1 tablespoon milk
For the icing:
40g/1½ oz butter
25g/1 oz cocoa, sieved
3 tablespoons evaporated milk
100g/4 oz icing sugar, sieved

Grease an oblong tin about 33 × 18cm/11 × 7 inches, 2.5-cm/1-inch deep. Sieve together flour, salt and cocoa. In another bowl beat butter and sugar until light and creamy. Add eggs a little at a time, beating well after each addition. Fold sieved ingredients into mixture with milk. Mix well. Turn into prepared tin.

Bake in a moderately hot oven for about 35 minutes until centre of sponge springs back when lightly pressed. Allow to cool in tin.

Melt butter for icing. Add cocoa. Cook over low heat for 1 minute. Remove from heat and add evaporated milk and icing sugar. Mix in thoroughly. Spread over cake in tin and leave to set, then cut cake into 15 squares.

QUICK TIP

If the blanched almonds break when you try to split them, leave soaking in hot water for half an hour or so to allow them to soften first.

QUICK TIP

Cocoa gives a strong chocolate flavour. It is essential to cook it for all recipes and to add sweetening. Chocolate powder is already sweetened and does not require cooking in recipes; the resulting flavour is less chocolatey.

75 Strawberry cream tarts

76 Flapjacks

You will need . . .

100g/4 oz plain flour
¼ level teaspoon salt
65g/2½ oz butter
15g/½ oz castor sugar
For the filling:
150ml/¼ pint double cream
225g/8 oz fresh strawberries
3 level tablespoons redcurrant jelly

Preparation time
15 minutes

Cooking time
15 minutes

Oven setting
190°C; 375°F; Gas Mark 5

Make rich short crust pastry (see recipe 80; add the sugar to the rubbed-in butter and flour). Roll it out on a lightly floured table. Cut nine circles with a 5-cm/2-inch fluted cutter. Use to line patty tins. Prick and then chill for 15 minutes. Line each with greaseproof paper and baking beans, or foil. Bake the cases in a moderately hot oven for about 15 minutes. Remove paper and beans, or foil, for last 5 minutes. Cool on a wire tray.

Whip cream until it forms soft peaks and divide it between the pastry cases. Arrange strawberries on top.

Melt the redcurrant jelly over a low heat in a small pan. Heat gently, stirring occasionally, until smooth. Spoon glaze over tartlets.

You will need . . .

100g/4 oz margarine
4 level tablespoons golden syrup
75g/3 oz granulated sugar
225g/8 oz rolled oats
¼ level teaspoon salt

Preparation time
15 minutes

Cooking time
30 minutes

Oven setting
160°C; 325°F; Gas Mark 3

Grease a square, shallow tin, about 19-cm/7½-inches. Put margarine and syrup in a pan and leave over a low heat until margarine has melted. Remove from heat and add sugar, oats and salt. Mix thoroughly.

Turn mixture into prepared tin and cook in a very moderate oven for 30 to 40 minutes until golden brown.

Leave to cool in tin for 5 minutes then cut into 12 bars (*see Quick Tip below*). Place on a wire tray to finish cooling.

QUICK TIP

Chilling pastry before baking helps to prevent the pastry shrinking in the oven. Too much water in the pastry also causes shrinkage.

QUICK TIP

Cut up the flapjacks in the tin whilst they are still warm. If they are allowed to get completely cold, they will be too crisp and will just break into small pieces.

77 Almond macaroons

78 New Zealand biscuits

You will need . . .
2 large egg whites
100g/4 oz ground almonds
175g/6 oz castor sugar
25g/1 oz ground rice
few drops almond essence
8 almonds, blanched

Preparation time
15 minutes

Cooking time
25-30 minutes

Oven setting
150°C; 300°F; Gas Mark 2

Line two large baking trays with rice paper or, if this is not available with non-stick household parchment or greaseproof paper. Put 1 teaspoon egg white into a small bowl and put on one side for glazing.

Whisk remaining egg white until it forms soft peaks. Fold in ground almonds, sugar, ground rice and almond essence. Mix well. Put 16 heaped teaspoons of the mixture on to rice paper and smooth them slightly with the back of a spoon. Put half a blanched almond in the centre of each macaroon. Brush the tops with egg white.

Bake for 25-30 minutes in a cool oven until the macaroons are pale golden. Allow to cool slightly before removing from the baking tray. Tear away excess rice paper from around the edge of the macaroons. If using non-stick household parchment peel it carefully away. When they are quite cold, store in an airtight tin.

You will need . . .
50g/2 oz golden syrup
150g/5 oz butter
100g/4 oz castor sugar
75g/3 oz rolled oats
50g/2 oz desiccated coconut
100g/4 oz plain flour
2 level teaspoons bicarbonate of soda

Preparation time
15 minutes

Cooking time
20 minutes

Oven setting
160°C; 325°F; Gas Mark 3

Grease 2 baking trays. Put the syrup, butter and castor sugar into a pan and leave to melt over a low heat. Remove the pan from the heat and stir in the dry ingredients. Dissolve the bicarbonate of soda in a bowl in 1 tablespoon hot water. Add to the other ingredients and leave to cool for a few minutes.

Divide into 30 portions, roll into balls and place on the baking trays, leaving plenty of room between each.

Bake for about 20 minutes or until the biscuits have browned evenly. Remove from the oven and leave on the baking trays for a few minutes to harden. Cool on a wire tray.

QUICK TIP

When a trifle calls for ratafias to mix with the sponge used crushed almond macaroons instead. They taste the same and are quicker to make.

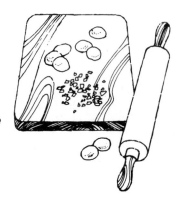

QUICK TIP

These biscuits are fun for children to make. They love rolling the balls of mixture before baking. If mum does the weighing out first they are easy to finish, so let these biscuits be your child's first step in cookery.

79 Cherry cake

You will need . . .
225g/8 oz glacé cherries
75g/3 oz self-raising flour
75g/3 oz plain flour
pinch salt
175g/6 oz butter

Preparation time 175g/6 oz castor sugar
15 minutes finely grated rind of 1 lemon
3 eggs, beaten
Cooking time 75g/3 oz ground almonds
1 hour 20 minutes little milk if necessary

Oven setting
180°C; 350°F; Gas Mark 4

Grease an 18-cm/7-inch cake tin and line with greased grease-proof paper. Rinse cherries (*see Quick Tip below*). Cut each cherry in half. Sieve the flours and salt together twice then toss the cherries in a little of the flour. Cream butter, sugar and lemon rind together until the mixture is pale and creamy. Add beaten egg a little at a time, beating well after each addition and keeping mixture stiff. Add a tablespoon of flour with last amount of egg. Fold in flour, cherries and ground almonds adding a little milk to make a fairly stiff dropping consistency; the stiff consistency will help cherries to remain suspended evenly in cake while it is baking.

Turn mixture into prepared tin and bake in a moderate oven for about 1 hour 20 minutes, or until a skewer inserted in centre of cake comes out clean.

Leave cake to cool in tin for 5 minutes then turn it out on to a wire tray to finish cooling; remove paper. When cold, wrap in foil or store in an airtight tin.

QUICK TIP

To remove the syrup from glacé cherries before using, put into a sieve and rinse under running water. Drain well and dry very thoroughly on absorbent kitchen paper.

80 Bakewell tart

You will need . . .
175g/6 oz plain flour
¼ level teaspoon salt
40g/1½ oz butter
40g/1½ oz lard
For the filling:
Preparation time 100g/4 oz butter
20 minutes 100g/4 oz castor sugar
1 egg
Cooking time 25g/1 oz ground almonds
30 minutes 75g/3 oz ground rice
½ teaspoon almond essence
Oven setting 1 heaped tablespoon raspberry *or*
200°C; 400°F; Gas Mark 6 strawberry jam

Sieve flour and salt into a bowl. Cut fats in small pieces and rub into the flour until mixture resembles fine breadcrumbs. Mix to a firm dough with water. Roll pastry out thinly on a lightly floured table. Use to line a 20-cm/8-inch plain flan ring, placed on a baking sheet; reserve trimmings. Prick the base. Cool for 10 minutes.

Heat butter for filling until it has just melted, but is not brown. Stir in sugar and cook for 1 minute, then add egg, ground almonds, rice and essence. Spread jam in base of flan case and pour filling on top. Roll strips from pastry trimmings and arrange in a lattice pattern on top of the tart, fixing with milk.

Bake tart for about 30 minutes in a hot oven until well risen and golden brown. The filling should spring back into shape when lightly pressed with a finger. Remove flan ring. Cool on a wire rack.

QUICK TIP

When using butter for pastry, make sure it is hard by keeping it in the refrigerator until just before use. Cut up fats with two knives, using a scissor action before rubbing in.

81 Rock cakes

82 Easter cake

You will need . . .

225g/8 oz plain flour
½ level teaspoon salt
2 level teaspoons baking powder
65g/2½ oz butter
65g/2½ oz sugar

Preparation time
15 minutes

100g/4 oz dried fruit
¼ teaspoon ground nutmeg
1 egg
2 tablespoons milk

Cooking time
15-20 minutes

Oven setting
200°C; 400°F; Gas Mark 6

Sieve flour, salt and baking powder together. Rub fat into the flour until the mixture resembles fine breadcrumbs. Stir in sugar, fruit and nutmeg.

Beat egg with milk and add to flour mixture. Mix well with a fork; the mixture should be stiff but not too sticky and should leave the sides of the mixing bowl clean.

Divide the mixture into 12 and place on a greased tray; rough up with a fork. Bake in a moderately hot oven for 15 to 20 minutes. Cool on a wire tray.

You will need . . .

350g/12 oz plain flour
½ level teaspoon salt
¾ level teaspoon *each* mixed spice and ground cinnamon
250g/9 oz butter

Preparation time
30 minutes

250g/9 oz soft brown sugar
5 large eggs, lightly beaten
rind of 1 lemon, grated
175g/6 oz stoned raisins

Cooking time
2 hours 45 minutes

100g/4 oz each sultanas and currants
75g/3 oz each glacé cherries and candied peel

Oven setting
180°C; 350°F; Gas Mark 4
160°C; 325°F; Gas Mark 3

50g/2 oz almonds, blanched and chopped
about 4 tablespoons milk
2 level tablespoons apricot jam, sieved
275g/10 oz almond paste

Grease and line a 23-cm/9-inch cake tin. Sieve flour, salt, spice and cinnamon. Halve cherries and chop peel. Cream butter and sugar until pale and creamy, add lemon rind. Gradually beat in eggs. Add 3 tablespoons of flour towards end to prevent mixture curdling. Fold in remaining flour, fruit and enough milk to make a soft dropping consistency. Spoon half mixture into tin and spread evenly.

Make almond paste in usual way (*see Quick Tip below*). Roll one half of paste to a 23-cm/9-inch circle. Place on top of mixture in tin. Wrap remainder of paste in foil. Spoon in remaining mixture and hollow out centre slightly. Bake in a moderate oven for 30 minutes then in a very moderate oven for 2¼ hours. Cool in tin for 15 minutes. Turn out on to a wire tray. Remove paper.

Brush centre and edge of cake with apricot jam. Roll remaining almond paste into strips and plait; place round edge of cake and in the centre. Decorate with coloured eggs.

QUICK TIP

Rock cakes are not rich and are therefore best eaten on the day of baking. For a crunchy topping, sprinkle with demerara sugar before baking.

QUICK TIP

To make almond paste combine 275g/10 oz ground almonds with 275g/10 oz castor sugar, then mix to a stiff paste with juice of half a lemon and one large egg.

83 Madeira cake

You will need . . .

225g/8 oz self-raising flour
¼ level teaspoon salt
100g/4 oz butter
150g/5 oz castor sugar
2 eggs
few drops vanilla essence
about 3 tablespoons milk
For the top:
3 slices citron peel

Preparation time
15 minutes

Cooking time
1 hour

Oven setting
180°C; 350°F; Gas Mark 4

Sift together the flour and salt and set aside. Cream the butter and sugar until soft and light. Gradually beat in the blended eggs and essence, adding a little flour with the last few additions. Using a metal spoon, fold in the remaining flour and enough milk to mix to a soft consistency.

Spoon the mixture into a greased and lined 15-cm/6-inch round deep cake tin. Place in the centre of a moderate oven and bake for 1 hour. After 50 minutes place the slices of peel on the top of the cake (*see Quick Tip below*). Return to oven for the remaining 10 minutes. When baked, the cake should feel firm to the touch and a warmed skewer pushed into the centre should come out cleanly.

Allow the baked cake to cool for 5 minutes in the tin before cooling on a wire tray.

QUICK TIP

After 50 minutes place peel on the cake gently, where the crack appears. The peel is not put on the raw mixture as, being heavy, it would just sink into the cake.

84 Coffee ginger cake

You will need . . .

4 eggs
75g/3 oz castor sugar
75g/3 oz plain flour, sieved
For the buttercream filling:
350g/12 oz icing sugar, sieved
1 tablespoon coffee essence
2 tablespoons rum
175g/6 oz butter
50g/2 oz crystallised ginger, chopped
For the icing:
175g/6 oz icing sugar, sieved
1 tablespoon coffee essence
50g/2 oz almonds

Preparation time
35 minutes

Cooking time
20-25 minutes

Oven setting
190°C; 375°F; Gas Mark 5

Grease two 19-cm/7½-inch straight-sided sandwich tins and line bases with circles of greased greaseproof paper. Put eggs and sugar in a bowl placed over a pan of hot water. Whisk until mixture is pale and mousse-like. Remove from heat and carefully fold in flour. Divide mixture between tins and bake for 20 to 25 minutes in a moderately hot oven until centre of each sponge springs back when lightly pressed. Turn out and cool on a wire tray. Cut each cake in two.

Blend together icing sugar, coffee essence and rum. Cream butter until it is soft, then gradually add icing sugar mixture, beating well. Mix chopped ginger with three-quarters of filling and use to layer cakes together. Thinly spread the sides.

Make a fairly thick glacé icing with icing sugar, coffee essence and a little water. Use to cover top of cake. Blanch, chop and lightly toast almonds and press against sides of cake. Use remaining filling to pipe rosettes round top edge of cake.

QUICK TIP

To prevent crystallised ginger or other glace fruits sticking to the knife when chopping or slicing, use a wet knife remembering to shake off any excess water.

85 Meringues

You will need . . .

4 egg whites
225g/8 oz castor sugar
little extra castor sugar
For the filling:
150ml/¼ pint double cream
1 tablespoon drinking chocolate

Preparation time
15 minutes

Cooking time
1½-2 hours

Oven setting
110°C; 225°F; Gas Mark ¼

Oil 3 large baking trays thoroughly, or line with non-stick household parchment.

Put the egg whites into a china or ovenglass mixing bowl. Whisk with a rotary whisk until they are very stiff. Continue to whisk, adding the sugar a teaspoon at a time, and whisking well after each addition until all the sugar has been added. Using two wet dessertspoons, spoon the meringue on to the prepared baking trays, or pipe in rosettes using a large star tube.

Sprinkle with castor sugar and dry off in a very cool oven for 1½ to 2 hours or until they are crisp. Remove from the oven and cool on a wire tray. Whip the cream and add the chocolate. Sandwich two meringues together with filling. Store unused meringues in an airtight tin until they are required.

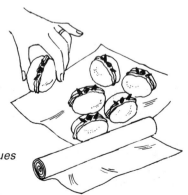

QUICK TIP

Silicone paper is specially treated to make it non-stick for sugar confections such as meringues and brandy snaps.

86 Glacé pineapple ring

You will need . . .

225g/8 oz self-raising flour
175g/6 oz butter
175g/6 oz castor sugar
3 eggs, beaten
3 tablespoons milk
65g/2½ oz glacé cherries, quartered
25g/1 oz glacé pineapple, chopped
For the topping:
40g/1½ oz icing sugar, sieved
glacé pineapple, quartered
glacé cherries

Preparation time
20 minutes

Cooking time
55-60 minutes

Oven setting
180°C; 350°F; Gas Mark 4

Well grease and line a savarin mould. Sieve flour into a bowl. In another bowl cream together butter and sugar until pale and creamy. Beat in egg a little at a time, beating well after each addition. Add a tablespoon of flour with last amount of egg. Fold rest of flour into mixture, then add milk, cherries and pineapple.

Turn mixture into prepared tin and bake in a moderate oven for 55 to 60 minutes. Turn ring out and cool on a wire tray.

Mix icing sugar with enough warm water to make a thin glacé icing. Spread a layer on top of ring, and arrange the pineapple and cherries. Then trickle remaining icing over fruit letting some run down the sides. Leave icing to set before putting into a cake tin.

QUICK TIP

If glacé pineapple is not available use chopped almonds, raisins and cherries in the mixture. Decorate with chopped almonds.

87 Victoria sandwich

You will need . . .
100g/4 oz butter
100g/4 oz castor sugar
2 large eggs, lightly beaten
100g/4 oz self-raising flour, sieved
For the filling and top:

Preparation time
10 minutes
2 tablespoons strawberry jam
2-3 level teaspoons castor sugar

Cooking time
20 minutes

Oven setting
180°C; 350°F; Gas Mark 4

Well grease two 15- or 18-cm/6 or 7-inch sandwich tins. Cream butter and sugar until pale and creamy, then beat in the eggs. Add a tablespoon of flour with the last amount of egg to prevent curdling. Fold in the rest of the flour with a metal spoon, then divide the mixture equally between the two tins.

Bake in a moderate oven for about 20 minutes. When the cake is cooked the colour should be pale golden and the mixture shrinking away from the edges of the tins and, when lightly pressed with a finger, should spring back into shape. Turn out to cool on a wire tray.

When completely cold, sandwich together with jam and dust with castor sugar.

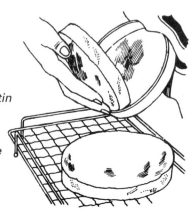

QUICK TIP

Leave the cake to cool in the tin for about 5 minutes before turning out to allow it to shrink and therefore be easier to remove from the tin.

88 Treacle tart

You will need . . .
100g/4 oz plain flour
pinch salt
25g/1 oz lard
25g/1 oz butter
For the filling:

Preparation time
15 minutes
225g/8 oz golden syrup
50g/2 oz fresh white breadcrumbs
grated rind of 2 lemons
2 teaspoons lemon juice

Cooking time
25 minutes

Oven setting
200°C; 400°F; Gas Mark 6

Sieve flour and salt into a bowl. Add fats cut into small pieces and rub them into flour until mixture resembles fine breadcrumbs. Add water and mix to a firm dough. Roll out pastry thinly on a floured table and use to line an 18-cm/7-inch ovenglass flan dish. Re-roll pastry trimmings and cut in circles with a 2-cm/¾-inch fluted cutter. Brush underside of each with water and arrange, overlapping, round edge of dish.

Mix together syrup, breadcrumbs, lemon rind and juice. Spoon filling into flan.

Bake in a moderately hot oven for about 25 minutes, until the pastry is pale golden.

QUICK TIP

When using an ovenglass dish, to make sure the underneath of a tart or double pastry pie is brown, place on a metal baking sheet that has been heated in the oven whilst baking.

89 Swiss roll

90 Orange almond cake

You will need . . .

3 large eggs
75g/3 oz castor sugar, warmed
75g/3 oz self-raising flour, sieved
For the filling and top:
4 level tablespoons raspberry jam
castor sugar

Preparation time
15 minutes

Cooking time
7-10 minutes

Oven setting
220°C; 425°F; Gas Mark 7

Grease and line a shallow Swiss roll tin 23 × 30cm/9 × 12 inches. Take eggs at room temperature and whisk with sugar until mixture is light and creamy and leaves a trail when the whisk is lifted out of the mixture. Fold in flour, using a metal spoon.

Turn into prepared tin and smooth level with a palette knife. Bake in a hot oven for 7 to 10 minutes until sponge begins to shrink from edges of the tin and is pale golden.

Turn out on to a sheet of greaseproof paper dredged with castor sugar. Trim edges of sponge, spread with warmed jam and roll up tightly. Dredge with castor sugar and cool on a wire tray.

You will need . . .

100g/4 oz butter
100g/4 oz castor sugar
grated rind of 1 orange
2 eggs, beaten
100g/4 oz self-raising flour, sieved
about 1 tablespoon milk
For the icing:
150g/5 oz butter
275g/10 oz icing sugar, sieved
1 tablespoon orange juice
75g/3 oz almonds

Preparation time
25 minutes

Cooking time
15-20 minutes

Oven setting
180°C; 350°F; Gas Mark 4

Grease two 18-cm/7-inch sandwich tins and line bases with a circle of greased greaseproof paper. Beat the butter, sugar and orange rind until the mixture is pale and creamy. Beat in the egg a little at a time, add a tablespoon of the flour with last amount of egg to prevent curdling. Fold in the rest of the flour and enough milk to make the mixture a soft dropping consistency. Divide between the tins and bake in a moderate oven for 15 to 20 minutes, or until the cakes spring back when lightly pressed with a finger. Turn out and cool on a wire tray.

Blanch, shred and lightly toast almonds (*see Quick Tip below*). Cream butter for buttercream icing until it is soft. Beat in icing sugar and orange juice. Sandwich cakes together with about one third of the icing.

Spread remaining icing over top and sides of the cake. Scatter almonds over top and base of sides.

QUICK TIP

For a smaller Swiss roll baked in an 18 × 33cm/ 7 × 11 inch tin use: 2 large eggs, 50g/2 oz castor sugar, 50g/2 oz self-raising flour. Heat the jam just until it is easy to spread; if it is too hot it will soak into the sponge.

QUICK TIP

Toasting almonds: take care not to do this too quickly, otherwise the edges over brown and taste bitter. Gently brown under a medium grill, turning frequently.

91 Family fruit cake

You will need . . .

150g/5 oz plain flour
150g/5 oz self-raising flour
225g/8 oz butter
225g/8 oz soft brown sugar
grated rind of 1 orange
5 eggs
450g/1 lb mixed fruit
100g/4 oz peel, finely chopped
100g/4 oz glacé cherries, quartered
1 tablespoon black treacle

Preparation time
15 minutes

Cooking time
2 hours 30 minutes

Oven setting
150°C; 300°F; Gas Mark 2

Grease and line a 20-cm/8-inch square or 23-cm/9-inch round cake tin with greased greaseproof paper. Sieve the flours together.

Cream together the butter, sugar and orange rind until the mixture is pale and creamy. Add the eggs a little at a time, beating well after each addition. Fold in the flour alternately with the dried fruit, peel and cherries. Finally, blend in the treacle. Turn the mixture into the prepared tin and bake in a very moderate oven for 2½ hours or until a skewer inserted in the centre comes out clean.

Remove the cake from the oven and leave to cool in the tin for 10 minutes. Turn it out on to a wire tray to finish cooling; remove paper.

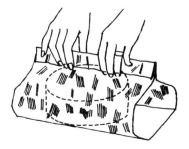

QUICK TIP

This cake makes far better eating when it has been well cooled, then stored and matured for at least a week in a cake tin or wrapped in foil.

92 Orange shortbread

You will need . . .

100g/4 oz plain flour
50g/2 oz cornflour
100g/4 oz butter
50g/2 oz castor sugar
grated rind of 1 orange
castor sugar

Preparation time
25 minutes

Cooking time
35 minutes

Oven setting
160°C; 325°F; Gas Mark 3

Sieve flour and cornflour together. Cream butter until it is soft then add the 50g/2 oz castor sugar and beat until the mixture is pale and creamy. Add orange rind then work in flour mixture a tablespoon at a time.

Lift shortbread on to a large baking tray. Roll out to a 20-cm/8-inch circle. Pinch the edges and prick the shortbread well with a fork. Cut through into 12 sections with the back of a knife, then sprinkle with a little castor sugar.

Leave to chill in the refrigerator for 15 minutes, then bake in a very moderate oven for 35 minutes or until pale golden brown. Cool on the baking tray for a few minutes, then lift on to a wire tray to finish cooling.

QUICK TIP

If you like a coarser textured shortbread use 50g/2 oz rice flour or semolina instead of the cornflour. As a change, soft brown sugar makes a caramel coloured shortbread, and this goes well with the orange flavour.

93 Traditional Christmas cake

You will need . . .

250g/9 oz plain flour
¼ level teaspoon salt
1 level teaspoon mixed spice
350g/12 oz stoned raisins
350g/12 oz sultanas
350g/12 oz currants
50g/2 oz candied peel, chopped
75g/3 oz glacé cherries, quartered
50g/2 oz almonds, blanched and chopped
225g/8 oz butter
225g/8 oz soft brown sugar
4 eggs, lightly beaten
1½ level tablespoons black treacle
2 tablespoons brandy

Preparation time
30 minutes

Cooking time
4 hours

Oven setting
150°C; 300°F; Gas Mark 2
140°C; 275°F; Gas Mark 1

Line base and sides of a 20-cm/8-inch round cake tin with a double layer of greaseproof paper, then tie a double band of brown paper 2.5cm/1-inch wider than the depth of the tin, round the outside. Sieve flour, salt and spice into a large bowl. Cream butter and sugar until pale and creamy. Beat in a little egg at a time.

Stir in treacle, then flour, dried fruit, peel, cherries and almonds. Turn mixture into prepared tin and bake in a cool oven for 3 hours, then reduce oven to very cool and bake for 1-1½ hours, or until skewer inserted in centre comes out clean.

Leave cake to cool in tin for 10 minutes, then turn it out on to a wire tray; remove paper. When almost cold turn it upside down, pierce with a skewer and spoon brandy over. When completely cold wrap in greaseproof paper and foil, or store in an airtight tin.

QUICK TIP

Make the cake at least a month before Christmas; this gives it time to mature. Before almond pasting spoon a little more brandy over the top of the cake.

94 Viennese biscuits

You will need . . .

100g/4 oz butter, warmed
25g/1 oz icing sugar, sieved
150g/5 oz plain flour
For the buttercream:
50g/2 oz butter
100g/4 oz icing sugar, sieved
25g/1 oz cooking chocolate, melted

Preparation time
15 minutes

Cooking time
10-15 minutes

Oven setting
190°C; 375°F; Gas Mark 5

Cream butter with icing sugar until it is soft (*see Quick Tip below*). Stir in sieved flour and mix well. If the mixture seems stiff, a few drops of milk may be added. Put the mixture into a piping bag fitted with a large star tube and pipe on to a greased baking sheet in small circles, rosettes or fingers, making sure that there are an even number of each different shape.

Leave in the refrigerator, or cold place, for at least 15 minutes to chill. Bake in a moderately hot oven for 10 to 15 minutes or until they are just beginning to turn golden brown. Cool on a wire tray.

Cream together the butter and icing sugar for the filling. Add the chocolate and mix well. When the biscuits are cold, sandwich together in parts with the buttercream, and dust the tops with sieved icing sugar.

QUICK TIP

It is most important to cream the butter and sugar until really soft otherwise, when the flour is added, the mixture would be too stiff to pipe.

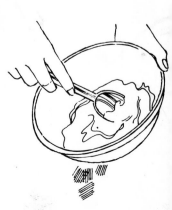

95 Chocolate button cake

96 Christmas cake icing

You will need . . .

150g/5 oz self-raising flour
25g/1 oz cocoa
75g/3 oz plain chocolate
175g/6 oz butter
175g/6 oz castor sugar

Preparation time
25 minutes

3 eggs, beaten
For the buttercream:
175g/6 oz butter
175g/6 oz icing sugar
50g/2 oz chocolate powder
25g/1 oz chocolate buttons

Cooking time
1 hour 15 minutes

Oven setting
180°C; 350°F; Gas Mark 4

Line base and sides of a 20-cm/8-inch cake tin with a double thickness of greaseproof paper and grease well. Sieve flour and cocoa into a bowl and put on one side. Put chocolate into a polythene bag, tie firmly and place in a bowl of hot water to melt chocolate. Beat butter and sugar until light and fluffy. Beat in egg a little at a time. Fold in flour and cocoa then stir in melted chocolate. Turn mixture into prepared tin and bake in a moderate oven for 1 hour 15 minutes, or until centre of cake springs back when pressed with a finger. Cake top will have a light crust.

Turn cake on to a wire tray to cool. Beat butter and icing sugar for buttercream until light and fluffy. Then beat in chocolate powder.

When cake is completely cold cut in three. Sandwich layers together again with two-thirds of buttercream. Spread top of cake with remaining buttercream swirling decoratively and decorate with chocolate buttons.

You will need . . .

For the almond paste:
350g/12 oz ground almonds
175g/6 oz castor sugar
175g/6 oz icing sugar, sieved
3 egg whites
few drops almond essence
3 tablespoons apricot jam, sieved
For the royal icing:
4 egg whites
1kg/2 lb icing sugar, sieved
4 teaspoons lemon juice
2 teaspoons glycerine

Preparation time
1 hour

Mix almonds and sugar in a bowl, then blend in egg whites and almond essence to make a soft paste. Knead until it is smooth, divide in three equal portions. Roll one piece on a sugared board to a 20-cm/8-inch circle. Roll remaining two-thirds to a strip the same depth as cake, and long enough to go all the way round edge. Brush sides of cake with apricot jam. Place long strip round sides and press firmly to join. Place circle of paste on top of cake. Allow to dry for at least 3 days before icing.

Whisk egg whites for royal icing until they become frothy. Add sugar, a tablespoon at a time, and beat well after each addition. Finally beat in lemon juice and glycerine. To prevent the icing hardening, cover bowl with a damp cloth.

Spread icing thickly over top and round sides of cake and draw it up in peaks with the handle of a teaspoon. Leave for a day to set then place decoration on top.

QUICK TIP

Buttercream keeps well for up to three weeks covered in the refrigerator. Make up a quantity at a time and add flavourings when you want to ice or fill a cake.

QUICK TIP

Using glycerine in the icing ensures that it is not hard. The lemon juice adds flavour and also helps to make a softer icing.

Fish and shellfish

There are few families in England, surrounded by sea, where fish is not served at least once a week. In this chapter, some excellent and original recipes are given for many kinds of fish and shellfish. Saltwater fish, such as cod, herring and plaice can be given a new, exciting appearance when prepared in the ways suggested here, and make a welcome change. Freshwater fish is represented by, among others, the tempting baked stuffed trout. Some of the many ways in which shellfish can be served, as hors d'oeuvre, in a salad or as a main course, will give you an opportunity to provide a variety of unusual and inexpensive dishes for many occasions.

98 Devilled lobster

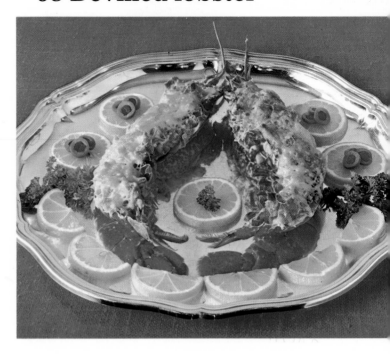

97 Prawn vol-au-vent

(illustrated on front cover)

You will need . . .
450g/1 lb frozen puff pastry
25g/1 oz butter
25g/1 oz plain flour
300ml/½ pint milk
salt and pepper

Preparation time
20 minutes

600ml/1 pint prawns, keep 4 in shells
1 large red pepper, cored, deseeded, diced and fried in 25g/1 oz butter for 2-3 minutes

Cooking time
35 minutes

1 small teaspoon anchovy essence
juice of ½ lemon

Oven setting
230°C; 450°F; Gas Mark 8

Roll pastry to oblong 20 × 40cm/8 × 16 inches, 1cm/½ inch thick. Cut out two 20-cm/8-inch ovals. Place one oval on baking tin, rinsed with cold water. Cut out 12.5-cm/5-inch oval from centre of 2nd oval. Dampen edges of oval on baking tin, put oval ring on top, press gently. With knife flake edge of pastry, prick base. Mark a criss-cross pattern over the top of the small oval. Place on the baking tin. Bake in a hot oven for 10 minutes, reduce to 200°C, 400°F, Gas Mark 6. Remove the small oval and cool. Cook large case for further 25 minutes.

Make sauce with butter, flour and milk by roux method. Season. Mix in prawns, pepper, anchovy essence and juice.

Cool pastry case on wire rack, remove centre and fill with prawn mixture. Top with lid and serve hot or cold, garnished with the 4 prawns in their shells. *Serves 4.*

QUICK TIP

To make an equally delicious version of this recipe that is less expensive, use half white fish and half prawns in the sauce mixture.

You will need . . .
1 small lobster, boiled
50g/2 oz butter, melted
50g/2 oz white breadcrumbs
2 tablespoons thick cream
1 teaspoon cayenne pepper

Preparation time
10 minutes

2 lemons
25g/1 oz cheese, grated
few stuffed olives, sliced

Cooking time
20 minutes

few sprigs parsley

Oven setting
180°C; 350°F; Gas Mark 4

Remove claws from lobster and pick out meat. Cut shell in half lengthwise, remove intestinal cord and sac (the grey, greenish matter from head end). Carefully remove white meat and chop finely with claw meat. Wash and dry shells.

Mix the meat, butter, 40g/1½ oz breadcrumbs, cream and cayenne pepper together. Pile mixture back into shells and sprinkle with remaining breadcrumbs, juice of 1 lemon and cheese.

Bake in centre of preheated oven for 20 minutes. Serve hot, garnished with lemon slices, olives and parsley. *Serves 4.*

QUICK TIP

If no fresh lobster is available, make up the recipe with canned lobster. Put the mixture into scallop shells and bake for 12-15 minutes.

99 Baked stuffed trout

100 Cod with orange salad

You will need . . .

4 trout
100g/4 oz breadcrumbs
50g/2 oz butter
grated rind of ½ lemon
juice of 1 lemon

Preparation time
20 minutes

salt and pepper
1 egg yolk
75g/3 oz butter

Cooking time
30 minutes

25g/1 oz plain flour
little milk
2 teaspoons capers

Oven setting
180°C; 350°F; Gas Mark 4

1 stuffed olive, sliced
4 small tomatoes
few sprigs parsley

Gut the fish, remove fins, gills and eyes. Wash well. Make the stuffing: Mix the breadcrumbs, butter, lemon rind and half the juice, seasonings and egg yolk together. Beat well until smooth. Spread a quarter in each fish. Secure opening with cocktail sticks. Place in greased dish. Dot with 25g/1 oz butter, cover and cook in centre of preheated oven for 30 minutes.

Make the sauce: Melt remaining butter, add flour, mix well and cook for 2-3 minutes. Pour liquor from fish into a jug. Make up to 300ml/½ pint with milk, gradually add to pan and bring to the boil, stirring until thickened. Add remaining lemon juice and capers. Cook for 2-3 minutes.

Arrange fish on large serving platter with a slice of olive in each eye socket. Garnish with tomatoes and parsley. *Serves 4.*

You will need . . .

4 cod cutlets
salt and pepper
25g/1 oz butter
25g/1 oz white breadcrumbs
25g/1 oz cheese, grated
3 small oranges

Preparation time
15 minutes

1 tablespoon oil
1 teaspoon lemon juice
1 bunch watercress

Cooking time
10 minutes

Wipe the fish and season well. Dot with half the butter and grill for 5 minutes. Mix breadcrumbs and cheese together. Turn cutlets and cover with cheese mixture, dot with remaining butter and grill for another 5 minutes.

Meanwhile, peel oranges, removing all pith. Cut into thin slices and mix with oil and lemon juice.

Arrange cutlets on long serving platter. Drain oranges and arrange around the fish. Garnish with watercress. *Serves 4.*

QUICK TIP

To keep the pan clean as well as retaining the fish odour, line the tin with foil. Cover with another piece and press edges together.

QUICK TIP

Frozen cod steaks are an excellent alternative to fresh fish. They are easy to cook and stay a good shape because of their individual wrappers. Use them when in a hurry.

101 Baked mackerel

You will need . . .

4 mackerel
salt and pepper
1 onion, sliced
4 tablespoons vinegar
1 bay leaf

Preparation time
15 minutes

few cos lettuce leaves
2 tomatoes, cut into quarters

Cooking time
40 minutes

Oven setting
200°C; 400°F; Gas Mark 6

Bone the fish by removing head, entrails, gills and fins. Wash fish well under cold, running water. Make a slit from belly to tail, place slit side down on board. Press backbone firmly with knuckles, turn over and remove backbone. Season inside of fish well. Roll fish from head to tail, keeping tail in the air.

Place in deep ovenproof dish, cover with water, add onion, vinegar and bay leaf. Cover and cook for 40 minutes. Lift carefully from liquor and allow to cool.

Arrange lettuce leaves on large serving dish, place fish on top and garnish with tomatoes. *Serves 4.*

QUICK TIP

If preferred, the prepared fish can be left whole and baked in a shallow dish. It goes well with creamed potatoes and pickled red cabbage.

102 Crab balls

You will need . . .

175g/6 oz crab meat
75g/3 oz white breadcrumbs
salt and pepper
1 egg yolk
1 teaspoon lemon juice
1 egg
browned breadcrumbs
deep fat for frying

Preparation time
15 minutes

Cooking time
5-6 minutes a batch

Chop crab meat finely, with the breadcrumbs, salt, pepper, egg yolk and lemon juice. Beat until smooth. Divide into 8 portions and shape each into a ball.

Beat egg and coat each ball twice with egg and browned breadcrumbs. Fry in batches for 5-6 minutes or until golden brown.

Drain on crumpled kitchen paper and serve hot or cold.
Serves 4.

QUICK TIP

These are ideal for buffet parties if they are made a bit smaller. Make about twenty-four from the same mixture and spear each one with a cocktail stick. Serve with dips.

103 Prawns in batter

You will need . . .

600ml/1 pint prawns
salt and black pepper
50g/2 oz plain flour
2 teaspoons oil
4 tablespoons cold water
½ cucumber, diced
1 red pepper, cut into strips
25g/1 oz butter
50g/2 oz brown sugar
3 tablespoons vinegar
300ml/½ pint stock
1 tablespoon cornflour
deep fat for frying
1 egg white
1 × 340g/12 oz can beansprouts

Preparation time
20 minutes

Cooking time
4-5 minutes a batch

Pick prawns and season well. Sift flour into a small bowl. Season. Add oil and water, beating until smooth. The mixture should be thick.

Make the sauce. Fry cucumber and strips of pepper in butter until soft. Add sugar, vinegar and stock. Bring to the boil and cook for 5 minutes. Mix cornflour to smooth paste with a little water. Add to sauce. Bring back to the boil, stirring until thickened.

Heat deep fat until a faint haze appears. Whisk egg white and fold gently into batter. Dip two or three prawns together in batter and fry immediately in hot fat for 4-5 minutes or until golden brown. Drain fritters on crumpled kitchen paper and serve piled up on a bed of beansprouts. Pour sauce over and serve immediately. *Serves 4.*

QUICK TIP

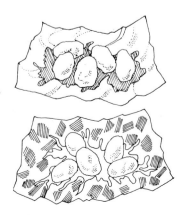

Crumpled kitchen paper will absorb the excess grease from the fritters very well. Alternatively, drain on crumpled kitchen foil to catch the fat in the creases of the foil.

104 Lobster cocktail

You will need . . .

175g/6 oz lobster meat
4 tablespoons mayonnaise
2 teaspoons tomato juice
salt and pepper
pinch mace
1 lettuce heart
4 lemon slices
pinch paprika

Preparation time
20 minutes

Chop lobster meat roughly. Mix mayonnaise, tomato juice, salt, pepper and mace together. Mix well, add a little to the lobster meat to moisten it and keep the rest aside.

Wash and dry lettuce. Shred finely and divide evenly between four glasses. Divide the lobster meat between the glasses and pour the remaining mayonnaise mixture over.

Cut the lemon slices from the edge to the centre and twist one on the side of each glass. Sprinkle top of mayonnaise mixture with paprika. Serve very cold with thinly sliced bread and butter. *Serves 4.*

QUICK TIP

Serve with bread and butter 'cigars': cut bread very thinly using a hot knife. Trim off crusts, butter bread and roll tightly. Pack into a tin and cover with a damp cloth. They will keep fresh for 1-2 days.

105 Mackerel en papillotes

You will need . . .

4 mackerel
salt and pepper
50g/2 oz butter
grated rind and juice of 1 orange
dash garlic salt

Preparation time
10 minutes

1 small onion
1 orange, cut in wedges
4 sprigs parsley

Cooking time
30 minutes

Oven setting
190°C; 375°F; Gas Mark 5

Remove head, entrails, fins and gills. Clean fish under cold, running water. Season well.

Beat butter until soft. Add orange rind and juice, beating until smooth. Add garlic salt. Peel and grate or chop onion, add to butter and beat well. Divide between the mackerel and spread inside each fish. Place each on square of greased foil, making a double fold along the top and at each end. Place on baking tin and bake for 30 minutes in preheated oven.

Carefully fold back the foil, crimping the edges decoratively. Garnish each fish with orange wedges and parsley. Serve hot or cold. *Serves 4.*

QUICK TIP

These are ideal for picnics. Serve them cold with a creamy horseradish sauce. Mix a little cream with the horseradish to make it a little less strong.

106 Tuna bake

You will need . . .

1 × 198g/7 oz can tuna fish
1 × 295g/10 oz can condensed mushroom soup
25g/1 oz white breadcrumbs
50g/2 oz butter

Preparation time
10 minutes

few mushrooms
1 sprig parsley

Cooking time
10 minutes

Drain fish and flake. Heat soup in small pan, add fish and cook for 2-3 minutes.

Pour mixture into baking dish. Sprinkle with breadcrumbs and dot with half the butter. Grill for 5 minutes or until golden brown.

Meanwhile, melt the remaining butter in a small pan. Wash the mushrooms, add to the butter and cook gently for 5 minutes. Use to garnish tuna mixture, along with parsley. *Serves 4.*

QUICK TIP

The fish and soup mixture can be thinned down with a little single cream. Beat the mixture until it is smooth and use it as a party dip for crisps.

107 Scallops au gratin

108 Crunchy topped fish bake

You will need . . .

4 scallops
600ml/1 pint milk
50g/2 oz butter
50g/2 oz plain flour
salt and pepper

Preparation time
20 minutes

50g/2 oz grated cheese
1 tablespoon browned breadcrumbs
1 tomato

Cooking time
20 minutes

bunch watercress

Gently cook scallops in milk for 10 minutes. Drain and reserve milk. Melt butter and add flour. Mix well. Cook for 2-3 minutes. Remove from heat and gradually add milk. Bring to the boil, stirring until thickened. Add half the cheese, seasoning, mix well and heat until melted.

Place a scallop in each of four deep shells, pour sauce over each and sprinkle with breadcrumbs and remaining cheese. Grill for 5 minutes or until golden brown.

Meanwhile, make tomato waterlily. With a sharp knife make slits in tomato in a criss-cross pattern almost to the base. Pull segments apart gently. Garnish scallops with waterlily and watercress.

Serves 4.

You will need . . .

4 plaice fillets
1 × 295g/10 oz can condensed mushroom soup
100g/4 oz grated cheese
50g/2 oz butter

Preparation time
10 minutes

1 teaspoon grated onion
dash Worcester sauce
dash garlic salt

Cooking time
35 minutes

1 small bag crisps
few anchovies

Oven setting
180°C; 350°F; Gas Mark 4

Put fillets in greased ovenproof dish. Spread with soup and top with cheese.

Melt butter, add onion, Worcester sauce and garlic salt. Mix well. Add crushed potato crisps and mix again.

Spread mixture over fillets and bake in centre of oven for 35 minutes. Garnish with criss-cross of anchovies and serve with tomato salad.

Serves 4.

QUICK TIP

Cook the scallops in a little dry white wine. This will give a much richer, more subtle flavour and make this into a more sophisticated dish.

QUICK TIP

Grate more cheese than you need. It will keep well in a screw-top jar and save you time when next preparing a recipe using grated cheese.

Herrings
109 with mustard sauce

You will need . . .

4 large herrings
salt and pepper
25g/1 oz butter
25g/1 oz plain flour
2 teaspoons mustard
pinch curry powder
300ml/½ pint fish stock *or* water
1 lemon, cut into wedges
few sprigs parsley

Preparation time
15 minutes

Cooking time
15 minutes

Remove heads and entrails from fish. Wash well. Remove scales, cut off fins and gills. Season well. Make 2 slits on each side of fish and grill for 10 minutes.

To make sauce, melt butter, add flour, mustard and curry powder. Mix well and cook for 2-3 minutes. Remove pan from heat and add stock or water, stirring all the time. Return to heat and bring to the boil, stirring until thickened. Correct seasoning.

Arrange fish on large platter. Garnish with lemon wedges or slices and parsley sprigs. Pour sauce into a decorative line over fish. *Serves 4.*

QUICK TIP

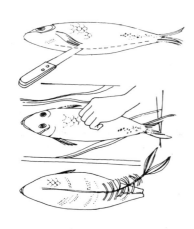

To bone fish before cooking: make a slit from the belly to the tail. Remove entrails and swim bladder. Place the fish, cut side down, on a board and press knuckles along the backbone. Invert the fish and lift out the bones, from the tail end.

110 Prawn and potato salad

You will need . . .

1 × 283g/10 oz can potatoes
2 tablespoons oil
salt and pepper
pinch dry mustard
pinch castor sugar
100g/4 oz peeled prawns
1 bunch watercress

Preparation time
10 minutes

Cooking time
5 minutes

Cook the potatoes in their liquid for 5 minutes. Drain while still hot. Put into a dish with the oil, salt, pepper, mustard and sugar. Mix well and leave until cold.

Reserve a few prawns for garnish and add the rest to the potatoes. Mix well.

Pile the potato mixture on a serving plate. Wash the watercress and remove the stalks. Shake dry and arrange on top and round the heap of potatoes and prawns. Garnish with remaining prawns. *Serves 4.*

QUICK TIP

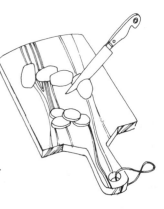

If you are using new potatoes, cut them into slices before cooking to make them go further and to shorten the cooking time.

Cucumber
111 crunchy herrings

You will need . . .

4-6 small herrings
salt and pepper
pinch mustard
approx. 25g/1 oz medium oatmeal
½ cucumber

Preparation time
10 minutes

150g/5 oz soured cream
grated rind and juice of 1 orange
orange segments

Cooking time
5 minutes

Clean and bone fish by removing head, entrails, gills and fins. Wash fish well under cold, running water. Make a slit from belly to tail and place slit down on board. Press backbone firmly with knuckles, turn over and remove backbone. Season well with salt, pepper and mustard. Roll each in oatmeal. Fry or grill for 20 minutes, turning frequently.

Peel cucumber and dice. Put into bowl with 2 level teaspoons salt. Toss and leave for 15 minutes. Mix cream with orange rind and juice. Rinse and drain cucumber. Add cream and well.

Arrange herrings on serving platter. Garnish with orange segments. Serve cucumber mixture separately from a bowl.
Serves 4.

112 Potted shrimps

You will need . . .

1.2 litres/2 pints shrimps
100g/4 oz butter
juice of ½ lemon
pinch ground mace
75g/3 oz butter, clarified
1 bunch watercress

Preparation time
20 minutes

Clean the shrimps, chop and mix with the butter. Beat well. Add the lemon juice and mace, beat well.

Divide the mixture into small pots, press firmly and cover with clarified butter (*see Quick Tip below*). Allow to cool.

Cover pots and keep in cold place. To serve, place moulded shrimps into bed of lettuce leaves or shredded lettuce or arrange pots on a small tray. Garnish with watercress.
Serves 4.

QUICK TIP

Plain yogurt can be used successfully instead of cream for this sauce. Yogurt is lighter than cream, and still gives a delicious flavour.

QUICK TIP

To clarify butter, heat it very gently in a wide, shallow pan. Carefully pour off the clear liquid into an earthenware or stone container, leaving the whitish deposits in the pan.

113 Plaice rolls

You will need . . .

Prepared list:

4 large plaice fillets
salt and pepper
grated rind and juice of 1 lemon
1 teaspoon chopped parsley
4 rashers streaky bacon

Preparation time
20 minutes

25g/1 oz butter
1 tablespoon milk
1 small onion

Cooking time
30 minutes

1 small tin tomatoes
dash Worcester sauce

Skin the fillets. Season well with salt and pepper. Lay each fillet skinned side up. Sprinkle with lemon rind, juice and parsley. Roll up head to tail. Remove the bacon rinds and wrap a rasher around each fillet. Dot each with butter using not more than 15g/½ oz altogether, place on plate and add milk. Steam over a pan of hot water for 20 minutes.

Melt remaining butter in small pan. Peel and grate onion, add to butter and fry until transparent. Add tomatoes, Worcester sauce and seasoning of choice, e.g. basil, mixed herbs or dash garlic salt. Cook rapidly for 5 minutes.

Carefully remove fish rolls, turn on to side and grill for 2-3 minutes to brown bacon. Arrange the tomato mixture in a serving dish and place fish rolls in centre. *Serves 4.*

114 Salmon chaudfroid

You will need . . .

4 salmon steaks
25g/1 oz breadcrumbs
lemon juice
150ml/¼ pint mayonnaise
150ml/¼ pint aspic jelly (made from packet crystals)

Preparation time
40 minutes

½ fresh red pepper, blanched
few capers

Cooking time
10 minutes

1 lettuce
bunch watercress

Steam fish on greased plate over pan of hot water for 10 minutes. Drain, remove skin and centre bone, keeping the fish whole. Leave to cool. Mix breadcrumbs with enough lemon juice to bind, use to fill cavity in each steak.

Mix mayonnaise with half the aspic. Leave until cold and beginning to set. Stand fish on wire rack with plate underneath and pour sauce over, coating evenly. When set, gently pour remaining aspic over, catching the surplus for later use. Leave until set.

Cut pepper into strips and arrange over chaudfroid, place capers between pepper strips. Shred lettuce and arrange on large serving dish. Place salmon steaks on lettuce and garnish with watercress in centre. Serve very cold. *Serves 4.*

QUICK TIP

To skin the fish:
Hold the fish by the tail.
Skin from tail to head with
quick, short strokes keeping
the edge of the blade close
to the surface of the skin so
that no fish is wasted.

QUICK TIP

The jelly will set more quickly
if you add just enough hot
water to dissolve the crystals.
Make up the rest with cold
water. Pour the mixture into a
bowl and let stand in
cold water.

115 Fish curry

You will need . . .

1kg/2 lb coley
salt and pepper
juice of ½ lemon
1 onion
50g/2 oz butter
50g/2 oz plain flour
1 tablespoon curry powder
600ml/1 pint stock or water
1 small cauliflower
1 teaspoon chopped parsley

Preparation time
15 minutes

Cooking time
25 minutes

Skin the fish and cut into small pieces. Season well. Sprinkle with lemon juice. Peel and grate or chop the onion. Fry in butter until transparent. Add fish and fry gently for 5 minutes. Remove fish and keep to one side.

Add flour and curry powder to butter, mix well and cook for 5 minutes, stirring frequently. Remove pan from heat and gradually add stock or water. Return to heat and bring to the boil, stirring until thickened. Cook for 5 minutes. Add fish to sauce and cook for further 10 minutes.

Cook cauliflower sprigs in salted, boiling water. Drain and arrange around edge of dish. Pour fish and sauce into centre. Garnish with parsley. *Serves 4.*

116 Whitebait

You will need . . .

225g/8 oz whitebait
25g/1 oz plain flour
salt and pepper
deep fat for frying
juice of 1 lemon
few lemon wedges
few sprigs parsley

Preparation time
5 minutes

Cooking time
3-4 minutes a batch

Rinse fish under cold water. Pat dry on cloth. Toss fish in flour mixed with salt and pepper. Place in frying basket, shake off excess flour and plunge basket into very hot fat. Cook for 3-4 minutes.

Drain fish on crumpled kitchen paper and sprinkle immediately with lemon juice.

Pile fish on to serving dish and garnish with lemon wedges and parsley. Serve very hot. *Serves 4.*

QUICK TIP

This mixture is delicious when it is spread on hot, buttered toast and popped under a hot grill for 3-4 minutes. Top with a little chutney and serve hot.

QUICK TIP

Fresh sprats can be cooked in the same way as whitebait. Remove the heads of the sprats before washing. Cook them in small batches, about four or five at a time.

117 Fish envelopes

118 Whiting meunière

You will need . . .

450g/1 lb frozen puff pastry
25g/1 oz butter
225g/8 oz cod fillet
salt and pepper
juice of ½ lemon
1 tablespoon chopped parsley
1 egg
4 sprigs parsley

Preparation time
15 minutes

Cooking time
15 minutes

Oven setting
230°C; 450°F; Gas Mark 8

Roll out pastry thinly. Cut out 4 20-cm/8-inch squares, place on baking tin and leave in cold place while making filling.

Melt butter in pan. Skin fish and cut into small pieces, add to butter with salt, pepper, lemon juice and parsley. Mix well, cover and cook for 5 minutes, shaking pan often. Beat the egg, add half to the fish and mix well. Divide the mixture between the pastry, keeping it well in the centre.

Dampen the edges of the pastry and bring the four corners to the centre, pressing well to seal. Brush with remaining egg. Bake in top of preheated oven for 10 minutes, or until golden brown. Serve hot or cold, garnished with parsley.   *Serves 4.*

You will need . . .

2 whiting, filleted
plain flour
salt and pepper
100g/4 oz butter
few lemon slices
few beetroot slices
juice of ½ lemon
2 teaspoons chopped parsley

Preparation time
15 minutes

Cooking time
10 minutes

Wipe the fish and dust well with flour, salt and pepper. Melt the butter and fry the fillets on both sides for about 10 minutes. Remove to a dish and keep hot.

Arrange the lemon slices around the edge of a large platter. Place the fish in the centre. Cut the beetroot into diamonds and arrange between the lemon slices.

Lightly brown remaining butter in the pan, add lemon juice and parsley, mix well and pour over the fish. Serve immediately.   *Serves 4.*

QUICK TIP

Place the mixture on one half of the pastry and seal by folding over the edge. This will not give so decorative a result but is quicker.

QUICK TIP

To melt butter without burning it, add a small amount of cooking oil. The fat then can be raised to a much higher temperature without burning.

119 Crab mayonnaise

Bream and 120 almond scallop

You will need . . .

175g/6 oz crab meat
2 hard-boiled eggs
150ml/¼ pint mayonnaise
coral if available *or* anchovies
watercress

Preparation time
15 minutes

Chop crab meat roughly. Chop eggs and mix with meat. Arrange the mixture in a neat pile in a shallow glass dish. Pour mayonnaise over.

Arrange the coral or anchovies in a pattern over the mayonnaise and garnish with watercress around the edge.

Serve with a wreath of thinly sliced brown bread and butter.

Serves 4.

You will need . . .

75g/3 oz butter
450g/1 lb cooked bream, flaked
salt and pepper
2 tablespoons dry sherry
2 eggs
8 tablespoons evaporated milk
1 tablespoon chopped parsley
50g/2 oz fresh white breadcrumbs
25g/1 oz blanched almonds

Preparation time
10 minutes

Cooking time
25 minutes

Oven setting
180°C; 350°F; Gas Mark 4

Melt 25g/1 oz butter and gently cook fish for 3 minutes. Season. Add sherry. Mix well.

Beat the eggs, add evaporated milk and parsley, stirring well. Add to fish and mix. Toss crumbs well in remaining melted butter.

Pour fish mixture into greased ovenproof dish, sprinkle with crumbs and almonds. Bake in centre of oven for 20 minutes.

Serves 4.

QUICK TIP

If home-made mayonnaise is not available, add 4 tablespoons whipped cream and 1 whisked egg white to 300ml/½ pint of bottled mayonnaise. This will increase the bulk and diminish the acid flavour of the bought mayonnaise.

QUICK TIP

Bream is a firm, fleshy fish, so if it is not available, the recipe can be made up with either halibut or turbot.

Chicken, turkey and duck

We are all familiar with the roast turkey that takes pride of place on many Christmas tables and we all know roast chicken. But the possibilities do not end there and the recipes in this section show that there are many other ways to cook poultry, to make tasty dishes. Why not try turkey in aspic as an hors d'oeuvre, for a change? Chicken can be given a specially festive look when served with almonds or an exotic air when prepared with pineapple and sauce, as in the recipe for Malayan chicken. Try duck for a change in new ways, with celery for example, or as a terrine of duck.

121 Roast turkey with apples

(illustrated on frontispiece)

You will need . . .	1 turkey (5.5kg/12 lb)
	salt and pepper
	1kg/2 lb chestnuts
	300ml/½ pint milk
	450g/1 lb cooking apples
Preparation time	50g/2 oz castor sugar
20 minutes	225g/8 oz pork sausage meat
	100g/4 oz butter
Cooking time	1 apple per person and pork sausage
3½-4 hours	meat for garnish
	2 sprigs parsley

Oven setting
180°C; 350°F; Gas Mark 4

Prepare turkey for oven. Season well with salt and pepper. Peel the chestnuts, put into a pan with the milk, bring to the boil, cover and cook for 20 minutes.

Peel, core and slice apples. Cook them in a pan with sugar and 1 tablespoon water. Shake pan to prevent sticking. Drain chestnuts and chop finely, add to apples and sausage meat, mix well and season with salt and pepper. Add 25g/1 oz butter and beat until smooth. Stuff the turkey with this mixture and spread turkey with remaining 75g/3 oz butter. Bake in centre of oven for 3½-4 hours. Baste turkey frequently with juices.

For garnish, bake 1 apple per person on shelf underneath turkey, fill centres with chopped pork or sausage meat. Place turkey on serving dish, garnish with apples and parsley.

QUICK TIP

To make a decorative finish to the apples: cut the skins from top to bottom in several places instead of once round so that when they split the result is petal shaped.

122 Aspic chicken

You will need . . .	1 small roasting chicken (1.5kg/3 lb)
	salt and pepper
	1 onion, peeled
	1 bay leaf
	50g/2 oz butter
Preparation time	1 packet aspic jelly
10 minutes	few sprigs parsley
	few lemon wedges
Cooking time	few green pepper rings
1 hour 15 minutes	

Oven setting
200°C; 400°F; Gas Mark 6

Wipe the chicken, remove the bag of giblets and season well with salt and pepper. Put onion and bay leaf inside chicken, rub breast with butter and cook chicken in centre of oven for 1¼ hours. Baste often during cooking.

Make up aspic jelly according to instructions on packet, pour into a shallow dish and allow to set. (*See Quick Tip below*). Wash parsley and drain.

Cool chicken on wire rack, then place on large serving dish. Chop the jelly roughly or cut into cubes and arrange round the chicken with parsley and lemon wedges. Arrange the pepper rings on top.   *Serves 4.*

QUICK TIP

In order to cut the aspic jelly more easily into squares or other shapes, dip the knife into some very hot water before making each incision.

123 Chicken parcels

You will need . . .

4 chicken joints
salt and pepper
1 small onion
100g/4 oz mushrooms
juice of ½ lemon
50g/2 oz butter

Preparation time

10 minutes

Cooking time

1 hour

Oven setting

200°C; 400°F; Gas Mark 6

Season the chicken well with salt and pepper. Slice the onion thinly, wash the mushrooms.

Place a chicken joint in the centre of a square of foil, divide onions and mushrooms between each parcel, sprinkle with lemon juice and dot with butter.

Make a double fold along the top of the parcel, and double folds at each end. Place on baking tin and bake for 1 hour. Open foil 10 minutes before the end and continue to cook uncovered. Serve from the foil for picnics. *Serves 4.*

124 Chicken and sweetcorn

You will need . . .

4 chicken joints
75g/3 oz butter
1 bunch spring onions, trimmed
1 × 283g/10 oz can new potatoes, drained
1 × 198g/7 oz can sweetcorn
25g/1 oz flour
300ml/½ pint milk
salt and pepper
few parsley sprigs
few lemon wedges

Preparation time

15 minutes

Cooking time

20 minutes

Rub the chicken with 50g/2 oz butter. Grill or fry until golden brown all over for 15-20 minutes.

Make the sauce. Sauté the onions and potatoes in remaining butter, add the sweetcorn and mix well. Add the flour. Mix and cook for 2-3 minutes. Remove from the heat and gradually add the milk. Bring to the boil, stirring all the time until thickened. Cook for 5 minutes longer. Season well.

Pour the mixture into a shallow dish. Arrange the joints on top of the sauce. Garnish with parsley and lemon wedges. *Serves 4.*

QUICK TIP

The addition of one tablespoon single cream to each parcel makes this a delectable dish. The same amount of soured cream or plain yogurt with a few chopped chives added can also be used to vary the flavour.

QUICK TIP

The sauce can quite safely be made up to two days in advance and kept well-covered in the refrigerator until you are ready to use it.

125 Chicken with sherry sauce

126 Chicken crème

You will need . . .

4 chicken joints
salt and pepper
100g/4 oz butter
100g/4 oz mushrooms
25g/1 oz plain flour

Preparation time
15 minutes

2 tablespoons sherry
300ml/½ pint stock
150ml/¼ pint single cream

Cooking time
35 minutes

few slices bread
oil and butter for frying
2 sprigs parsley

Season the chicken well. Melt the butter and fry the chicken for 25 minutes. Remove and keep hot. Add the mushrooms, whole, and cook for 2-3 minutes. Remove and keep to one side.

Add the flour to the remaining fat. Mix well and cook for 2-3 minutes. Remove the pan from the heat, add the sherry and stock gradually, stirring all the time. Return to the heat, bring to the boil, stirring continually until thickened. Add the cream, mix and heat through, but do not boil. Return the mushrooms to the sauce, heat through again.

Make the croutons by cutting out shapes from slices of bread, using small, fancy cutter. Fry until crisp in oil and butter. Arrange the chicken on a large serving dish, pour the sauce over and garnish with fried croutons and parsley. *Serves 4.*

You will need . . .

450g/1 lb cooked chicken
salt and pepper
100g/4 oz lean ham
1 packet aspic jelly
2 teaspoons gelatine

Preparation time
30 minutes
plus setting time

150ml/¼ pint double cream
juice of ½ lemon
8 radishes
chicory leaves
1 small can asparagus tips
½ bunch watercress

Mince the chicken finely. Season well with salt and pepper. Mince the ham and mix with the chicken. Make up the aspic according to the directions on the packet. Mix gelatine with aspic jelly, stir until dissolved. Whip the cream until thick, but not stiff.

Mix the aspic with the mixture, cool and when almost set, fold in the cream and lemon juice. Mix well. Pour the mixture into a greased 15-cm/6-inch straight sided cake tin and allow to set. Meanwhile, make the radish roses. Cut radish from the tip downwards but not quite to the base. Let radishes stand in iced water for about 30 minutes to open out.

Prepare the chicory and arrange on large serving dish. Remove the crème from tin on to bed of chicory. (*See Quick Tip below*). Garnish with asparagus tips and radish roses and watercress. *Serves 4.*

QUICK TIP

If you are using leftover chicken for this dish, add the cream to a can of condensed mushroom soup and cook as in the recipe.

QUICK TIP

To remove the mould easily from the tin, dip the tin in hot water up to the rim, place a serving plate on top of the tin and invert the plate and tin. Shake the tin sharply to release vacuum and lift off.

127 Roast duck with celery

128 Terrine of duck

You will need . . .

1 duck (1.75-2.25kg/4-5 lb)
salt and pepper
50g/2 oz butter
2 tablespoons oil
1 head celery
bouquet garni
300ml/½ pint stock or water with stock cube
1 × 227g/8 oz can red cherries
small bunch watercress

Preparation time
20 minutes

Cooking time
2 hours 15 minutes

Oven setting
200°C; 400°F; Gas Mark 6

Prepare the duck for cooking. Season well with salt and pepper. Melt the butter with the oil and heat gently. Fry duck for 10 minutes, turning often to brown evenly. Remove the duck and keep to one side.

Wash the celery, remove outer stalks and leaves. Cut into strips, dry and fry for 15 minutes in the remaining fat. Drain and keep to one side. Return duck to pan, add bouquet garni and stock, season well, cover and cook for about 1½ hours.

Pour off liquid, add the cherries and cook with duck and celery for further 10 minutes in top of oven, uncovered, to brown. Skim off excess fat from liquid. Boil juices rapidly for 10 minutes and pour around duck. Garnish with watercress. Serve very hot. *Serves 4.*

You will need . . .

1 fresh duck (1.75-2.25kg/4-5 lb)
salt and pepper
1 level teaspoon mixed herbs
225g/8 oz lean pork
100g/4 oz pork fat
1 small onion, chopped
1 egg
juice of 1 orange
few bay leaves
few orange slices

Preparation time
30 minutes

Cooking time
1-1½ hours

Oven setting
190°C; 375°F; Gas Mark 5

Skin duck, remove breast meat in thin slices and bone the rest of the duck. Mince the meat (except the slices). Season well. Mince the pork and fat, mix with the minced duck meat, onion, egg and orange juice. Beat until evenly blended.

Press half the mixture into a well-greased straight sided ovenproof dish, lay the sliced meat on top and cover with the rest of the minced meat. Press firmly. Cover the dish and stand in a shallow tin half filled with hot water. Bake in the centre of the oven for 1-1½ hours.

Cover meat with foil and press gently as it cools, to exclude all air bubbles. Serve cold from the dish garnished with bay leaves and orange slices. *Serves 4.*

QUICK TIP

As an alternative to strips of celery – cut the whole head of celery into slices. Some pieces will break, but most will stay round and these will make an attractive finish to the dish.

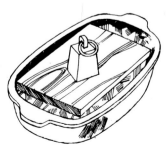

QUICK TIP

To press the meat evenly, cover it with aluminium foil and then with a flat object such as a board. Put a heavy weight on top to press the meat into a good flat shape.

Roast chicken
129 with almonds

You will need . . .

1 chicken (1.5kg/3½ lb)
1 clove garlic, peeled and chopped
1 onion
peel of ½ lemon
100g/4 oz butter

Preparation time
10 minutes

100g/4 oz blanched almonds
225g/8 oz button onions
25g/1 oz brown sugar

Cooking time
1 hour 30 minutes

450g/1 lb new potatoes *or* canned
potatoes
bunch watercress

Oven setting
200°C; 400°F; Gas Mark 6

Wipe the chicken and stand on a rack in a roasting tin. Make small nicks in the skin and insert a piece of garlic in each. Peel the onion and put inside the chicken with the lemon peel. Rub the chicken liberally with half the butter and bake in the centre of the oven for 1 hour 30 minutes. Baste well during cooking. Sprinkle with blanched almonds 15 minutes before end of cooking time.

Peel the onions and glaze in the remaining butter. Add the sugar and cook gently until browned and soft. Brown the potatoes in the same way.

Arrange chicken on serving dish with onions and potatoes round and almonds on top. Garnish with watercress. Serve with cooked carrots. *Serves 4.*

130 Turkey in aspic

You will need . . .

450g/1 lb cooked turkey breast
100g/4 oz pâté de foie
1 × 213g/7½ oz can mandarins, drained
600ml/1 pint aspic jelly
few cucumber slices
few sprigs watercress

Preparation time
20 minutes

Cut the turkey breast into neat slices. Spread each slice with pâté. Arrange the mandarins and turkey in a pattern over the base of a shallow tin. Pour over a little cold aspic and allow to set.

Pour on the rest of the aspic, mixed with any surplus turkey and mandarins. Allow to set.

Remove jelly from tin on to a serving dish. Serve garnished with cucumber slices and watercress. *Serves 4.*

QUICK TIP

To blanch almonds: put them into a pan of cold water, bring to the boil. Remove from the heat and drain. Cover the almonds with cold water and the skins will peel off quite easily.

QUICK TIP

Aspic sets more quickly in a metal container than in a china bowl. The metal container placed in a bowl of ice will make the aspic set even more quickly.

131 Chicken with mushrooms

Quick cream
132 of turkey soup

You will need . . .

- 4 chicken joints
- 75g/3 oz butter
- 100g/4 oz mushrooms, sliced
- 1 small onion, chopped
- 300ml/½ pint stock
- 1 tablespoon tomato purée
- ¼ teaspoon chopped herbs
- 1 teaspoon chopped parsley

Preparation time
20 minutes

Cooking time
35 minutes

Season chicken pieces and fry in butter for 20 minutes or until tender. Add mushrooms and cook for 2-3 minutes. Remove chicken pieces and keep hot.

Add the onion to the pan, cook until transparent. Add the stock and boil up, reduce the heat and cook for 5 minutes. Add the tomato purée and herbs. Correct the seasoning and cook 5 minutes longer.

Arrange the chicken on a serving dish and pour the sauce over. Sprinkle with chopped parsley. *Serves 4.*

You will need . . .

- 225g/8 oz cooked turkey meat
- 25g/1 oz butter
- 1 small onion, grated
- 1 rasher bacon
- 1 chicken stock cube
- 600ml/1 pint water
- 150ml/¼ pint cream
- 1 tablespoon chopped parsley

Preparation time
10 minutes

Cooking time
20 minutes

Remove the turkey skin and cut flesh into neat pieces. Melt the butter, fry onion and bacon for 5 minutes. Add stock cube and water, bring to the boil and simmer for 10 minutes. Remove bacon and chop finely. Reserve for garnish.

Add the turkey and bring back to the boil. Skim off excess fat. Add cream, stir gently, but do not boil.

Pour soup into tureens, sprinkle top with chopped parsley and bacon pieces. Serve with French bread. *Serves 4.*

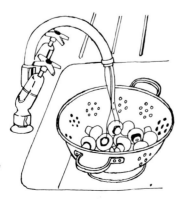

QUICK TIP

If using button mushrooms, there is no need even to slice them. Just wash, dry and add whole.

QUICK TIP

If you do not have any fresh cream available, an effective and delicious substitute is undiluted evaporated milk.

133 Turkey risotto

You will need . . .

450g/1 lb cooked turkey meat
50g/2 oz butter
2 onions, chopped
1 tablespoon curry powder
1 level teaspoon mixed herbs
salt and pepper
dash garlic salt
225g/8 oz Patna rice
1 chicken stock cube
450ml/¾ pint water
25g/1 oz stuffed olives, sliced
225g/8 oz frozen or canned peas
tomato quarters

Preparation time
15 minutes

Cooking time
45 minutes

Cut the meat into neat pieces. Melt the butter in a large sauce-pan, fry onion until transparent. Add curry powder, herbs, salt, pepper and garlic salt. Mix well and cook for 3 minutes. Add rice, mixing well.

Mix stock cube in water, pour over rice, bring to the boil, cover and cook for 35 minutes or until the rice has absorbed all the liquid. Add the turkey and olives. Stir thoroughly and heat gently for 5 minutes.

Arrange the risotto on a large platter, surround with cooked peas and garnish with tomato quarters. *Serves 4.*

134 Chicken mayonnaise

You will need . . .

450g/1 lb cold, cooked chicken
1 bunch spring onions
300ml/½ pint mayonnaise
1 lettuce
8 tomato quarters
dash paprika
parsley

Preparation time
20 minutes

Cut the chicken into neat pieces. Chop the onions finely and mix well with the chicken and half the mayonnaise.

Wash and dry the lettuce. Arrange leaves on a serving dish. Pile the chicken on top of the lettuce and coat with the remaining mayonnaise, leaving a border of lettuce showing.

Arrange the tomato quarters around the base of the mayonnaise. Sprinkle the top of the pyramid with paprika. Serve very cold. Garnish with parsley. *Serves 4.*

QUICK TIP

When cooking rice, use approximately double the amount of water to rice. A measuring jug is extremely helpful in doing this.

QUICK TIP

*A quick way to make mayonnaise if you have a liquidiser:
Put a whole egg, seasoning, 1 tablespoon lemon juice or vinegar into the liquidiser, switch on, pour up to 150ml/¼ pint oil gently through the top on to mixture. It takes only 10 seconds.*

135 Potted chicken

You will need . . .

2 chicken joints
salt and black pepper
juice of ½ lemon
few sprigs fresh tarragon *or* parsley
100g/4 oz butter
6 orange wedges
1 lettuce, shredded

Preparation time
20 minutes plus setting time

Cooking time
15 minutes

Season the chicken with salt and pepper. Grill for 15 minutes, turning frequently. Cool, remove all the meat and mince it finely.

Add the lemon juice and tarragon or parsley, reserving 1 sprig for the garnish. Check the seasoning. Pound the meat mixture until smooth and creamlike. Work in half the butter. Divide the mixture into small, ramekin dishes or foil containers (*see Quick Tip*) and leave until quite cold.

Melt remaining butter and pour a little over each one. Leave to set. When cold, serve turned out on bed of lettuce and garnished with orange wedges and tarragon or parsley.
Serves 4.

136 Chicken rissoles

You will need . . .

450g/1 lb cooked chicken
100g/4 oz fresh white breadcrumbs
salt and pepper
1 teaspoon lemon juice
2 eggs
approx. 50g/2 oz brown breadcrumbs
deep fat for frying
100g/4 oz button mushrooms
few sprigs parsley

Preparation time
20 minutes

Cooking time
20 minutes

Mince the chicken finely and add to the breadcrumbs. Season well, add lemon juice and 1 whole egg. Beat well until smooth. The mixture should be stiff.

Divide the mixture into 8 portions. Make into a sausage shape and dip in beaten egg. Toss in brown breadcrumbs. Do this twice.

Fry the rissoles, three at a time, in deep fat until golden brown and crisp. Drain on crumpled kitchen paper. Serve hot or cold, garnished with mushrooms and parsley. *Serves 4.*

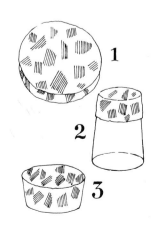

QUICK TIP

If no suitable moulds are available, make foil ones. Place a double thickness of foil over the base of a tumbler and press foil down the sides. Remove and use as required.

QUICK TIP

If you find that the mixture is too soft to make into the required shapes, put it into the refrigerator for about 30 minutes before shaping into rissoles.

137 Chicken with tomatoes

You will need . . .

4 chicken joints
salt and black pepper
3 tablespoons oil
4 large tomatoes
1 clove garlic
½ teaspoon each fresh thyme and basil
150ml/¼ pint white wine
12 black olives
1 teaspoon chopped parsley

Preparation time
15 minutes

Cooking time
35 minutes

Oven setting
180°C; 350°F; Gas Mark 4

Season the chicken joints well. Heat the oil and fry the chicken for 20 minutes, turning often. Transfer to an ovenproof dish, cover and continue to cook in the oven for 10 minutes.

Make the sauce. Skin the tomatoes and chop them finely. Peel and crush the garlic. Fry in the remaining fat, adding the thyme, basil and wine. Bring to boil. Cook gently until soft. Add the olives and mix well.

Arrange the chicken on a serving dish. Pour the sauce over and sprinkle with parsley. Serve with salad. *Serves 4.*

138 Chicken chaudfroid

You will need . . .

1 small whole chicken (1.5-1.75kg/ 3-3½ lb)
1 chicken stock cube
600ml/1 pint water
½ packet aspic jelly
300ml/½ pint mayonnaise
few anchovy fillets
1 box mustard and cress
6 stuffed olives, sliced

Preparation time
40 minutes

Cooking time
30 minutes

Joint the chicken into six pieces (*see Quick Tip below*). Put chicken into a pan with the stock cube and water, bring slowly to the boil, cover and simmer for 30 minutes. Drain and remove the skin. Stand the pieces on a wire rack with foil underneath. Leave until quite cold.

Make up the aspic as directed on the packet, cool and mix with the mayonnaise. Cut the anchovy fillets into thin strips. Cut roots off the mustard and cress and wash.

Spoon the setting sauce over each chicken piece. Allow to set completely, then repeat the process. Garnish with anchovy fillets and olive slices. Arrange the chicken pieces on a plate, with bunches of cress in between each piece. Serve immediately. *Serves 4.*

QUICK TIP

Instead of using fresh tomatoes, and especially when these are more expensive than usual, use canned tomatoes. A 397g/14 oz can will do nicely.

QUICK TIP

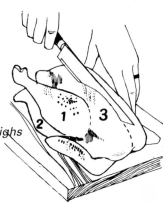

To joint a chicken into 6 pieces, separate the legs and thighs and cut the breast into 2 portions. Use the carcass and wings for stock or soup, as they are too difficult a shape to cover with sauce.

139 Malayan chicken

140 Chicken cobbler

You will need . . .

6 jointed chicken legs
salt and pepper
4 tablespoons oil
1 × 340g/12 oz can pineapple pieces
2 teaspoons soy sauce

Preparation time
10 minutes

2 teaspoons Worcester sauce
1 teaspoon arrowroot
1 red pepper

Cooking time
30 minutes

1 green pepper

Season the chicken well. Heat the oil in a large frying pan, add the chicken and cook for 10 minutes.

Drain the pineapple, add the pieces to the chicken with the soy sauce and Worcester sauce. Mix the arrowroot with a little of the juice until smooth, add the rest and add to the pan. Bring to the boil, stirring until slightly thickened. Cook for 20 minutes, stirring occasionally.

Arrange the chicken on a hot serving dish, pour the sauce over and garnish with strips of red and green pepper. *Serves 4.*

You will need . . .

2 chicken joints
40g/1½ oz butter
100g/4 oz mushrooms
300ml/½ pint milk
150ml/¼ pint water

Preparation time
25 minutes

1 chicken stock cube
1 teaspoon lemon juice
250g/9 oz plain flour

Cooking time
45 minutes

2 teaspoons baking powder
75g/3 oz margarine
2 sprigs parsley

Oven setting
220°C; 425°F; Gas Mark 7

Cut each chicken joint in half. Melt the butter and fry the chicken and mushrooms for 5 minutes. Remove the mushrooms. Add the milk, water, stock cube and lemon juice to the chicken, bring to the boil, cover and cook for 30 minutes. Mix 25g/1 oz flour to a smooth paste with a little water. Remove the chicken, cut off the flesh and return to the liquid with the flour paste. Bring to the boil, stirring until thickened. Add the mushrooms.

Make the scone topping. Sift the flour and baking powder together, add the margarine, cut into small pieces and rub in until the mixture resembles fine breadcrumbs. Add sufficient water to make a soft dough. Press out on a floured surface to 1-cm/½-inch thickness, and shape to size of dish.

Turn the chicken mixture into an ovenproof dish, place the scone mixture on top, mark into a criss-cross pattern, brush with milk and bake in the centre of the oven for 10 minutes or until well risen and golden brown. Serve garnished with parsley. *Serves 4.*

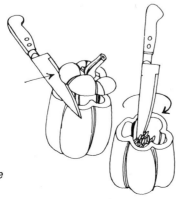

QUICK TIP

To seed pepper: first cut off top. Then run the point of a knife round the inside. The seeds and core will then lift out easily.

QUICK TIP

To prevent the knife from sticking to the cobbler topping when making the criss-cross pattern, dip the knife into some flour before making each incision.

141 Chicken potato pie

You will need . . .

25g/1 oz butter
1 chicken (1.5kg/3 lb)
1 × 295g/10 oz can condensed vegetable soup
1 large packet instant potato
50g/2 oz Gruyère cheese, grated

Preparation time
20 minutes

Cooking time
40 minutes

Oven setting
190°C; 375°F; Gas Mark 5

Melt the butter in a large flameproof dish. Cut the chicken into eight pieces and fry in the butter until golden brown. Add the soup and quarter can of water. Mix well, cover the dish and cook in the centre of the oven for 30 minutes.

Make up the potato as directed on the packet. Put into a piping bag fitted with a star nozzle. Pipe the potato over the top of the chicken mixture. Sprinkle with cheese.

Grill or bake for a further 10 minutes or until the top is golden brown. *Serves 4.*

142 Pimento turkey

You will need . . .

450g/1 lb cooked turkey meat
25g/1 oz butter
2 onions, sliced
1 × 227g/8 oz can pimentoes
1 chicken stock cube
600ml/1 pint hot water
salt and pepper
1 teaspoon cornflour

Preparation time
10 minutes

Cooking time
20 minutes

Cut the turkey meat into neat pieces. Melt butter and fry onion until transparent. Drain the pimentoes and cut into strips. Add to the onion and cook for 5 minutes.

Dissolve stock cube in water, add to pan and bring to the boil. Reduce the heat and simmer for 10 minutes. Season well.

Mix the cornflour to a smooth paste with a little cold water, add to pan and stir until thickened. Add the turkey meat and heat through. Arrange in a serving dish with the sauce poured over.
Serves 4.

QUICK TIP

If no piping nozzle is available, make a foil piping bag by rolling a double thickness of foil into a cone. Put the potatoes in, cut off the end and pipe through this hole. This gives an irregular but very attractive finish.

QUICK TIP

If pimentoes are not available, use as an alternative two aubergines, sliced, or four courgettes, cut into thin slices or strips.

143 Quick chicken soup

You will need . . .

1 chicken joint
25g/1 oz butter
1 small onion, chopped
2 teaspoons flour
600ml/1 pint water
1 chicken stock cube
salt and pepper
juice of ½ lemon
slices of toast cut into very
small squares (sippets)
2 teaspoons chopped parsley

Preparation time
15 minutes

Cooking time
25 minutes

Fry the chicken in butter for 10 minutes. Drain and cut off all the meat. Fry the onion in remaining butter until transparent. Add the flour, mix well and cook for 2-3 minutes. Gradually add the water, bring to the boil, stirring until thickened. Add stock cube and chicken pieces.

Return the chicken bones to the pan, season well and add lemon juice. Cover the pan and cook for 10 minutes longer. Meanwhile make the sippets of bread.

Remove the chicken bones. Check seasoning, adding more if required. Pour soup into shallow soup plates and serve sprinkled with sippets of bread and parsley. *Serves 4.*

144 Chicken mornay

You will need . . .

1 whole chicken (1.5kg/3 lb)
salt and pepper
100g/4 oz butter
25g/1 oz flour
300ml/½ pint milk
50g/2 oz cheese, grated
1 teaspoon French mustard
1 tablespoon crushed cornflakes

Preparation time
20 minutes

Cooking time
55 minutes

Oven setting
200°C; 400°F; Gas Mark 6

Joint the chicken into four, season well and place in an oven-proof dish. Dot with 50g/2 oz butter and bake in the centre of oven for 45 minutes.

Make the white sauce. Melt 25g/1 oz butter, add flour, mix well and cook for 2-3 minutes. Remove from heat and gradually add milk. Add 25g/1 oz cheese and the mustard, mix well and cook for 2-3 minutes. Beat in the remaining butter a little at a time. Cook gently for 5 minutes.

Pour off excess liquid from chicken, cover with sauce, and sprinkle with cornflakes and remaining cheese. Grill for 5-10 minutes or until bubbling. Serve very hot. *Serves 4.*

QUICK TIP

To give a more attractive appearance, the croutons can be cut into fancy shapes such as hearts and diamonds, by using very small cocktail cutters.

QUICK TIP

To give an even more savoury flavour to this dish, crushed potato crisps can be used instead of cornflakes.

Rice and pasta

Rice and pasta form the staple diet in many countries all over the world, and although we think of rice mainly to be used as a sweet dish—the old-fashioned rice pudding for example—a colourful rice hors d'oeuvre or the famous sweet 'n' sour pork served with plain boiled rice are well worth trying!

There are many kinds of pasta in all sorts of enchanting shapes and in most grocery shops a large choice can be found, such as pasta shells and bows.

These recipes also show how pasta can be used in quite new ways: why not try a sweet apple macaroni pudding instead of the usual savoury macaroni dish?

145 Sweet 'n' sour pork

(illustrated on frontispiece)

You will need . . .

	350g/12 oz belly of pork
	50g/2 oz plain flour
	1 tablespoon oil
	1 egg white
	1 × 70g/2¾ oz can frozen orange juice
Preparation time	1 tablespoon brown sugar
20 minutes	3 tablespoons vinegar
	1 tablespoon soy sauce
Cooking time	1 fresh orange
20 minutes	salt and pepper
	2 teaspoons cornflour
	275-350g/10-12 oz boiled long grain rice

Remove rind from pork and cut flesh into neat cubes. Mix flour, oil and 5 tablespoons water to a smooth paste. Season to taste. Whisk egg white until stiff and fold into the flour mixture using a metal spoon. Dip each piece of pork in batter and fry in hot, deep fat for a few minutes until golden brown and crisp. Drain on kitchen paper.

Put orange juice, sugar, vinegar and soy sauce into a small pan. Heat gently, adding enough water to make up to 300ml/½ pint. Thickly peel orange, cut into segments and add to the sauce with salt and pepper to taste.

Mix cornflour to a smooth paste with a little cold water, add to the sauce and bring to the boil, stirring until thickened. Pile pork into a bowl, pour sauce over and serve with a bowl of plain boiled rice and chutney. *Serves 4.*

You will need . . .

	75-100g/3-4 oz Carolina rice
	600ml/1 pint milk
	50g/2 oz castor sugar
	25g/1 oz butter
	pinch ground nutmeg

Preparation time
5 minutes

Cooking time
2 hours

Oven setting
160°C; 325°F; Gas Mark 3

Grease a 1.2-litre/2-pint pie dish. Then put in rice, milk and sugar. Stir well and dot the top with butter. Bake in centre of preheated oven for 2 hours.

Sprinkle top with grated nutmeg after 1 hour.

If a richer pudding is desired, add 150ml/¼ pint single cream or small tin evaporated milk. *Serves 4.*

QUICK TIP

After cooking rice, place in a colander and pour hot water over to separate and loosen the grains. If the pork and sauce is not quite ready, put the rice on a dish in the oven to keep hot.

QUICK TIP

To make this really rich and creamy tasting: if any skin forms from the milk during the first hour of cooking, stir it into the rice with a fork before sprinkling with nutmeg, and continue the slow cooking.

147 Quick spaghetti carbonara

You will need . . .

275g/10 oz quick cooking spaghetti
50g/2 oz butter
1 can egg and ham Hot Toast Savoury
few shakes garlic salt, if liked
parsley sprigs

Preparation time
5 minutes

Cooking time
15 minutes

Cook spaghetti in a large saucepan of salted, boiling water for 12 minutes, or until tender.

Drain and place in a large hot serving dish. Add butter and hot toast savoury, mix gently with a fork until butter and savoury has softened.

Sprinkle with garlic salt, garnish with parsley, and serve immediately. Serve with a green salad.　　　　*Serves 4.*

QUICK TIP

To keep hot if there are late-comers: the hot toast savoury and butter can be put into a large saucepan with the spaghetti when cooked for up to 30 minutes, allowing the butter to melt slowly.

148 Lasagne pie

You will need . . .

½ packet lasagne verde
1 large can minced beef
1 tablespoon tomato purée
garlic salt
pinch black pepper
150ml/¼ pint single cream
50g/2 oz grated cheese

Preparation time
10 minutes

Cooking time
30 minutes

Oven setting
200°C; 400°F; Gas Mark 6

Cook lasagne for 5 minutes in a large pan of salted, boiling water. Drain and keep hot. Empty meat into a saucepan with tomato purée, garlic salt and black pepper to taste. Cook for 5 minutes, stirring well.

Arrange the lasagne and meat in layers in a shallow, oven-proof dish, finishing with a layer of meat. Cover dish and cook for 15 minutes in centre of preheated oven.

Remove covering and pour cream over top. Sprinkle with cheese and return to oven for a further 10 minutes, or brown under a hot grill for 3-4 minutes. Serve immediately.
　　　　Serves 4.

QUICK TIP

A delicious alternative: use canned chunky stewed steak instead of minced beef and either plain or green lasagne. Season the steak and spread between the partly cooked lasagne. While the pie bakes make a quick tomato sauce to go with it.

149 Noodles with kidney sauce

150 Peach tart

You will need . . .

50g/2 oz butter
1 onion
2 lambs kidneys
1 × 198g/7 oz can sweetcorn
1 × 283g/10 oz can kidney soup

Preparation time
10 minutes

225g/8 oz noodles
½ teaspoon chopped parsley

Cooking time
15 minutes

Melt butter and fry chopped onion until transparent. Cut kidneys in half, remove skin and tubes and cut flesh into small pieces. Add to the pan and fry for 5 minutes. Drain corn, add to pan with the soup. Bring slowly to the boil and simmer for 1 minute.

Cook noodles in a large saucepan of salted, boiling water for 7-8 minutes. Drain and arrange on a large, hot serving dish.

Pour the sauce in the centre and serve sprinkled with chopped parsley. *Serves 4.*

You will need . . .

175g/6 oz short crust pastry
1 × 439g/15½ oz can creamed rice
1 × 213g/7½ oz can peach slices
1 teaspoon arrowroot
1 tablespoon honey
1 glaće cherry

Preparation time
20 minutes

Cooking time
15 minutes

Oven setting
220°C; 425°F; Gas Mark 7

Roll out pastry to fit a 20-cm/8-inch deep pie plate. Line plate, trim edges (*see Quick Tip below* for unusual pastry edge) prick base and bake blind for 15 minutes. Cool on a wire rack.

Empty rice into flan case. Drain peaches, reserving the juice. Arrange slices around edge of rice.

Mix arrowroot with a little of the juice to make a smooth paste, add more to make up to 4 tablespoons. Add honey and mix well. Bring slowly to the boil, stirring until thickened. Pour over the rice and peaches and serve very cold. Decorate with a glacé cherry. *Serves 4.*

QUICK TIP

For preparation prior to a party; the cooked noodles can be kept moist for a few hours in a large polythene bag, with a little oil added to them to prevent sticking. To serve: reheat in a large saucepan with lid, or in a slow oven in a covered dish.

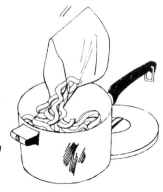

QUICK TIP

For this unusual pie edging fluted round cutters may be used: first cut rounds, using a 4-cm/1½-inch fluted cutter. Then cut crescents from the fluted circles and place the crescents round the edge of the pastry tart. Press well to seal.

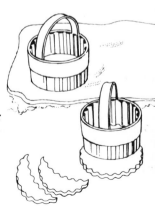

151 Rice salad

You will need . . .

225g/8 oz cooked long grain rice
salt and pepper
1 tablespoon oil
2 oranges
1 clove garlic

Preparation time 225g/8 oz cooked tongue
20 minutes 2 heads chicory

Put the rice into a large bowl. Season well with salt and pepper. Put the oil into a small bowl. Peel the oranges thickly and cut the flesh into segments, add to the oil. Crush the garlic and add to the orange mixture. Season and mix well.

Cut meat into neat cubes and add to the rice. Toss well. Cut one head of chicory into thin slices, so that when it separates it becomes small crescent shapes. Add to the rice with the orange mixture and mix well.

Arrange remaining chicory leaves around edges of a salad bowl and pile salad in the centre. Garnish with more fresh orange slices if liked. *Serves 4.*

152 Lasagne rolls

You will need . . .

½ packet lasagne verde
salt and pepper
2 cans chicken Hot Toast Savoury
50g/2 oz button mushrooms
25g/1 oz butter

Preparation time 25g/1 oz plain flour
10 minutes 300ml/½ pint milk
1 egg

Cooking time few tomatoes, cut in wedges
15 minutes few sprigs parsley

Cook lasagne in salted boiling water for 5 minutes. Drain and lay flat on a tea towel.

Spread hot toast savoury over each one and roll up loosely. Place in an ovenproof dish and keep warm in oven.

Melt butter and fry mushrooms for 2-3 minutes. Drain and keep hot, for garnish. Add flour to the remaining butter, and mix. Cook for 3 minutes. Remove from heat, gradually add milk and bring to the boil, stirring until thickened. Beat egg and add to the sauce. Season with salt and pepper. Heat gently but do not boil. Pour sauce over lasagne and garnish with mushrooms, tomatoes and parsley. *Serves 4.*

QUICK TIP

For extra speed or if oranges are out of season: use tinned mandarin oranges and pour a little lemon juice over the slices to give a sharper flavour.

QUICK TIP

If lasagne are inclined to stick together when cooked, separate them after draining by placing under hot running water, or dip in a pan of hot water for a few seconds. This also makes them easier to roll up.

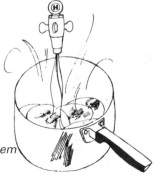

153 Bacon savoury rice

154 Salmon salad

You will need . . .

50g/2 oz butter
6 rashers bacon
100g/4 oz mushrooms
1 small onion
225g/8 oz long grain rice
salt and pepper
watercress

Preparation time
15 minutes

Cooking time
25 minutes

Melt butter in a large saucepan. Remove rinds from bacon and chop two rashers into small pieces, cut remaining rashers in half and roll tightly. Fry all the bacon in butter until crisp. Remove the rolls and keep to one side. Wash and slice the mushrooms and fry in remaining butter. Remove mushrooms and bacon pieces and put to one side.

Peel and finely chop the onion. Fry with the rice for 10 minutes in remaining butter. Add 600ml/1 pint water, salt and pepper. Bring slowly to the boil and simmer for 15 minutes, or until the rice is tender and the water absorbed. Return mushrooms and bacon pieces, mix well.

Put rice on to a serving dish and garnish with bacon rolls, mushrooms and watercress. *Serves 4.*

You will need . . .

225g/8 oz pasta shells
4 tablespoons oil
1 tablespoon vinegar
salt and pepper
1 teaspoon mixed herbs
225g/8 oz cooked or canned salmon
1 lettuce
½ cucumber, sliced

Preparation time
10 minutes

Cooking time
15 minutes

Cook the shells in salted fast boiling water for 15 minutes. Drain, rinse under cold water and put into a bowl.

Mix oil, vinegar, salt, pepper and herbs together. Pour over shells, toss well and leave until quite cold. Flake the salmon.

Arrange lettuce leaves around the edge of a large serving dish. Pile salmon and shells in the centre. Arrange cucumber between salmon mixture and lettuce. Pour excess oil over and serve immediately. *Serves 4.*

QUICK TIP

For a special treat at breakfast: if there is any left-over cold cooked rice, this dish can be prepared by quickly cooking the bacon and mushrooms, then frying the chopped onion and adding the ready cooked rice. Heat through and serve.

QUICK TIP

To drain shells thoroughly: after cooking and rinsing, wrap in a clean tea towel for a few minutes to remove excess water, remove from tea towel, then make oil and vinegar dressing and pour over them and toss in the bowl. The dressing will then be more readily absorbed.

155 Rice and orange mould

You will need . . .
1.2 litres/2 pints milk
75g/3 oz rice
25g/1 oz sugar
2 oranges
15g/½ oz gelatine
50g/2 oz almonds, blanched and browned

Preparation time
15 minutes

Cooking time
30 minutes

Put milk, rice and sugar into a large saucepan. Bring to the boil and simmer for 30 minutes, stirring occasionally to prevent sticking. Leave to cool.

Grate the orange rind. Mix rind and juice of one orange and stir in the gelatine. Heat gently until gelatine dissolves. Beat into rice mixture. Chop nuts finely and add to rice mixture.

Pour into a 1.2-litre/2-pint ring mould and allow to set. Remove pith from the remaining orange and cut the flesh into thin slices. Invert the pudding on to a glass serving dish and decorate with orange slices. *Serves 4.*

156 Stuffed peppers

You will need . . .
4 medium-sized peppers
225g/8 oz cooked rice
1 clove garlic
100g/4 oz black olives
1 × 50g/1¾ oz can anchovy fillets
salt and pepper
1 × 140g/4.9 oz can condensed tomato soup

Preparation time
15 minutes

Cooking time
20 minutes

Oven setting
190°C; 375°F; Gas Mark 5

Remove tops from each pepper. Scoop out seeds, put shells into a pan of cold water and bring to the boil. Drain and stand peppers in an ovenproof dish.

Mix rice, crushed garlic, chopped olives and chopped anchovies together. Season well and fill each pepper with the mixture. Top each with a whole anchovy fillet.

Dilute soup with half a tin of water and pour around the peppers. Cover dish with a tight fitting lid or piece of foil and bake in centre of preheated oven for 15 minutes. *Serves 4.*

QUICK TIP

To save time when serving: arrange slices of fresh orange in the base of the mould before pouring in the rice mixture. When turned out, the orange slices form a colourful decoration, and none other is needed.

QUICK TIP

To give a professional finish: if the peppers are uneven or rounded at the base end, cut a slice off the bottom so that they are upright when filled, and standing in the sauce.

157 Paella

158 Apple macaroni pudding

You will need . . .

- 8 chicken legs
- 4 tablespoons oil
- 4 tomatoes
- 1 teaspoon paprika
- 275g/10 oz Patna rice
- 4 giant prawns
- 150g/5 oz frozen green beans
- salt
- pinch saffron

Preparation time
15 minutes

Cooking time
about 35 minutes

Trim the chicken legs and fry in oil until golden brown. Remove and keep to one side.

Peel and chop tomatoes. Fry in remaining oil, stir in paprika and add 2 pints water. Bring to the boil, reduce to simmering and return chicken and rice to the pan. Stir well and cook for 10 minutes. Add halved prawns and beans, season well with salt and simmer until all water has been absorbed.

Add saffron, mix well and serve from the dish in which it was cooked. *Serves 4.*

You will need . . .

- 100g/4 oz quick cooking macaroni
- 50g/2 oz butter
- 75g/3 oz brown sugar
- 1 × 295g/10 oz can apple purée
- dessert apple slices

Preparation time
10 minutes

Cooking time
20 minutes

Oven setting
200°C; 400°F; Gas Mark 6

Cook macaroni as directed for 7 minutes. Drain.

Melt half the butter in a saucepan, add macaroni and half the sugar. Toss well until sugar has dissolved. Pile half the mixture in a greased ovenproof dish. Add half the apple purée, cover with remaining macaroni and finally apple purée. Sprinkle top with rest of brown sugar. Top with slices of apple.

Dot with remaining butter and bake in oven for 10 minutes to heat apple and caramelise the sugar. Serve very hot.
Serves 4.

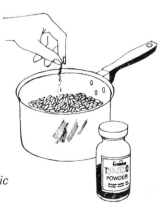

QUICK TIP

To make rice yellow: if saffron (which is sometimes scarce and expensive) is unavailable, use turmeric powder to colour the rice. Use just a pinch, otherwise you will have turmeric flavoured paella!

QUICK TIP

To cut down on preparation time: if in a great hurry, add the apple purée to the cooked macaroni with the sugar and butter in a shallow dish. Mix well and brown under the grill.

159 Rice cheesecakes

Spaghetti
160 with green beans

Rice cheesecakes

You will need . . .

75g/3 oz Patna rice, cooked
1 egg
75g/3 oz grated cheese
1 tablespoon chopped parsley
pinch mustard powder
25g/1 oz plain flour
50g/2 oz browned breadcrumbs

Preparation time
10 minutes

Cooking time
5 minutes each

Mix rice, half the beaten egg, cheese, parsley and mustard powder together. Add a little flour if necessary to stiffen the mixture. Beat well until evenly blended.

Divide into 8 portions and shape each into a flat cake. Dust liberally with flour. Coat with remaining egg and toss in brown breadcrumbs.

Fry in shallow fat for 2-3 minutes on each side. Serve very hot with green salad. *Serves 4.*

Spaghetti with green beans

You will need . . .

350g/12 oz spaghetti
salt and pepper
50g/2 oz butter
150g/5 oz frozen green beans
175g/6 oz cooked salt beef
1 × 150g/5 oz carton soured cream
1 bunch watercress

Preparation time
10 minutes

Cooking time
25 minutes

Cook the spaghetti in a large saucepan of salted, boiling water for 12 minutes or until tender. Drain and keep hot.

Meanwhile melt butter and fry defrosted beans for 5 minutes. Chop meat or cut into neat strips and add to pan with salt, pepper and the soured cream. Heat gently without boiling for 5 minutes.

Put the spaghetti into a serving dish and add the sauce. Arrange watercress in a ring round the dish. Serve immediately. *Serves 4.*

QUICK TIP

With fuel bills in mind: if you are using a moderate oven, 180°C, 350°F, Gas Mark 4, place the cheesecakes in a shallow tin, dribble with butter and bake for 20 minutes. They will rise slightly and have a lighter texture.

QUICK TIP

To save cooking time: boil the defrosted beans in with the spaghetti for the last 5 minutes of its cooking time. Heat the meat in the butter with seasoning and soured cream and mix into the drained spaghetti and beans.

161 Spaghetti milanese

162 Chocolate shell pudding

You will need . . .

275g/10 oz spaghetti
salt and pepper
25g/1 oz butter
1 onion
25g/1 oz plain flour
300ml/½ pint water
1 × 65g/2¼ oz can tomato purée
¼ teaspoon dried herbs
175g/6 oz ham
100g/4 oz mushrooms

Preparation time
20 minutes

Cooking time
15 minutes

Cook the spaghetti in a large saucepan of salted, boiling water for 10 minutes or until soft. Drain and keep hot.

Melt butter in a large pan. Peel and finely chop onion and fry until transparent. Add flour, mix well and cook for 2-3 minutes. Remove pan from heat and gradually add the water. Return to heat and add tomato purée and herbs. Bring to the boil, stirring all the time until thickened.

Chop ham roughly and add to sauce. Slice mushrooms and add to sauce. Season to taste. Cook gently for 5-10 minutes. Put spaghetti in large serving dish, pour sauce over, toss and serve very hot. *Serves 4.*

You will need . . .

100g/4 oz pasta shells
600ml/1 pint milk
25g/1 oz cocoa powder
little extra milk
2 tablespoons soft brown sugar
2 eggs
100g/4 oz castor sugar

Preparation time
10 minutes

Cooking time
40 minutes

Oven setting
190°C; 375°F; Gas Mark 5

Put shells and milk into a large saucepan, bring to the boil stirring to prevent sticking. Simmer for 20 minutes. Mix cocoa to a smooth paste with a little cold milk, add brown sugar and mix well. Stir into shell mixture and bring to the boil, stirring all the time until smooth. Add egg yolks and beat well. Pour mixture into an ovenproof dish.

Whisk egg whites until stiff and standing in peaks. Add half castor sugar and whisk again until thick. Add remaining sugar, folding in with a metal spoon.

Pipe mixture in a pattern over filling and bake in centre of oven for 15 minutes to lightly brown the meringue. *Serves 4.*

QUICK TIP

An alternative way of making the tomato sauce: use a can of condensed tomato soup. Add the soup and herbs to the fried onion and bring to the boil. Add the chopped ham, sliced mushrooms and seasonings, and cook as in original recipe.

QUICK TIP

To ensure that your meringue sets firmly add just a pinch of cream of tartar to the sugar before whisking with the egg whites.

Macaroni
163 and tuna layer pie

164 Pork and tomato savoury

You will need . . .

225g/8 oz cooked macaroni
salt and pepper
1×198g/7 oz can tuna fish
25g/1 oz butter
25g/1 oz flour

Preparation time
10 minutes

300ml/½ pint milk
100g/4 oz grated cheese
1 tablespoon brown breadcrumbs

Cooking time
20 minutes

Oven setting
200°C; 400°F; Gas Mark 6

Season macaroni well with salt and pepper. Flake tuna fish.

Melt butter in a small pan, add flour, mix well and cook for 2-3 minutes. Remove pan from heat and gradually add milk. Return to heat and bring to the boil, stirring until thickened. Add half the cheese and season well. Cook 2-3 minutes.

Arrange macaroni, tuna and sauce in layers in a shallow oven-proof dish, finishing with a layer of sauce. Sprinkle with the remaining cheese and coat with breadcrumbs. Dot with butter and bake in centre of preheated oven for 15 minutes, or until top is golden brown. Serve very hot. *Serves 4.*

You will need . . .

350 g/12 oz spaghetti
25 g/1 oz pork dripping
1 onion
100 g/4 oz belly of pork
450 g/1 lb tomatoes, skinned
100 g/4 oz grated Parmesan cheese

Preparation time
15 minutes

Cooking time
15 minutes

Cook the spaghetti in a large saucepan of salted, boiling water for 12 minutes or until tender. Drain and keep hot in a large serving dish.

Meanwhile make the sauce. Melt dripping and fry finely chopped onion for a few minutes. Cut pork into tiny strips and fry until browned. Cut tomatoes into rough pieces and add to pan. Season well. Cook 10 minutes, stirring to break up the tomatoes.

Pour sauce over the spaghetti and serve immediately. Hand cheese separately. *Serves 4.*

QUICK TIP

To bear in mind when planning the week's work and menus: this dish can be made a day in advance and stored in the refrigerator. It takes only 25 minutes cooking before you intend to serve it.

QUICK TIP

To remove tomato skins if unpeeled tomatoes are used: at the end of the cooking time boil the mixture rapidly for a few minutes. The skins will rise to the top and can be skimmed off with a perforated spoon.

165 Rice hors d'oeuvre

166 Rice imperial

You will need . . .

450g/1 lb Patna rice
salt and pepper
50g/2 oz cooked peas
2 tomatoes
1 × 106g/3¾ oz can brisling
50g/2 oz peeled prawns
1 stick celery, sliced
2 tablespoons sweet corn
1 piece of canned pimento
1 tablespoon cream
½ teaspoon parsley
1 clove garlic, crushed
2 tablespoons oil
½ tablespoon wine vinegar
1 bunch watercress

Preparation time
30 minutes

Cooking time
12 minutes

Cook rice in a large saucepan of salted, boiling water for 12 minutes. Drain, season well and press into a large oblong tin.

Put peas into a small bowl. Skin tomatoes and cut into small pieces. Put into another bowl. Put brisling into another bowl with their oil. Put prawns into a bowl. Peel and dice celery. Cut pimento into strips and mix with the celery. Mix sweet corn with cream and parsley. Mix garlic, oil, vinegar, salt and pepper together. Pour a little into each of the bowls and turn well.

Turn the rice mould on to a large serving dish or board. Place each mixture in a pile on top to give a decorative appearance. Arrange watercress around the rice. *Serves 4.*

You will need . . .

100g/4 oz Carolina rice
600ml/1 pint milk
25g/1 oz castor sugar
1 × 411g/14 oz can pears
1 tablespoon arrowroot
few drops pink colouring
few drops green colouring
angelica, cut into diamond shapes.

Preparation time
10 minutes

Cooking time
30 minutes

Put rice and milk into a large saucepan with sugar, bring slowly to the boil, stirring occasionally. Cover and simmer for 30 minutes or until all milk has been absorbed and rice is tender. Turn rice into a greased 20-cm/8-inch round sandwich tin, press and cool. Set and invert on to a flat serving dish.

Drain pears and keep the juice. Place pears, cut side down, on a wire rack. Blend arrowroot with a little of the juice. Add the rest and bring slowly to the boil, stirring until thickened. Put half into a bowl and add a little pink colouring, colour the other half pale green.

Coat half the pears green and half pink. When set arrange them on top of the flat rice mould and garnish with angelica. Serve very cold. *Serves 4.*

QUICK TIP

An attractive and easy dish for a party: prepare double the quantities of rice and also the toppings. To serve, spread the rice evenly on a large tray and then arrange small quantities of the different mixtures in indentations to make a colourful pattern.

QUICK TIP

To coat the pears professionally: place a piece of foil beneath the wire cooling rack. The foil will catch any surplus coating which will be left behind when transferring the pears to the rice mould.

167 Butterfly layer cake

You will need . . .

75g/3 oz Carolina rice
300ml/½ pint milk
pinch nutmeg
1 tablespoon sugar
2 eggs
50g/2 oz castor sugar
50g/2 oz plain flour
1 × 397g/14 oz can blackcurrant pie
filling

Preparation time
20 minutes

Cooking time
40 minutes

Oven setting
200°C; 400°F; Gas Mark 6

Put rice and milk into a large saucepan with nutmeg and sugar, bring slowly to the boil, stirring occasionally. Cover and simmer for 30 minutes or until all milk has been absorbed and rice is tender. Turn rice into a greased 20-cm/8-inch round sandwich tin, press and cool.

Whisk eggs and castor sugar together until thick enough to leave an impression of the whisk. Add flour, folding it in with a metal spoon. Turn into a 20-cm/8-inch greased sandwich tin and bake in centre of preheated oven for 10 minutes, or until firm and golden. Cool on a wire rack.

Spread cake with two-thirds pie filling, taking it right to the edges. Invert the rice on top of the filling, removing the tin. Decorate the top with remaining pie filling and spread in the shape of butterfly wings. *Serves 4.*

QUICK TIP

To speed up the preparation and setting time: use a tin of creamed rice, and stir in 1 tablespoon gelatine dissolved in 2 tablespoons hot water. Put to set in a sandwich tin.

168 Cheesy buttered noodles

You will need . . .

225g/8 oz plain noodles
salt and pepper
75g/3 oz unsalted butter
75g/3 oz hard cheese, grated

Preparation time
5 minutes

Cooking time
8 minutes

Cook noodles in a large saucepan of salted, boiling water for 7-8 minutes or until soft. Drain well and pile into a large, hot serving dish. Season well with salt and pepper.

Cut butter into small pieces and mix into noodles with the cheese.

Serve more unsalted butter and a large piece of cheese separately. *Serves 4.*

QUICK TIP

If no grated cheese is at hand, use semi-soft cheese, and simply cut it into small cubes. The hot noodles will melt it almost as quickly as grated hard cheese.

Pies and flans

There can hardly be anything more satisfying to a housewife than the excitement on the faces of her family when a bright and colourful fruit flan is put on the table. Recipes for such delightfully fresh and light flans can be found in this chapter.

Besides sweet flans, pies and tarts, there is also a choice of savoury flans, pies and smaller snacks, some of which can be served cold and are also particularly useful to take for picnics. With these recipes, all of which are bound to be popular with those who like pastry, every housewife can give her family the pleasure of enjoying delicious home-baking.

169 Peach bands

(illustrated on frontispiece)

You will need . . .
1 × 368g/13 oz packet frozen puff pastry
1 egg yolk
1 × 213g/7½ oz can peach slices
1 teaspoon arrowroot

Preparation time
20 minutes

Cooking time
10 minutes

Oven setting
220°C; 425°F; Gas Mark 7

Roll out pastry into oblong 30 × 10cm/12 × 4 inches. Cut out eight strips each 4 × 10cm/1½ × 4 inches. Flake edges using the back of a knife and cut into top of each band, 5mm/¼ inch from edge. Beat egg yolk and brush over the pastry. Bake in top part of oven for about 10 minutes or until well risen and golden brown. Cool on a wire rack.

Chop peaches roughly. Mix arrowroot to a smooth paste with a little of the juice. Add more juice to make up to 150ml/¼ pint. Bring to the boil, stirring until thickened. Cook until transparent.

Remove lids from each band. Scoop out uncooked pastry and fill with chopped peaches. Coat with glaze and serve cold.
Serves 4.

170 Corn and ham flan

You will need . . .
175g/6 oz short crust pastry
1 × 170g/6 oz can evaporated milk
25g/1 oz plain flour
50g/2 oz butter
1 small onion

Preparation time
20 minutes

75g/3 oz ham, diced
1 × 198g/7 oz can sweetcorn
1 teaspoon mustard

Cooking time
30 minutes

salt and pepper
75g/3 oz grated cheese
few sprigs parsley

Oven setting
200°C; 400°F; Gas Mark 6

Line a 20-cm/8-inch flan ring with the pastry. Trim the edges and bake blind for 20 minutes. Allow to cool. Make the milk up to 300ml/½ pint with water. Whisk in flour and add half the butter. Bring to the boil, stirring until thickened.

Chop the onion finely and fry in remaining butter until soft. Add to the mixture with the ham and drained corn, mustard, salt and pepper. Mix well.

Pour into prepared flan case, sprinkle with cheese and grill until browned. Serve cold, garnished with parsley. *Serves 4.*

QUICK TIP

Leftover egg whites can be stored in the refrigerator for at least a week. Keep until you have enough to make an angel cake (12 egg whites) meringue (only 2 egg whites) or use as a nutritive addition to jellies (1 egg white will do).

QUICK TIP

To prevent the pastry from stretching, wrap it round a floured rolling pin. Then lift up and place gently into flan case. It will unroll very easily into place.

171 Spinach cups

172 Lamb and mushroom pie

You will need . . .

8 slices white bread
50g/2 oz butter
150g/5 oz frozen leaf spinach
25g/1 oz margarine
2 eggs

Preparation time
20 minutes

100g/4 oz cottage cheese
25g/1 oz Parmesan cheese
15g/½ oz powdered milk and 150ml/¼
pint water

Cooking time
35 minutes

salt and black pepper
pinch paprika

Oven setting
180°C; 350°F; Gas Mark 4

2 tomatoes, cut into quarters

Remove crusts. Butter each slice and place, buttered side down, in 8 patty tins.

Cook spinach in the margarine, drain and place in cup cases spreading it up the sides to make a nest.

Whisk eggs and all other ingredients (except tomatoes) together. Pour into cases. Bake in centre of moderate oven for 20 minutes. Garnish cups with tomato quarters. Serve very hot.
Serves 4.

You will need . . .

1 Spanish onion
100g/4 oz mushrooms
25g/1 oz butter
450g/1 lb lamb
300ml/½ pint beef stock

Preparation time
20 minutes

salt and pepper
pinch mace
100g/4 oz frozen puff pastry

Cooking time
60 minutes

1 egg, beaten

Oven setting
200°C; 400°F; Gas Mark 6
180°C; 350°F; Gas Mark 4

Peel and chop onion. Wash and roughly chop mushrooms. Fry both gently in butter until soft.

Cut meat into 2.5-cm/1-inch pieces and add to pan. Cook for 10 minutes. Add stock and seasoning. Cover and simmer for 20 minutes.

Place mixture in pie dish, cover with pastry, trim edges and flute. Brush with beaten egg and bake in centre of oven for 30 minutes. Reduce temperature to 180°C; 350°F; Gas Mark 4 after 15 minutes.
Serves 4.

QUICK TIP

If you are using fresh spinach you will need to cook about 450g/1 lb to obtain the amount required for the recipe. Cook gently in a little butter. Do not add any water as the spinach will provide enough of its own liquid.

QUICK TIP

Left-over cooked lamb can also be used effectively for this recipe. Chop up the lamb and cook it gently for five minutes with the mushroom mixture.

173 Danish asparagus shells

You will need . . .

125g/4½ oz plain flour
pinch salt
75g/3 oz butter, cut into small pieces
1 egg
1 tablespoon Danish cream
4 scallop shells
1 packet white sauce mix
75g/3 oz shrimps
1 × 10½ oz can asparagus tips
1 tablespoon sherry
1 tablespoon lemon juice
pinch pepper

Preparation time
30 minutes plus 2 hours cooling time

Cooking time
20 minutes

Oven setting
220°C; 425°F; Gas Mark 7

Sift flour and salt, add butter cut into small pieces and mix lightly with flour. Add egg and cream. Mix lightly to make a soft dough. Leave in the refrigerator for 2 hours to harden.

Roll out very thinly. Grease the back of each shell and cover with pastry. Trim the edges and bake in centre of oven for 10-12 minutes. Allow to cool.

Make up the sauce mix as directed. Add most of the shrimps and the drained asparagus, reserving a little for garnish. Season well, add sherry, lemon juice and pepper. Heat gently. Pour into hot shells and serve immediately garnished with shrimps and asparagus. *Serves 4.*

QUICK TIP

To make smaller shapes for cocktail savouries or snacks, cover bases of patty tins with pastry and bake them. These small shells are ideal for buffet parties and can be filled with a wide variety of savoury fillings.

174 Apple meringue

You will need . . .

4 eggs
175g/6 oz castor sugar
50g/2 oz plain flour
4 teaspoons cocoa
450g/1 lb cooking apples
few cherries
few pieces angelica

Preparation time
20 minutes

Cooking time
20 minutes

Oven setting
200°C; 400°F; Gas Mark 6
220°C; 425°F; Gas Mark 7

Whisk 2 eggs and 50g/2 oz castor sugar together until thick enough to leave an impression of the whisk for a few seconds. Fold in the sifted flour and cocoa powder. Turn into a greased and floured 15-cm/6-inch flan tin. Bake in centre of oven for 10-12 minutes. Turn on to a wire rack and cool. Increase oven heat to 220°C; 425°F; Gas Mark 7.

Peel and core apples. Stew in a very little water until pulpy. Sweeten to taste. Separate remaining eggs. Beat yolks into the cooled apple mixture. Pour into the flan case and place on a fireproof plate.

Whisk egg whites until stiff and fold in remaining sugar. Pile on top of the apples and return to the oven for 3 to 4 minutes. Decorate with cherries and angelica. *Serves 4.*

QUICK TIP

To ensure that the meringue is stiff enough, whisk the whites until standing up in peaks. Start tilting the basin and shake gently – the whites will stay put if stiff enough. If the whites come away from the bowl, whisk a little longer.

175 Mushroom cream flan

You will need . . .

Preparation time
25 minutes

Cooking time
20 minutes

Oven setting
200°C; 400°F; Gas Mark 6

For the pastry:
175g/6 oz plain flour
pinch salt
40g/1½ oz butter, cut into small pieces
40g/1½ oz lard, cut into small pieces
For the filling:
2 hard-boiled eggs
2 teaspoons lemon juice
1 × 113g/4 oz packet cream cheese
100g/4 oz mushrooms
1 tablespoon milk
15g/½ oz butter
1 green pepper
1 tablespoon oil

Sift flour and salt into a bowl, add both fats and rub in until mixture resembles fine breadcrumbs. Add enough water to make a stiff paste. Roll out to fit a 20-cm/8-inch flan ring or baking tin. Line ring, trim edges and bake blind for 20 minutes. Allow to cool.

Chop eggs and mix with lemon juice and cheese. Wash and slice mushrooms, cook in milk and butter until soft. Wash and core pepper, cut into strips and fry in oil until soft. Drain mushrooms and pepper on kitchen paper.

Spread cheese mixture into flan case and arrange mushrooms and pepper over the top. *Serves 4.*

176 Gougère

You will need . . .

Preparation time
20 minutes

Cooking time
50 minutes

Oven setting
200°C; 400°F; Gas Mark 6

175g/6 oz plain flour
salt and pepper
300ml/½ pint water
50g/2 oz butter
3 eggs
225g/8 oz leeks
50g/2 oz butter
300ml/½ pint milk
pinch dry mustard
50g/2 oz grated cheese

Sift together 150g/5 oz flour and salt. Bring water and butter to the boil, add flour and beat well until smooth and mixture forms a ball. Add eggs one at a time, beating until smooth after each addition. Spread a little of the mixture in an ovenproof dish. Pipe the rest around the edge.

Wash and slice leeks. Fry for 5 minutes in butter. Add remaining flour, mix well and cook for 2-3 minutes. Remove from the heat and gradually add milk. Return to heat and bring to the boil, stirring all the time until slightly thickened. Add mustard and cheese.

Pour mixture into centre of the flan and bake for 40 minutes. *Serves 4.*

QUICK TIP

If you cut the fat into the flour with two knives before rubbing, you will find that it rubs in much more quickly.

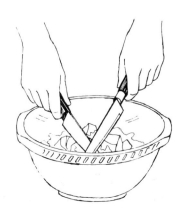

QUICK TIP

This mixture could be spread and piped on to a sheet of well-greased foil on a baking sheet instead of being cooked in a dish. Put the filling in before cooking, to speed up the preparation.

177 Crunchy top fruit pie

You will need . . .

1kg/2 lb cooking apples
225g/8 oz pitted prunes
juice of 1 lemon
75g/3 oz castor sugar
100g/4 oz plain flour

Preparation time
20 minutes
pinch salt
50g/2 oz butter, cut into small pieces
25g/1 oz brown sugar

Cooking time
30 minutes
pinch cinnamon

Oven setting
200°C; 400°F; Gas Mark 6

Peel, core and slice the apples, put into a pan with the prunes, lemon juice and castor sugar. Heat gently for about 20 minutes until apples begin to soften. Put fruit into an ovenproof dish.

Sift flour and salt, add butter and rub in until the mixture resembles fine breadcrumbs. Add brown sugar, and cinnamon, mixing well. Sprinkle the mixture over apples.

Bake in centre of oven for 10 minutes. Serve hot or cold decorated with fresh apple slices. *Serves 4.*

QUICK TIP

To save time, use canned apple filling (omitting the castor sugar) and packet crumble mix.

178 Danish flan

You will need . . .

175g/6 oz short crust pastry
1 × 340g/12 oz can chopped ham with pork
6 gherkins
½ teaspoon mustard

Preparation time
25 minutes
pinch pepper
pinch nutmeg
15g/½ oz gelatine

Cooking time
20 minutes
1 × 170g/6 oz can cream
3 egg whites
1 red pepper, cut into rings

Oven setting
200°C; 400°F; Gas Mark 6
1 green pepper, cut into rings
1 × 198g/7 oz can sweetcorn
few pickled onions

Roll out pastry to fit a 20-cm/8-inch flan tin. Trim the edges and bake blind for 20 minutes. Cool.

Chop the meat finely. Chop 3 gherkins and add to the meat with mustard, pepper and nutmeg. Dissolve gelatine in 2 tablespoons hot water. Add to the mixture with the cream. Mix well. Whisk egg whites and fold into the mixture when beginning to set. Pile into prepared flan case.

Arrange red and green pepper rings, corn and onions in a decorative pattern round the flan. Garnish top of flan with gherkin fans (*see Quick Tip below*). Serve very cold. *Serves 4.*

QUICK TIP

To make gherkin fans: cut narrow strips lengthwise with a sharp knife to about 1-cm/½-inch from the base. Then spread gently into fan shape.

179 Macaroon mincemeat tarts

You will need . . .

175g/6 oz plain flour
pinch salt
75g/3 oz pre-whipped fat
2 tablespoons water
3 tablespoons mincemeat
2 egg whites
75g/3 oz castor sugar
75g/3 oz ground almonds
few drops almond essence

Preparation time
15 minutes

Cooking time
30 minutes

Oven setting
190°C; 375°F; Gas Mark 5

Put flour, salt, fat and water into a large bowl, mixing to a dough with a fork. Turn on to a floured surface and knead lightly until smooth. Roll out pastry. Using 4-cm/1½-inch round cutter, cut out 40 rounds. Line 8 patty tins with 5 rounds each to make flour shapes. Bake in centre of oven for 10 minutes.

Spread base of each tartlet with mincemeat. Whisk egg whites until stiff. Fold in sugar, almonds and almond essence. Pile on to mincemeat and sprinkle with flaked almonds if liked.

Bake in centre of oven for 20 minutes. Serve with thick cream.
Serves 4.

180 Tuna fish pie

You will need . . .

40g/1½ oz butter
40g/1½ oz plain flour
300ml/½ pint milk
2 hard-boiled eggs, chopped
1 × 198g/7 oz can tuna, drained
grated rind of 1 lemon
1 × 368g/13 oz packet frozen puff pastry

Preparation time
20 minutes

Cooking time
25 minutes

Oven setting
220°C; 425°F; Gas Mark 7

Melt butter and stir in flour. Mix well and cook for 2-3 minutes. Remove from heat and gradually add milk. Return to heat and bring to the boil stirring until thickened. Add egg, flaked tuna fish and lemon rind. Mix well.

Roll out pastry and cut into two 20 × 10cm/8 × 4-inch oblongs. Place one on a baking sheet. Cover with filling, damp edges of the pastry and cover with other oblong. Make slits across the top. Press edges together to seal. Trim and flute. Brush with egg. Bake in centre of oven for 25 minutes.

Serve very hot.
Serves 4.

QUICK TIP

These tarts can be varied by using the following mixture, which makes a very good alternative to mincemeat: the juice and the grated rind of 1 lemon mixed with 4 tablespoons lemon curd.

QUICK TIP

To prevent dark rings forming round egg yolks, drain off boiling water, crack the shells immediately and then cover with cold running water until the eggs are completely cold.

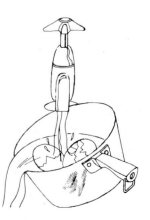

181 Cherry ginger crunch

You will need . . .

175g/6 oz ginger biscuits
75g/3 oz butter
1 teaspoon powdered ginger
1 × 170g/6 oz can evaporated milk
20g/¾ oz cornflour
25g/1 oz castor sugar
few drops vanilla essence
1 × 397g/14 oz can cherry pie filling

Preparation time
10 minutes

Cooking time
5 minutes

Crush biscuits into crumbs. Melt butter, add biscuits and ginger. Mix well. Press into a 20-cm/8-inch flan tin and allow this to set.

Make milk up to 300ml/½ pint with water. Mix cornflour and sugar together with a little milk. Bring rest to the boil and pour over cornflour mixture, stirring well. Return to pan and bring to the boil, stirring until thick. Add vanilla essence.

Spread half the pie filling in base of case, cover with cornflour mixture. Top with remaining pie filling. *Serves 4.*

182 Orange cream flan

You will need . . .

For the flan:
75g/3 oz butter or margarine
75g/3 oz castor sugar
2 eggs
75g/3 oz self-raising flour
For the filling:
1 × 312g/11 oz can mandarins
grated rind and juice of 1 orange
75g/3 oz sugar
25g/1 oz cornflour
2 eggs
15g/½ oz butter

Preparation time
20 minutes

Cooking time
20 minutes

Oven setting
180°C; 350°F; Gas Mark 4

Grease and flour a 21-cm/8½-inch sponge flan tin. Cream butter or margarine and sugar together until light and fluffy. Add the eggs one at a time, beating well after each addition. Fold in flour and turn mixture into prepared tin. Bake in centre of oven for 20 minutes. Turn out and cool on wire rack.

Drain mandarins. Add orange rind with juice to the mandarin juice. Make up to 300ml/½ pint with water. Mix sugar, cornflour and egg yolks together. Bring orange juice to the boil, pour over egg mixture, stirring well. Return to pan and bring back to the boil, stirring until thickened. Add butter and beat well. Allow to cool.

Whisk egg whites and fold into mixture. Pile into flan case. Decorate with mandarins. *Serves 4.*

QUICK TIP

When making a crushed biscuit crust for a flan, put the biscuits into a polythene bag and close it tightly. Crush the biscuits with a rolling pin and there will be no wastage or mess.

QUICK TIP

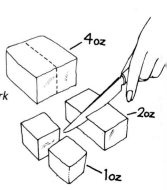

Even 15g/½ oz butter can be measured without weighing. Mark off each 250g/8.82 oz in grams/ounces with a knife and half again until you reach the required amount.

Tomato 183 bacon and egg pies

184 Curry and rice ring

You will need . . .

225g/8 oz short crust pastry
2 eggs
75g/3 oz bacon rashers, chopped
3 tomatoes, skinned
75g/3 oz Cheddar cheese, grated
¼ teaspoon dry mustard
1 × 170g/6 oz can evaporated milk

Preparation time
10 minutes

Cooking time
30 minutes

Oven setting
200°C; 400°F; Gas Mark 6

Roll out pastry to 3-mm/⅛-inch thickness. Cut out 6 rounds to fit 6 old saucers. Trim the edges.

Beat eggs and add bacon. Chop tomatoes roughly and add to egg with cheese, mustard and milk. Pour into the prepared pastry cases. Place on baking sheet and bake in centre of oven for 30 minutes.

Serve hot or cold. *Serves 4.*

You will need . . .

175g/6 oz Patna rice
salt and pepper
25g/1 oz butter
100g/4 oz bacon
1 banana, sliced
1 packet white sauce mix
2 teaspoons curry powder
350g/12 oz cold cooked chicken
150g/5 oz sweet corn kernels, drained

Preparation time
20 minutes

Cooking time
25 minutes

Cook the rice in a large saucepan of salted, boiling water for 12 minutes. Drain, mix with salt, pepper and butter. Press into a 20-cm/8-inch sponge flan tin. Keep hot.

Remove bacon rind, cut bacon into strips and fry gently in own fat. Drain and reserve a few pieces for garnish. Fry banana in remaining bacon fat. Keep a few pieces for garnish. Make up the sauce as directed, add curry powder and cook for 5 minutes. Add chicken, bacon, banana and sweet corn. Heat through.

Turn the rice mould on to a large serving dish, pour sauce mixture into the centre and garnish with remaining bacon and banana. Serve very hot. *Serves 4.*

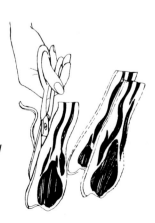

QUICK TIP

Use sharp kitchen scissors instead of a knife for removing the bacon rind. Scissors are easier for removing the small bones as well.

QUICK TIP

The rice mould can be made up two days in advance if necessary. Store it in its tin, wrapped in aluminium foil, or a polythene bag, in the refrigerator.

185 Picnic loaf

Cheese and
186 onion potato flan

You will need . . .

1 onion
450g/1 lb belly of pork
100g/4 oz ham
chicken stock cube made up with
300ml/½ pint water

Preparation time
30 minutes

350g/12 oz plain flour
salt
100g/4 oz lard
150ml/¼ pint hot water

Cooking time
1 hour

4 hard-boiled eggs
little milk for brushing

Oven setting
200°C; 400°F; Gas Mark 6

Chop onion finely. Mince pork and ham. Mix with onion and stock. Sift flour and salt into a large bowl. Heat lard and water until boiling. Add flour and beat well until the mixture forms a ball. Separate one third and keep hot.

Knead the rest lightly until smooth. Shape into a greased 450g/1 lb loaf tin, fill with half the meat mixture, place eggs on top and cover with rest of the mixture.

Shape remaining dough to fit the top of the tin. Press the edges together and flute. Brush with milk and bake in centre of oven for 1 hour. Serve cold with tomato salad (*see Quick Tip below*).
Serves 4.

You will need . . .

1 packet instant potato
50g/2 oz plain flour
salt and pepper
50g/2 oz butter
2 large onions

Preparation time
20 minutes

300ml/½ pint milk
100g/4 oz grated cheese

Cooking time
30 minutes

Oven setting
200°C; 400°F; Gas Mark 6

Make up the potato as directed. Add 25g/1 oz flour, salt, pepper and butter. Beat well until smooth. Place the mixture on an ovenproof plate and shape into an 20-cm/8-inch round. Build up sides to hold the filling.

Peel, chop and fry onions in the remaining butter. Add 25g/1 oz flour, mix well and cook for 2-3 minutes. Remove from heat and gradually add milk. Return to the heat and bring to the boil, stirring all the time until thickened. Season well.

Add cheese and heat until melted. Pour into the prepared flan case and bake in the centre of the oven for 25 minutes.
Serves 4.

QUICK TIP

To make a quick tomato salad – skin and slice the tomatoes, put them into shallow dish. Mix 3 parts oil with 1 part vinegar or lemon juice, season and shake in a screw-top jar. Pour over the tomatoes and sprinkle with fresh or dried basil.

QUICK TIP

Instead of fresh onions, use 1 tablespoon dried onion flakes to make this recipe even more quickly.

187 Kipper and egg flan

You will need . . .

For the pastry:
100g/4 oz plain flour
pinch salt
50g/2 oz margarine
50g/2 oz cheese, finely grated

Preparation time
15 minutes

For the filling:
1 × 200g/7 oz packet kipper fillets
4 eggs
50g/2 oz grated cheese
salt and pepper
green pepper rings

Cooking time
35 minutes

Oven setting
200°C; 400°F; Gas Mark 6
180°C; 350°F; Gas Mark 4

Sift flour and salt into a large bowl. Add margarine and rub in until mixture resembles fine breadcrumbs. Add cheese and mix well. Mix to a stiff consistency with water. Line a 20-cm/8-inch flan ring. Bake blind for 20 minutes.

Flake kippers finely. Arrange over base of flan case. Separate eggs and beat yolks until smooth. Add half the cheese and pour over kippers. Season.

Whisk whites until stiff, add remaining cheese and pile on top of flan. Bake in centre of oven for 15 minutes. Garnish with green pepper rings. Serve hot or cold. *Serves 4.*

QUICK TIP

If you are using fresh kippers, first of all remove as many of the bones as possible. Then liquidise the kippers with the egg yolks. The liquidising process will break down any bones that remain.

188 Mushroom wheel

You will need . . .

100g/4 oz short crust pastry
1 onion
50g/2 oz mushrooms
25g/1 oz butter
1 × 200g/7 oz can luncheon meat
2 eggs
salt and pepper
1 × 170g/6 oz can evaporated milk
watercress

Preparation time
20 minutes

Cooking time
30 minutes

Oven setting
200°C; 400°F; Gas Mark 6
180°C; 350°F; Gas Mark 4

Line an 18-cm/7-inch flan ring with the pastry. Trim edges and prick base.

Chop onion finely. Wash and slice mushrooms. Fry both in butter until soft. Place in base of flan case. Cut luncheon meat into fingers and arrange like the spokes of a wheel over vegetables.

Beat eggs until smooth, season and add milk. Pour over the mixture and bake in centre of oven for 15 minutes. Reduce heat and cook for a further 15 minutes. Serve cold with salad. *Serves 4.*

QUICK TIP

To give the flan a shiny appearance, brush with a little beaten egg yolk just before baking.

189 Raspberry meringue flan

You will need . . .

4 eggs
250g/9 oz castor sugar
25g/1 oz cornflour
300ml/½ pint evaporated milk
few drops vanilla essence
450g/1 lb frozen raspberries

Preparation time
20 minutes

Cooking time
2-3 hours

Oven setting
110°C; 225°F; Gas Mark ¼

Separate eggs and whisk whites until stiff and standing in peaks. Add 100g/4 oz of the sugar and whisk again until thick. Fold in another 100g/4 oz sugar, using a metal spoon. Put the mixture into a large piping bag fitted with a star nozzle. Pipe a large round on a baking tin (*see Quick Tip below*) and spread inwards to make a base. Pipe around edge of circle to build up sides. Bake on lowest shelf of oven for 2-3 hours or until completely dried out.

Mix cornflour and remaining sugar with a little of the milk to make a smooth paste. Bring remaining milk to the boil and pour over cornflour. Return to pan and bring back to the boil, stirring until thickened. Cook for 2-3 minutes. Add egg yolks and vanilla essence. Beat well and heat gently, but do not boil. Leave until cold.

Drain raspberries. Spread cold vanilla cream into case and arrange the raspberries on top. *Serves 4.*

190 Egg custard tart

You will need . . .

175g/6 oz short crust pastry
egg white for brushing
25g/1 oz powdered milk
2 eggs
½ teaspoon vanilla essence
15g/½ oz sugar
½ teaspoon nutmeg

Preparation time
15 minutes

Cooking time
50 minutes

Oven setting
220°C; 425°F; Gas Mark 7
160°C; 325°F; Gas Mark 3

Roll out pastry to fit an 18-cm/7-inch flan tin. Line the tin and brush base with a little egg white. Prick base and bake in hot oven for 10 minutes.

Make the powdered milk up to 300ml/½ pint with water. Add eggs, vanilla essence and sugar. Beat well until smooth. Pour into prepared pastry case and sprinkle with nutmeg.

Bake in centre of very moderate oven for 40 minutes or until firm. Cool, remove ring and serve flan very cold. *Serves 4.*

QUICK TIP

Line the baking sheet with foil and pipe the meringue on to the foil. This way the foil will not release the meringue until it is completely cooked.

QUICK TIP

This mixture can be used for a variety of other sweets, crèmes for instance. Pour the mixture into greased cups and stand these in a tin of water. Bake in the oven for about 30 minutes.

191 Tarte florette

192 Vegetable pie

You will need . . .

For the pastry:
175g/6 oz plain flour
pinch salt
75g/3 oz margarine, cut into small pieces
1 teaspoon castor sugar
1 egg yolk

Preparation time
30 minutes

For the filling:
2 eggs
50g/2 oz sugar
25g/1 oz flour
300ml/½ pint milk
few drops vanilla essence
150ml/¼ pint double cream
3 tablespoons apricot jam
15g/½ oz plain chocolate

Cooking time
25 minutes

Oven setting
200°C; 400°F; Gas Mark 6

Sift flour and salt, add margarine and rub into flour until mixture resembles fine breadcrumbs. Add sugar and egg yolk with enough cold water to make a stiff paste. Roll out to fit a 20-cm/8-inch flan case. Bake blind for 20 minutes. Cool.

Make the custard. Blend 1 egg and 1 egg yolk with sugar and flour. Gradually add milk and vanilla essence. Bring to the boil slowly. Reduce heat and cook 2-3 minutes. Cover and allow to cool.

Whip cream until thick, but not stiff. Whisk egg white until stiff and fold into the cream. Spread jam over base of flan case. Pour over custard and top with piped cream. Decorate with grated chocolate. *Serves 4.*

You will need . . .

225g/8 oz carrots
100g/4 oz button mushrooms
225g/8 oz button onions
50g/2 oz butter
225g/8 oz runner beans, sliced and cut into small pieces

Preparation time
30 minutes

250g/9 oz plain flour
100g/4 oz mixed fats, cut into small pieces
75g/3 oz grated cheese
1 egg yolk
1 egg, beaten
sprig parsley

Cooking time
1 hour

Oven setting
200°C; 400°F; Gas Mark 6

Prepare carrots and cook in salted boiling water for 20 minutes. Drain and reserve 300ml/½ pint liquid. Wash mushrooms. Peel onions and fry with mushrooms in butter until soft. Add carrots and beans. Mix well. Add 25g/1 oz flour, mix well and cook for 2-3 minutes. Gradually add carrot liquid. Bring to the boil, stirring until thickened. Put mixture into a greased pie dish.

Sift remaining flour, add fats and rub in until mixture resembles fine breadcrumbs. Add cheese and mix well. Add egg yolk and enough cold water to make a stiff paste. Roll out to fit top of pie dish. Trim edges and flute.

Roll out trimming and cut into strips. Use to make a lattice pattern over top of pie. Brush with egg and bake for 30 minutes in centre of oven. Serve garnished with parsley. *Serves 4.*

QUICK TIP

To prevent a skin forming on custard, cover the surface immediately it is cooked with damp greaseproof paper.

QUICK TIP

If no pastry wheel is available for cutting the strips, then use a plain knife dipped into flour.

Salads and snacks

An attractive, colourful hors d'oeuvre to a festive main meal, a quickly prepared snack, a filling omelette or a delightful mixed salad – there are plenty of possibilities to choose from.

The delicious recipes in this chapter are particularly useful when hungry mouths have to be fed at short notice.

There is a choice of cold and hot snacks and salads to be served on their own or as part of a meal. As none of these recipes is difficult to prepare and all can be ready to serve in a short time, they will also prove to be a great help to a housewife faced with unexpected guests.

193 Chicken liver savoury

(illustrated on back cover)

You will need . . .	225g/8 oz long grain rice
	1 large onion
	450g/1 lb chicken livers
	25g/1 oz butter or margarine
	2 tablespoons corn or olive oil
Preparation time	100g/4 oz button mushrooms
5 minutes	salt and pepper to taste
	25g/1 oz extra butter
Cooking time	1 tablespoon chopped parsley
15 minutes	

Cook the rice in plenty of boiling salted water until just tender (about 12 minutes). Drain in a colander, carefully pour through fresh hot water to separate the grains.

While rice is cooking, peel and finely chop onion (*see Quick Tip below*). Slice mushrooms, reserving a few for decoration. Cut chicken livers into bite-sized pieces, discarding any stringy membranes. Melt 25g/1 oz fat and the oil; cook onion gently until transparent but not brown. Add chicken livers and sliced mushrooms, stirring occasionally for 10 minutes or until livers are cooked; season to taste.

Return rice to the saucepan, reheat gently, stirring in chicken mixture lightly to blend. Toss reserved mushrooms in melted extra ounce of butter for 1 minute. Adjust seasoning if necessary. Serve the savoury piled in a hot dish decorated with mushrooms and parsley. *Serves 4.*

194 Chicken aspic towers

You will need . . .	150g/5 oz frozen mixed vegetables
	1 bunch radishes
	1 chicken stock cube
	1 level tablespoon aspic jelly crystals
	100g/4 oz cold chicken (or lamb), diced
Preparation time	1 small lettuce, shredded
30 minutes	1 tablespoon dry sherry (optional)

Thaw vegetables, blanch in boiling water for 3 minutes and drain well. Top and tail radishes, slice 8 thinly and add to vegetables. From remaining radishes, make radish roses (*see Quick Tip below*). Pour 450ml/¾ pint boiling water over stock cube, add jelly crystals, stir until dissolved and allow to cool. Add sherry.

Rinse out 8 small coffee cups or dariole moulds with cold water. When aspic is syrupy and beginning to set, pour 1 tablespoon into each mould. Stir vegetables and diced chicken or meat into the rest of the aspic jelly and as soon as first jelly layer is set, spoon in the remaining jelly mixture, chill until set.

To serve, wring out a tea towel in very hot water and press around each mould or cup and turn out on to a bed of shredded lettuce. Decorate with radish roses. *Serves 4.*

QUICK TIP

To chop onion: cut peeled onion in half. Place flat side on board and hold at stalk end with a fork. Slice finely first lengthwise then across. Rinse hands in cold water immediately, or the smell will cling to them.

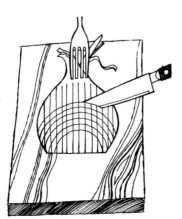

QUICK TIP

Making radish roses: cut radish across from the tip down to within 5-mm/¼-inch from base. Repeat 3 times. Leave radishes in cold water for half an hour, to open out.

195 Savoury tartlets

You will need . . .

2 hard-boiled eggs
175g/6 oz short crust pastry
25g/1 oz butter
25g/1 oz flour
1 × 170g/6 oz can evaporated milk
100g/4 oz fresh or frozen prawns, peeled
50g/2 oz peas, cooked
salt and pepper to taste
1 dessertspoon lemon juice

Preparation time
20 minutes

Cooking time
20 minutes

Oven setting
180°C; 350°F; Gas Mark 4

Shell and chop hard-boiled eggs roughly. Roll out pastry thinly. Cut out 12 tartlet cases with a 7.5-cm/3-inch fluted cutter (*see Quick Tip below*). Use to line patty tins. Bake 'blind' in a moderately hot oven for 20 minutes.

Meanwhile, melt the butter, stir in the flour and cook, stirring, for 2 minutes. Remove from the heat, add evaporated milk made up to 300ml/½ pint with water. Return to heat and cook for a further few minutes, stirring. Add chopped hard-boiled egg, half the prawns and the cooked peas. Stir in seasoning to taste and lemon juice. (Use more lemon juice if liked.)

Pour filling into empty tartlet cases. To decorate, top the tartlets with reserved prawns.
Note: Filling can be varied. Chopped ham can be substituted for prawns, or cooked mushrooms for the egg, for instance.
Serves 4.

QUICK TIP

To cut out clean shapes: dip fluted cutter into flour each time before using. If a plain cutter is used, give a slight twist when cutting.

196 Chicken Waldorf salad

You will need . . .

4 red-skinned apples
2 tablespoons lemon juice
4 celery sticks
225g/8 oz cold chicken, diced
50g/2 oz walnuts, halved
150ml/¼ pint mayonnaise or salad cream
1 large lettuce
225g/8 oz peas, cooked

Preparation time
15 minutes

Core and slice the apples and sprinkle with lemon juice. Reserve 12 slices for decoration and dice the rest.

Clean and chop the celery. Wash and drain lettuce, chop heart and mix with the diced chicken, chopped apple, celery, walnut halves and the mayonnaise. Line salad bowl with outer lettuce leaves and pile in salad.

Decorate with piles of peas divided by apple slices round the edge.
Basic Mayonnaise: Beat 1 teaspoon castor sugar, and ½ level teaspoon each of salt, pepper and dry mustard into 2 egg yolks. Add 1 teaspoon tarragon or wine vinegar or lemon juice. Pour 300ml/½ pint olive or corn oil into a measuring jug. Beat in a few drops at a time until sauce begins to get pale and thick, then increase the flow, beating all the time. Halfway through the process, thin with 1 tablespoon of vinegar or lemon juice.
Serves 4.

QUICK TIP

To improve salads: cut a garlic clove and rub inside of the salad bowl with the cut surface. This will give a subtle garlic flavour.

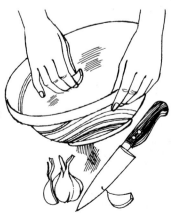

Cheese and 197 pineapple snack

You will need . . .

1 bunch radishes
1 × 227g/8 oz can pineapple chunks
1 × 65g/2½ oz can red pimentoes
225g/8 oz cream cheese
salt and pepper to taste

Preparation time
20 minutes

1 small French loaf
50g/2 oz butter
1 heaped teaspoon caraway seeds
1 bunch watercress

Top and tail radishes and make radish roses (*see Quick Tip, recipe 194*). Drain the pineapple chunks and cut into small pieces, reserving juice. Drain pimentoes and chop roughly. Beat 2 tablespoons pineapple juice into the cream cheese, gently fold in the chopped pineapple and pimentoes. Season to taste. Chill, if possible.

Make caraway bread (*see Quick Tip below*). When bread is ready, pile cheese mixture into one serving bowl, with the radish roses and watercress, in another.

Serve hot bread straight from the foil wrapper. Everyone helps himself to portions of the cheese dip and the bread.

Serves 4.

QUICK TIP

Making caraway bread: add 1 teaspoon caraway seeds to 75g/3 oz butter, blend well. Slice French bread at 1-2.5cm/ ½-1 inch intervals without cutting right through and butter well with the caraway butter. Wrap in foil. Heat in hot oven for 10-15 minutes.

198 Asparagus wheel flan

You will need . . .

225g/8 oz short crust pastry
25g/1 oz butter or margarine
25g/1 oz flour
150ml/¼ pint milk
1 × 411g/14 oz can green asparagus spears
salt and pepper to taste
50g/2 oz Cheddar cheese, grated

Preparation time
15 minutes

Cooking time
30 minutes

Oven setting
190°C; 375°F; Gas Mark 5
200°C; 400°F; Gas Mark 6

Roll out pastry thinly. Line a 20-cm/8-inch flan ring with the pastry and bake 'blind' (*see Quick Tip below*). Bake for 25 minutes altogether in a moderately hot oven.

Melt the butter, stir in the flour to form a *roux* (*see Quick Tip, recipe 212*). Cook, stirring, over a gentle heat for 2 minutes, remove from heat. Make up milk to 300ml/½ pint with liquid from can of asparagus. Season to taste. Add gradually to roux stirring all the time. Continue stirring, until sauce thickens, over a gentle heat.

Cool slightly, pour into flan, sprinkle half the cheese over, arrange the asparagus spears to form spokes of a wheel, and sprinkle over rest of the cheese. Return to a hot oven for a few minutes.

Serves 4.

QUICK TIP

To bake blind: prick bottom of flan to allow trapped air to escape. Place a circle of greaseproof paper on base. Cover with dried beans, rice or small crusts of bread. Remove paper and beans when the pastry is half cooked.

199 Monte Carlo salad

You will need . . .

225g/8 oz new potatoes, cooked
1 × 198g/7 oz can tuna fish
1 × 50g/1¾ oz can anchovy fillets
4 tablespoons lemon French dressing
4 tomatoes

Preparation time — 4 sticks celery
10 minutes — 8 black or green olives (optional)
1 heaped tablespoon mixed fresh herbs, chopped (parsley, chives, mint, as available)

Slice cooked potatoes thinly. Drain tuna fish and roughly flake. Drain anchovy fillets and chop. Add liquid from tuna fish and oil from anchovies to French dressing (*see method, recipe 208*). Slice tomatoes thinly. Clean and chop the celery.

Place a layer of potatoes in a salad bowl, sprinkle with half the dressing, top with a layer of tuna fish and anchovies, then a layer of celery and tomatoes. Repeat layers, ending with celery and tomatoes.

Decorate with the whole or halved olives and sprinkle with the chopped herbs.
Note: To make lemon French dressing, substitute 2½ table-spoons lemon juice for the 2 tablespoons vinegar in basic French dressing recipe. *Serves 4.*

200 Gourmet pork sausages

You will need . . .

450g/1 lb pork sausages
1 level tablespoon gravy browning
1 level teaspoon Continental mustard
1 rounded tablespoon redcurrant jelly
1 level teaspoon sweet paprika pepper

Preparation time — 1 rounded tablespoon sweet pickles,
10 minutes — chopped
1 tablespoon vinegar

Cooking time — salt and pepper to taste
15 minutes — 1 packet instant mashed potato (for 4)
1 tablespoon chopped parsley

Grill or fry sausages for about 15 minutes until golden brown all over.

Meanwhile, make the Gourmet sauce. Blend the gravy browning with a little cold water. Boil 300ml/½ pint water, stir in all the seasonings, then the gravy mix. Cook, stirring, until well blended, thick and smooth. Taste and adjust seasoning, if necessary. Allow to simmer and reduce slightly for 10 minutes.

Make up instant potato as directed on the packet. Spoon or pipe round the sides of a serving dish (*see Quick Tip below*). Arrange sausages in the centre. Pour over the sauce. Decorate with chopped parsley. *Serves 4.*

QUICK TIP

Making celery curls: cut celery into 5-cm/2-inch pieces. Cut into thin horizontal strips. Leave in cold water for half an hour; they will then curl.

QUICK TIP

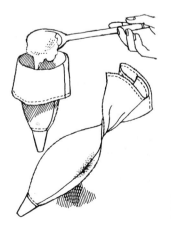

To fill a piping bag with potato, turn back the top of the bag to form a deep cuff. Fill the bag pushing well down with a wooden spoon. Pull up cuff and twist to remove any remaining air. Always use a large strong forcing bag.

201 Cheesy leek flan

202 Sweetcorn savoury

You will need . . .

225g/8 oz short crust pastry
450g/1 lb leeks
25g/1 oz butter or margarine
25g/1 oz plain flour
300ml/½ pint milk
salt and pepper to taste
1 level teaspoon made mustard
100g/4 oz strong Cheddar cheese, grated

Preparation time
15 minutes

Cooking time
25 minutes

Oven setting
190°C; 375°F; Gas Mark 5

Line a flan tin with the rolled out pastry, or use a fluted flan ring (*see Quick Tip below*). Bake 'blind' for 15 minutes in a moderately hot oven, then remove the paper and weights, and return to oven for a further 10 minutes.

Cut the leeks across in 5-mm/¼-inch rings and wash well. Melt 15g/½ oz butter and add the leeks, cover and cook over a moderate heat for *3 minutes only* (sufficient water will adhere to leeks from washing to prevent them burning).

Meanwhile, melt the remaining butter, stir in the flour over a gentle heat until completely absorbed. Add the milk and cook, stirring, until sauce is smooth and thick. Season to taste and stir in the mustard and grated cheese. As soon as cheese is melted, stir in leeks. Pour mixture into warm flan case and serve at once. *Serves 4.*

You will need . . .

1 bunch spring onions
1 × 329g/12 oz can corn niblets
1 × 298g/10½ oz can luncheon meat
25g/1 oz lard or dripping
salt and pepper to taste
4 slices white bread

Preparation time
10 minutes

Cooking time
10 minutes

Trim and finely chop the spring onions, reserving a few for decoration. Drain corn niblets. Dice the luncheon meat, fry gently in the lard until brown on all sides. Stir in the corn niblets and chopped onions. Season to taste.

Heat through and turn into a warmed serving dish.

Meanwhile, toast the bread, trim, cut into triangles and use to surround the dish (*see Quick Tip below*). Decorate with reserved spring onions. *Serves 4.*

QUICK TIP

Lining a fluted flan ring: work pastry carefully into each flute. Allow the rough edges to fall over the edge and with a sharp stroke of the rolling pin, roll across the ring. This will make a clean cut of the edges.

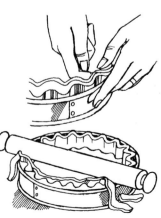

QUICK TIP

To make toast triangles: remove all crusts from toast leaving a square. Cut across corner to corner twice. Each slice makes four triangles.

Fried sardine
203 sandwiches

204 Tomato prawn cups

You will need . . .

8 large slices white bread
1 tablespoon peanut butter
1 × 120g/4⅜ oz can sardines
4 eggs
150ml/¼ pint milk

Preparation time
10 minutes

salt and pepper to taste
50g/2 oz butter or margarine
watercress

Cooking time
10 minutes

Remove crusts from the bread. Blend peanut butter with oil from the sardines and use to spread the bread. Mash sardines and spread on 4 of the slices.

Beat up 2 of the eggs, stir in 2 tablespoons milk. Season to taste. Melt 25g/1 oz butter, stir in eggs and scramble. Cool slightly. Spread over the sardine mixture. Press the other 4 slices in place firmly. Beat up the other 2 eggs with the rest of the milk. Pour into a soup plate and dip the sandwiches in this mixture (*see Quick Tip below*). Heat remaining butter in a frying pan and quickly fry the sandwiches on both sides until golden brown.

Serve each sandwich decorated with washed watercress.
Serves 4.

You will need . . .

100g/4 oz fresh or frozen prawns
8 large tomatoes
1 breakfast cup cooked long grain rice
2 tablespoons lemon juice
1 tablespoon chopped parsley
2 tablespoons mayonnaise or salad cream
salt and pepper to taste
½ cucumber, sliced
mustard and cress

Preparation time
20 minutes

Peel prawns, if using fresh ones, or defrost. Reserve 8 for decoration, chop the rest. Cut tops off tomatoes to make 'cups' (*see Quick Tip below*). Scoop out flesh and pips and keep flesh to fill omelettes or add to soups.

Mix the rice with lemon juice, parsley, mayonnaise or salad cream and the chopped prawns. Season to taste. Fill the tomato cups with this mixture and top each with a whole prawn.

Arrange circles of overlapping cucumber slices and stand each tomato cup in the centre of a circle. Decorate with mustard and cress.
Serves 4.

QUICK TIP

To coat sandwiches in egg: pour well beaten egg on plate. Dip sandwiches on each side by using tongs. Hold up and allow to drain before placing in frying pan. A little milk added to the egg will make it go further.

QUICK TIP

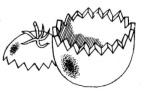

Making tomato cups: make 5-mm/¼-inch zigzag cuts using a sharp pointed knife near top of tomato. Pull cap off carefully and scoop out centre. Or merely slice top off tomato, and leave edge plain.

205 Sausage beanfeast

You will need . . .

1 bunch spring onions
1 × 100g/4 oz can pineapple rings
450g/1 lb pork sausages
15g/½ oz butter
1 × 450g/16 oz can baked beans with tomato sauce
2 dessertspoons vinegar
salt and pepper to taste

Preparation time
5 minutes

Cooking time
15 minutes

Wash the spring onions and chop. Halve 3 pineapple rings and reserve 5 halves, chop the rest. Grill the sausages until golden brown on all sides (*see Quick Tip below*). Reserve 5 and slice the rest.

Lightly fry the onions and chopped pineapple in the butter until tender. Add baked beans and the sliced sausages, vinegar and seasoning. Simmer for 5 minutes. Meanwhile fry the pineapple halves.

Pour baked bean mixture into serving dish. Decorate with the whole sausages and fried pineapple halves. *Serves 4.*

206 Rosy egg mayonnaise

You will need . . .

8 hard-boiled eggs
1 level tablespoon bottled tomato sauce
150ml/¼ pint mayonnaise
1 small can anchovy fillets
1 cucumber
4 medium tomatoes
pinch sweet paprika pepper
few sprigs parsley

Preparation time
20 minutes

Cool eggs under running water and shell them. Blend the tomato sauce with the mayonnaise. Drain oil from anchovies. Wipe and slice cucumber thinly. Make tomatoes into water-lilies. (*see Quick Tip below*).

Slice eggs in half lengthwise, arrange cut side down on over-lapping circles of cucumber slices. Coat each egg with a spoonful of mayonnaise. Cut each anchovy fillet in half and arrange over the eggs. Sprinkle paprika pepper over the top.

Arrange tomato waterlilies decorated with parsley round the serving dish. *Serves 4.*

QUICK TIP

To ensure that sausages keep their shape and do not split, first put in cold water and bring to the boil; immediately drain well. Then grill or fry the sausages in the normal way.

QUICK TIP

Making tomato waterlilies: make zigzag cuts through centre of tomato using a sharp pointed knife. Pull halves apart gently. Make 7 points.

207 Farmer's wife omelette

You will need . . .

1 large onion
2 tomatoes, peeled
25g/1 oz macaroni small shapes
4 rashers streaky bacon
25g/1 oz butter

Preparation time
5 minutes

4 eggs
salt and pepper to taste
4 tablespoons peas, cooked

Cooking time
10 minutes

Peel and chop the onion. Peel and roughly chop the tomatoes (*see Quick Tip below*). Cook macaroni as directed on the packet. Grill bacon rashers until crisp. Meanwhile, using a heavy 20-cm/8-inch frying pan, fry the onion in the butter until golden.

Whisk eggs with 2 tablespoons cold water and season to taste, pour over the onion. Sprinkle over the peas, chopped tomatoes and macaroni. Cook gently, stirring the centre and loosening the edges with a palette knife until set. Put under a hot grill for 1 minute.

Serve in quarters, each topped with a crisp slice of bacon.
Serves 4.

208 Vegetarian sunburst salad

You will need . . .

2 medium carrots
1 large lettuce
½ cucumber
225g/8 oz Cheddar cheese
1 heaped tablespoon peanut butter
2 tablespoons French dressing

Preparation time
10 minutes

Peel the carrots, wash and drain the lettuce, wipe the cucumber and slice thinly. Grate the carrots and cheese on a coarse grater. Beat the peanut butter into the French dressing; it will become quite thick. Line a salad bowl with lettuce leaves.

Arrange the cheese and carrots in alternate heaps around the bowl, so that each person may take a serving of carrot and cheese with some lettuce. Use cucumber slices as dividers.

After serving, pour dressing over each portion.
Basic French dressing: ½ teaspoon salt, ½ teaspoon sugar, ½ teaspoon dry mustard, ¼ teaspoon pepper. Add 2 tablespoons tarragon or wine vinegar and 6 tablespoons olive or corn oil. It will keep in a cool place for at least 1 week. *Serves 4.*

QUICK TIP

To peel tomatoes: place tomato on kitchen fork and hold over high gas jet until skin 'pops'. Keep turning. Alternatively, put tomatoes in basin, cover with boiling water, leave for half a minute only.

QUICK TIP

To make cucumber cones: do not remove the skin. Cut thin slices of cucumber. Make one cut on each slice to centre. Overlap cut edges to make cone.

209 All-seasons salad

Pears with
210 cream cheese balls

You will need . . .

4 thick slices white bread
100g/4 oz luncheon meat
1 × 2½ oz can red pimentoes
100g/4 oz button mushrooms
100g/4 oz long grain rice

Preparation time
5 minutes

4 tablespoons French dressing
¼ teaspoon garlic powder (optional)
50g/2 oz butter or margarine

Cooking time
12 minutes

salt and pepper to taste
few lettuce leaves

Cut bread and luncheon meat into 1-cm/½-inch dice. Cut pimentoes into thin strips; reserve some for decoration. Slice mushrooms.

Cook rice until just tender in boiling salted water, drain in a colander and carefully pour through fresh hot water to separate grains. While still hot, stir in French dressing (*see method, recipe 208*), luncheon meat, pimentoes and garlic if used. Meanwhile, toss mushrooms in melted butter until just cooked (about 2 minutes), remove. Cook bread dice in remaining fat. Add both to rice mixture. Season to taste. Chill, if possible.

Wash and drain lettuce leaves and pile up salad in lettuce leaf cups, decorating with pimento strips. *Serves 4.*

You will need . . .

75g/3 oz flaked almonds
225g/8 oz cream cheese
4 ripe pears
juice 1 lemon
4 tablespoons mayonnaise

Preparation time
15 minutes *plus*
1 hour to chill

1 tablespoon tomato ketchup or purée
1 tablespoon cream
dash of Tabasco sauce
dash of Worcestershire sauce
salt and pepper to taste
1 lettuce

Chop and toast the almonds. Form the cream cheese into small balls and roll in chopped, toasted almonds. Chill for 1 hour.

Peel, core and halve the pears, brush liberally with lemon juice, to prevent discolouration (*see Quick Tip below*). Combine the mayonnaise, ketchup or purée, cream, Tabasco Worcestershire sauce and seasoning.

Shred outer leaves of lettuce and place in centre of serving dish. Quarter the heart and place on top. Pile the cheese balls on to the pear halves, and arrange round the lettuce. Serve with the spicy mayonnaise sauce. *Serves 4.*

QUICK TIP

Chopping parsley quickly: put a few sprigs in a teacup, snip up with kitchen scissors, turning the cup with one hand as you work. It will take only about a minute to produce finely chopped parsley.

QUICK TIP

Preventing discoloration: if fresh ripe pears are used sprinkle with lemon juice immediately after peeling to preserve colour. The same method can be used to preserve apple slices.

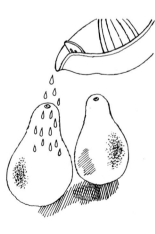

211 Pineapple crowns

You will need . . .

1 heaped tablespoon mustard pickles
4 large slices white bread
50g/2 oz lard or dripping
8 5-mm/¼-inch slices canned pork luncheon meat
4 pineapple rings

Preparation time
20 minutes

Chop mustard pickles very finely. Trim crusts from bread and fry golden brown on both sides in the lard. Drain well and keep hot.

In remaining fat, fry the slices of pork luncheon meat until brown and crisp. Remove and arrange 2 slices, side by side, on each slice of fried bread to cover it. Fry the pineapple rings *very lightly* on both sides, taking care they do not stick to the pan. Place 1 ring on top of each portion.

Decorate the pineapple rings with chopped mustard pickles.
Serves 4.

212 Creamy smoked haddock

You will need . . .

300ml/½ pint milk
1 chicken stock cube
4 portions smoked haddock or golden fillet
25g/1 oz butter or margarine
25g/1 oz flour
1 heaped tablespoon chopped parsley
8 slices hot buttered toast *or*
1 packet instant potato (for 4)
few sprigs parsley

Preparation time
5 minutes

Cooking time
20 minutes

Heat the milk in a saucepan with the stock cube until cube dissolves. Poach the fish gently in the milk, covered, for about 15 minutes until tender. Remove fish with straining spoon, flake roughly, put in a warm serving dish, or four scallop shells.

Chop the parsley. Melt butter in another saucepan, stir in flour until well blended, to make a *roux (see Quick Tip below)*. Pour in milk through a strainer. Cook, stirring, until it makes a thick smooth sauce. Stir in parsley and pour over fish.

Serve with plenty of freshly-made, hot buttered toast, or with instant mashed potato, spread or piped into a border.
Serves 4.

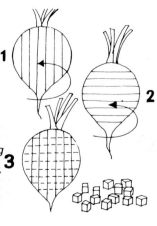

QUICK TIP

Dicing beetroots for salads: cut in 5-mm/¼-inch slices keeping beetroot whole in shape. Turn and cut beetroot into 5-mm/ ¼-inch slices again. Give a final turn. Cut again into 5-mm/ ¼-inch slices.

QUICK TIP

To make a smooth sauce: melt fat slowly over heat. Do not allow to brown. Stir in all the flour making a roux. When completely blended add liquid, one-third at a time, stirring continuously. Resulting sauce will be smooth and free from lumps.

213 Coleslaw

Salmon and
214 sweetcorn salad

You will need . . .
½ head crisp white cabbage (about 450g/1 lb)
1 large carrot
2 red-skinned apples
2 tablespoons lemon juice
1 heaped dessertspoon grated onion
300ml/½ pint mayonnaise
salt and pepper to taste

Preparation time
35 minutes

Remove hard stem and coarse outer leaves from cabbage. Shred finely and put in cold water to crisp for ½ hour. Scrape and grate carrot. Quarter and core the apples, grate or chop finely. Sprinkle with lemon juice (*see Quick Tip, recipe 210*).

Drain cabbage well, mix with onion, carrot and apple. Toss lightly in the mayonnaise until all the ingredients are coated. Season to taste.

Serve this salad with cold meat such as thinly sliced ham, roast beef or lamb. It keeps very well in a screwtop jar or polythene container in the refrigerator for several days.
*Note:*There are many variations of this recipe. You can include a few caraway seeds, some chopped sweet green pepper, chopped salted nuts; or make a different dressing with 8 tablespoons French dressing and 100g/4 oz soured cream.

Serves 4.

You will need . . .
3 large carrots
1 × 212g/7 oz can red salmon
1 × 198g/7 oz can sweetcorn kernels
1 cucumber
1 small sweet green pepper
4 tablespoons mayonnaise or salad cream
2 tablespoons lemon juice

Preparation time
20 minutes

Scrape carrots, make the carrot curls (*see Quick Tip below*) and grate the remainder of the carrots. Drain salmon and break up into bite-size pieces with a fork. Drain the sweetcorn. Wipe the cucumber and slice thinly. Wipe the pepper and remove stalk and seeds. Reserve 3 slices and chop the rest finely.

Mix the salmon, sweetcorn, grated carrot and pepper lightly together. Line a salad bowl with overlapping cucumber slices. Pile up the salmon mixture in the centre.

Thin the mayonnaise with the lemon juice. Pour over the salmon mixture. Decorate with the carrot curls and pepper slices.

Serves 4.

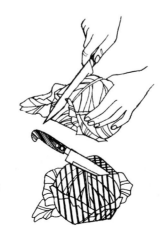

QUICK TIP

To slice cabbage: cut cabbage in half. Remove hard core from each half with a V-shaped cut. Place flat side down on board. Cut lengthwise into 2-cm/¾-inch strips, holding cabbage intact. Slice thinly across.

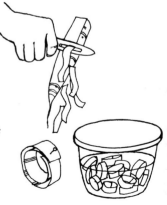

QUICK TIP

Making carrot curls: choose a large carrot. Remove thin slices with potato peeler. Curl and skewer with cocktail stick. Leave in cold water until required. Remove stick before serving.

215 Danish dressed salad

You will need . . .

50g/2 oz Danish blue cheese
6 tablespoons salad oil
4 tablespoons lemon juice
1 level teaspoon sugar
2 level teaspoons salt
100g/4 oz mild Cheddar cheese
1 medium onion
1 celery heart
few lettuce leaves
8 thin slices breakfast sausage or salami

Preparation time
20 minutes

Crumble up the blue cheese and put in a screwtop jar with oil, lemon juice, sugar and salt. Screw on lid and shake well. Chill if possible.

Cut Cheddar cheese into 1-cm/½-inch dice. Peel and grate or very finely chop the onion. Clean and roughly chop the celery. Mix all together. Wash and drain lettuce leaves. Line salad bowl with lettuce. Put in cheese mixture.

Pour dressing over. Decorate with sausage cones which are made by cutting half across a slice of sausage from edge to centre. Curl round one cut edge over the other to form a cone. Arrange two together at intervals round the salad bowl.

Serves 4.

216 Curried egg salad

You will need . . .

8 hard-boiled eggs
small knob butter
1 level tablespoon mayonnaise or salad cream
1 level teaspoon curry powder
salt to taste
½ cucumber
1 lettuce heart, quartered

Preparation time
20 minutes

Cool egg under running water and shell them. Slice in half across, scoop out yolks carefully with a teaspoon so as not to pierce whites. Cut a sliver from each rounded end so that the egg white 'cups' will stand firmly.

Mash the yolks with the butter, mayonnaise, curry powder and salt with a fork. Taste mixture and adjust seasoning, if necessary. Pipe back into the 'cups', dividing equally between them.

Wipe cucumber, score and slice 'turret' style (*see Quick Tip below*). Wash and drain the lettuce quarters carefully. Arrange stuffed eggs in the centre of a serving dish surrounded with the lettuce quarters, divided by cucumber slices. *Serves 4.*

QUICK TIP

To make a quick dressing: put oil and vinegar and seasoning in a screwtop jar – an empty mustard jar is ideal. Shake vigorously for about one minute or until oil has emulsified.

QUICK TIP

Making cucumber turrets: choose a well shaped cucumber. Make 3-mm/⅛-inch incisions lengthwise in skin of cucumber using sharp pointed knife. Remove alternate strips of skin. Slice cucumber.

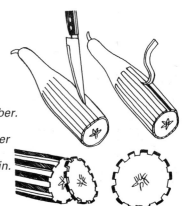

Lamb and pork

Many of our best-loved traditional dishes call for lamb or pork using different cuts varying from a big Sunday roast to an economical weekday stew. However, these familiar cuts can also be used in more imaginative, even exotic, dishes, some of which are presented in this chapter. A dish in which meat and fruit are combined will be greeted with delight on a hot day.

When the family shows signs of getting tired of the daily meat and two veg., or the weather seems not quite right for putting a casserole on the table, there is sure to be a recipe in this chapter that is just right for the occasion.

217 Harvest home casserole

(illustrated on back cover)

You will need . . .
- 2 onions
- 50g/2 oz lard
- 2 sweet green peppers
- 450g/1 lb courgettes
- 3 mushrooms, peeled and chopped
- 450g/1 lb belly pork, diced
- garlic salt
- salt and pepper to taste
- 1 tablespoon tomato purée
- 300ml/½ pint chicken stock, made up with ½ chicken stock cube

Preparation time
5 minutes

Cooking time
1 hour

Peel and slice the onions. Melt the lard and fry them in a saucepan for 5 minutes. Keep saucepan covered so onions remain soft.

Remove stalks and seeds from the peppers and chop. Wash and slice unpeeled courgettes thickly, and add these, with the mushrooms and pork, to the saucepan. Stir well and season to taste. Mix the tomato purée with the stock and add to the saucepan.

Cover with lid and simmer gently for 1 hour. This dish can also be cooked slowly in the oven. *Serves 4.*

218 Guard of honour

You will need . . .
- 2 matching joints best end neck of lamb
- 2 tablespoons melted dripping
- few cocktail cherries
- 450g/1 lb potatoes, peeled and halved
- few sprigs parsley

Preparation time
10 minutes

Cooking time
1 hour 15 minutes

Oven setting
180°C; 350°F; Gas Mark 4

Ask the butcher to chine the joints, remove surplus fat and skin from around the ends of the rib bones, so that bones protrude 2.5-cm/1-inch. Place the two joints on end in the roasting tin and close together, so that the bone tips cross each other like swords. Add dripping. Surround with the potatoes (*see Quick Tip below*).

Roast in a moderate oven for about 1¼ hours. To serve, take the joints just as they are from the roasting tin and stand on a serving dish. Surround with the potatoes, placing sprigs of parsley between.

Decorate the tips of the bones alternately with cutlet frills and cocktail cherries. *Serves 4-6.*

QUICK TIP

To retain juiciness and flavour of meat: coat in seasoned flour and fry gently to seal before adding liquid to the stew. If meat is naturally juicy, add flour when stew is cooked so that the meat juices enrich the gravy, instead of coating and frying first.

QUICK TIP

To roast potatoes: peel and cut medium-sized potatoes in half. Boil for two minutes, drain, shake well, and place round the joint. Spoon the hot fat over them. Bake for about an hour until golden brown. Baste once or twice.

219 Monday pie

Skewered
220 lamb with beetroot

219 Monday pie

You will need . . .

1 small onion, peeled and chopped
50g/2 oz mushrooms, sliced
15g/½ oz dripping
450g/1 lb cooked lamb, minced
½ teaspoon Worcestershire sauce
salt and pepper to taste
300ml/½ pint gravy
450g/1 lb potatoes, boiled and mashed
1 egg, lightly beaten

Preparation time
5 minutes

Cooking time
45 minutes

Oven setting
200°C; 400°F; Gas Mark 6

Fry the onion and mushrooms for a few minutes in the dripping. Reserve a few mushroom slices for decoration. Add the lamb, Worcestershire sauce, salt, pepper and gravy. Mix well and place in an ovenproof dish.

Pile the mashed potato on top and rough up with a fork – or pipe it on with a large forcing bag or tube. Brush the top with beaten egg (*see Quick Tip below*).

Cook in a moderately hot oven for about 40 minutes until golden brown. Decorate with mushroom slices and return to the oven to reheat for a few minutes. *Serves 4.*

220 Skewered lamb with beetroot

You will need . . .

450g/1 lb lean lamb, diced
3 tablespoons oil
3 tablespoons vinegar
pinch thyme
4 rashers bacon
1 × 100g/4 oz can pineapple cubes
1 small beetroot, cooked and peeled
salt and pepper to taste
clove of garlic (optional)
few strips sweet green pepper
350g/12 oz rice, cooked and buttered

Preparation time
10 minutes *plus*
1 hour to marinade

Cooking time
10 minutes

Make a marinade with the oil, vinegar, thyme and seasoning. Pour over the lamb and leave for at least one hour. Trim rind from bacon rashers, cut in half and form into bacon rolls. Dice cooked beetroot. Cut diamond shapes from green pepper.

Rub 4 skewers with the garlic clove. Thread on to the skewers the lamb alternately with pineapple, bacon rolls and beetroot, beginning and finishing with green pepper. Brush over with the marinade. Grill slowly turning the skewers several times for about 10 minutes.

Place skewers on a bed of buttered rice (*see Quick Tip, recipe 237*) to serve. *Serves 4.*

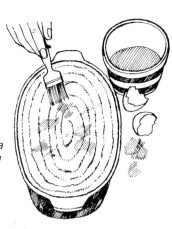

QUICK TIP

To give a golden brown finish to any potato topping and likewise to pastry, brush with a beaten egg yolk before putting in the oven. If no egg yolk is available, milk can be used though the result is not so golden.

QUICK TIP

To reheat rice: put into a covered saucepan with a few tablespoons water and heat gently. Shake the pan now and again and the rice will be as fluffy as when first cooked.

221 Lancashire hot pot

222 Layered lamb casserole

You will need . . .

750g/1½ lb middle or best end neck of lamb
2 lamb's kidneys, skinned and cored
salt and pepper
2 carrots, peeled and sliced
1 small turnip, peeled and sliced
225g/8 oz onions, peeled and chopped
1 leek, washed and chopped
450g/1 lb potatoes, peeled and sliced
300-450ml/½-¾ pint water or stock
25g/1 oz butter
sprig of parsley

Preparation time
10 minutes

Cooking time
2 hours

Oven setting
160°C; 325°F; Gas Mark 3
200°C; 400°F; Gas Mark 6

Cut the lamb and kidneys into neat pieces. Put layers of meat and vegetables into a casserole, seasoning to taste.

Finish with a layer of thickly sliced potatoes, overlapping. Pour in the water or stock, sufficient to come about a third of the way up the casserole, and cover top with little dabs of butter. Cover casserole and put into a very moderate oven for about 2 hours.

Uncover casserole for last half an hour and increase oven temperature to moderately hot, to brown the top layer of potatoes. If liked, the potato topping can be browned under a hot grill. Decorate with parsley. *Serves 4.*

You will need . . .

1kg/2 lb middle neck of lamb, chined
1 small white cabbage (about 750g/ 1½ lb)
1 heaped teaspoon caraway seeds
salt and pepper to taste
450g/1 lb potatoes, peeled
225g/8 oz small tomatoes, halved
25g/1 oz butter or margarine

Preparation time
10 minutes

Cooking time
1 hour 15 minutes

Cut the lamb into chops and trim off excess fat; place in bottom of a large strong saucepan or flameproof casserole. Shred the cabbage, discarding hard core. Wash well, drain, and put half on top of the fat trimmings. Arrange the chops on this bed of cabbage, sprinkle with caraway seeds and season. Top with potatoes and the rest of the cabbage, and dot with butter.

Cover pan and bring to the boil, then simmer for 1¼ hours. (No water need be added.)

Half an hour before the dish is ready, add tomato halves. A little water can be added at this stage if the pan seems dry. Cover and finish cooking. *Serves 4.*

QUICK TIP

To transform a plain stew into a hot pot, peel and slice thinly potatoes for the topping. Parboil for 2 minutes, strain and shake gently to make floury. Arrange overlapping on top of the stew, brush with meat dripping or oil and brown under grill.

QUICK TIP

To slice finely: vegetables, especially tomatoes, which are not quite firm enough are difficult to slice thinly with an ordinary knife. Use a knife with a serrated edge. You can buy slicing knives with part plain, part serrated blades.

223 Honey-glazed lamb

You will need . . .

1 small leg or shoulder of lamb
sprig of rosemary or bay leaf
pinch ground cinnamon
seasoned flour
1 carrot, peeled and sliced

Preparation time
10 minutes

1 onion, peeled and chopped
1 stick celery, washed and chopped
1 tablespoon thick honey

Cooking time
1 hour 40 minutes

4 fresh pears
50g/2 oz glacé cherries
few sprigs watercress

Oven setting
180°C; 350°F; Gas Mark 4

Rub the meat all over with a mixture of cinnamon and seasoned flour. Place the prepared vegetables in the bottom of a roasting tin, with the rosemary or bay leaf. Place the meat on top. Bake in a moderate oven allowing 25 minutes per pound plus 25 minutes over. After one hour turn the joint and baste well.

Half an hour before serving, lift out the meat and drain all fat from roasting tin. Replace meat, best side up, and spread with honey, add peeled and cored pear halves. Return to the oven and continue cooking, basting meat and pears once or twice.

Serve meat surrounded with pears and watercress. Place 2 cherries in each pear half. *Serves 4-6.*

224 Pork-in-a-blanket

You will need . . .

350g/12 oz pork fillet, cut in 1-cm/½-inch slices
2 red-skinned eating apples
1 large onion, peeled
50g/2 oz butter or margarine

Preparation time
10 minutes

25g/1 oz flour
1 chicken stock cube
150ml/¼ pint milk

Cooking time
20 minutes

salt and pepper to taste
1 packet instant potato (for 4)

Peel, core and chop one apple. Chop the onion finely. Melt the butter in a frying pan, place sliced pork in the centre and chopped onion round the edge. Cook very gently, covered, for 5 minutes. Turn pork slices, stir onions, and add chopped apple. Cover and cook for another 5 minutes. Remove pork to warm serving dish.

Stir flour into pan, cook for 2 minutes. Dissolve chicken stock cube in 150ml/¼ pint boiling water, add to pan with the milk. Cook until smooth and thick, stirring gently. Taste and correct seasoning. Pour sauce over pork.

Make up mashed potato, according to directions on packet. Pipe or spread round serving dish, slide under grill for 2 minutes to brown. Meanwhile core and slice remaining apple. Use to decorate. *Serves 4.*

QUICK TIP

To make gravy: pour off fat keeping back the meat juices. Add enough flour to absorb fat. Stir well over a gentle heat. Add water gradually from vegetables, boil and skim to remove grease. Season to taste and, if pale, add a little gravy browning using a skewer.

QUICK TIP

To make mashed potato smooth and creamy, beat in some butter and an egg yolk. If the potato is to be used for piping, sieve it first, as even very tiny lumps will tend to clog the tube.

225 Pan-fried pork

You will need . . .
450g/1 lb shoulder or belly pork, thinly sliced
1 egg, beaten and seasoned with salt and pepper
1 packet sage and onion stuffing *or*

Preparation time
10 minutes

100g/4 oz medium oatmeal
75g/3 oz lard
350g/12 oz potatoes, boiled

Cooking time
15 minutes

1 large onion
1 heaped tablespoon chopped parsley

Flatten the slices of pork with a rolling pin and cut into portions. Dip each slice into the seasoned beaten egg and toss in the dry stuffing or oatmeal. Fry in a little hot lard on both sides until brown and tender (about 15 minutes). Place in a hot serving dish.

Meanwhile, cut the potatoes into 1-cm/½-inch dice. Peel and chop the onion finely. Melt rest of lard, cook onions gently until just brown but not crisp. Stir in potatoes, increase heat and cook, stirring occasionally, until potatoes are brown. Sprinkle over the meat.

Decorate with parsley and serve with a green vegetable.
Serves 4.

226 March pork casserole

You will need . . .
1 small sweet green pepper
50g/2 oz bacon dripping
1 onion, peeled and chopped
1 leek, washed and chopped
50g/2 oz button mushrooms

Preparation time
10 minutes

1 teaspoon curry powder
½ teaspoon salt
½ teaspoon pepper

Cooking time
1 hour 45 minutes

25g/1 oz flour
750g/1½ lb hand or shoulder pork, diced
1 × 227g/8 oz can tomatoes

Oven setting
160°C; 325°F; Gas Mark 3

pinch mixed sweet herbs

Remove stalk and seeds from the pepper and chop it. Melt the fat and fry the onion, leek, pepper and mushrooms for 3 minutes. Transfer to a casserole.

Add the curry powder, salt and pepper to the flour, and then toss the pork in this mixture. Fry the coated pork for 5 minutes, stirring well, then put into the casserole with the vegetables, tomatoes and herbs.

Cover tightly and cook for 1¾ hours in a very moderate oven. Serve with jacket potatoes (*see Quick Tip below*). *Serves 4.*

QUICK TIP

To make sauté potatoes: boil the potatoes until almost cooked. Strain and cool. Cut into 5-mm/¼-inch slices and fry gently in a little butter. If liked, add a little finely chopped onion and sprinkle with chopped parsley.

QUICK TIP

To prepare jacket potatoes: scrub and dry equal-sized potatoes. Prick with a fork and brush with oil. Place on a baking tray and bake in a hot oven for 1½ hours or until tender. Cut a cross on the top, squeeze open and top with butter.

227 Old English pork casserole

You will need :. .

175g/6 oz leeks
25g/1 oz lard
500 g/1¼ lb shoulder of pork
50g/2 oz seasoned flour
300ml/½ pint brown ale
dash Tabasco sauce
piece lemon peel
75g/3 oz button mushrooms
bouquet garni
salt and pepper to taste

Preparation time
10 minutes

Cooking time
1 hour 20 minutes

Clean and chop the leeks. Melt the lard in a flameproof casserole. Fry the leeks for a few minutes.

Meanwhile, cut the pork into 2.5-cm/1-inch squares and toss in the seasoned flour. Add this to the leeks and cook for 5 minutes. Add the ale, Tabasco sauce, lemon peel, mushrooms and bouquet garni (*see Quick Tip below*). Bring to the boil. Put lid on and reduce heat. Simmer for 1¼ hours. Remove bouquet garni.

Season to taste. Serve with mashed potatoes and buttered carrots. *Serves 4.*

228 Lamb cobbler

You will need . . .

1kg/2 lb middle neck of lamb, trimmed
2 medium onions, peeled and chopped
3 tomatoes, skinned and sliced
1 carrot, peeled and sliced
1 parsnip, peeled and diced
25g/1 oz fat
25g/1 oz flour
1 beef stock cube
salt and pepper to taste
Scone Topping:
225g/8 oz self-raising flour
½ teaspoon mixed herbs
50g/2 oz margarine
150ml/¼ pint milk

Preparation time
10 minutes

Cooking time
1 hour 50 minutes

Oven setting
180°C; 350°F; Gas Mark 4
200°C; 400°F; Gas Mark 6

Melt the fat and fry the onions, carrot, parsnip and meat until lightly browned. Put with the tomatoes in layers in a casserole. Make up the stock cube with 450ml/¾ pint boiling water. Add the flour to the melted fat and cook for a few minutes; add the stock and seasonings, bring to the boil and pour over the meat. Cover.

Cook in a moderate oven for 1½ hours. Meanwhile make the scone topping.

Mix all the dry ingredients together and rub in the fat. Just before the meat is cooked add the milk to the dry ingredients and mix to a soft dough. Roll out and cut into scones. Place on top of the meat and cook in a hot oven for a further 20 minutes, uncovered. *Serves 4.*

QUICK TIP

To make a bouquet garni: place a few parsley stalks, sprig of thyme and bay leaf on a square of muslin. Tie into a bundle with strong thread, fixing thread ends to saucepan or casserole handle, and place bundle in dish. Remove before serving.

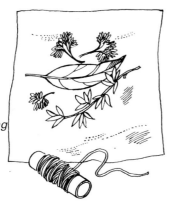

QUICK TIP

The flavour of a cobbler topping can be varied by seasoning with celery or garlic salt, or by adding 2 tablespoons grated cheese and a good pinch cayenne pepper to the flour. Cobblers can be glazed with beaten egg yolk or milk and sprinkled with grated cheese.

229 Piglets

Lamb with 230 herb dumplings

You will need . . .

350g/12 oz cooked pork, minced
2 heaped tablespoon sage and onion stuffing
2 eggs, lightly beaten
salt and pepper to taste

Preparation time
15 minutes

breadcrumbs for coating
fat for frying
1 bunch watercress

Cooking time
20 minutes

For the sauce:
1 × 65g/2¼ oz can tomato purée
1 beef stock cube
1 level dessertspoon cornflour
15g/½ oz butter or margarine
1 heaped teaspoon brown sugar

Mix together the minced pork, dry stuffing, seasoning and half the beaten egg. Add enough hot water to make a firm paste. Let stand for at least 10 minutes.

Meanwhile make the sauce. Dissolve stock cube in 300ml/½ pint boiling water, add tomato purée, sugar and butter. Cook together gently for 5 minutes. Blend cornflour with a little water, stir into sauce, and continue to cook, stirring for another 3 minutes.

Divide pork mixture into 12 even-sized balls. Coat in remaining egg and breadcrumbs. Deep fry (or shallow fry on both sides) in fat until rich golden brown. Serve with the sauce, and decorate with watercress. *Serves 4.*

You will need . . .

750g/1½ lb lamb, boned and chopped
2 tablespoons seasoned flour
1 tablespoon oil
2 large onions
100g/4 oz frozen peas

Preparation time
15 minutes

450ml/¾ pint water
1 chicken stock cube
450g/1 lb carrots, peeled and sliced

Cooking time
1 hour 15 minutes

For the dumplings:
100g/4 oz self-raising flour
50g/2 oz suet

Oven setting
190°C; 375°F; Gas Mark 5

1 tablespoon mixed herbs
salt and pepper to taste
little cold water

Remove excess fat and chop the meat into medium-sized pieces. Roll in seasoned flour. Fry onion lightly taking care not to brown. Add meat and fry lightly for two minutes.

Dissolve chicken stock cube in 450ml/¾ pint boiling water and add to onion and meat with the carrots. Turn into an ovenproof casserole. Cover and cook in a moderately hot oven for 1 hour.

To make dumplings, mix flour with suet, herbs and seasoning. Add sufficient cold water to make a stiff dough, form into balls. Stir peas into the meat, arrange the dumplings on top and return to the oven for a further 15 minutes. *Serves 4.*

QUICK TIP

To reduce baked crusts and odd pieces of bread to toasted breadcrumbs, spread out between two sheets of greaseproof paper and roll with a rolling pin into crumbs.

QUICK TIP

Dumplings can have other flavourings than herbs. Add grated orange or lemon rind for beef casseroles, a pinch of nutmeg and 1 tablespoon finely chopped onion for pork casseroles, and add 1 level teaspoon caraway seeds for tomato flavoured veal casseroles.

231 Crunchy stuffed pork

You will need . . .

Preparation time
15 minutes

Cooking time
2 hours

Oven setting
190°C; 375°F; Gas Mark 5

1.5kg/3 lb joint belly pork with skin
100g/4 oz soft white breadcrumbs
1 onion, peeled and grated
1 lemon rind, grated
1 stick celery, washed and chopped
½ teaspoon nutmeg
25g/1 oz walnuts, chopped
50g/2 oz seedless raisins
1 egg
25g/1 oz butter, melted
salt and pepper
lard

Score the pork skin and remove the bones from the joint.

To make the stuffing, mix together remaining ingredients except lard and season to taste. Flatten the meat, skin side down and spread with the stuffing. Roll and secure with a skewer. Put the joint in a roasting tin, brush the skin with a little melted lard and sprinkle liberally with salt. Roast for 30 minutes to the pound and 30 minutes over in a moderately hot oven.

Serve with apple sauce, buttered carrots and sprouts.

Serves 4-6.

232 Fricassée of lamb

You will need . . .

Preparation time
5 minutes

Cooking time
1 hour 30 minutes

Oven setting
180°C; 350°F; Gas Mark 4

750g/1½ lb lamb (leg or shoulder), diced
25g/1 oz seasoned flour
25g/1 oz butter
1 large carrot, peeled and sliced
1 large onion, peeled and sliced
1 small can button mushrooms
salt and pepper to taste
1 bay leaf
good pinch rosemary
1 tablespoon cream
1 tablespoon chopped parsley

Coat diced meat with seasoned flour. Fry onion and carrot gently in the butter for two minutes without allowing to brown. Add the meat, turn in the hot fat to seal. Sprinkle in rest of flour, stir well, turn into an ovenproof casserole and add sufficient water to cover. Add the bay leaf and rosemary, cover.

Cook in a moderate oven for 1½ hours, adding mushrooms for the last 15 minutes of cooking time. Taste and correct seasoning if necessary.

Remove lid, stir in cream, sprinkle with parsley and serve at once.

Serves 4.

QUICK TIP

When using stale breadcrumbs in stuffing, leave soaking in a little milk for about an hour before use. Squeeze moisture out before mixing. This improves the flavour and texture.

QUICK TIP

To remove excess fat when cheaper cuts of meat are used, cook the dish and allow to cool. Remove the solidified fat from the surface. Reheat to serve.

233 Pig-in-the-middle

You will need . . .

75g/3 oz mushrooms
50g/2 oz lard
4 spare rib or neck pork chops
50g/2 oz white breadcrumbs
25g/1 oz suet

Preparation time
10 minutes

salt and pepper
1 egg, lightly beaten
300ml/½ pint batter (*made from 100g/
4 oz flour, pinch salt, 1 egg and 300ml/
½ pint milk and water*)
few parsley sprigs

Cooking time
25 minutes

Oven setting
220°C; 425°F; Gas Mark 7

Chop the mushrooms. Melt the lard in an ovenproof dish. Trim and season the chops and place in the melted fat. Mix the breadcrumbs, suet and mushrooms together, season well and bind with the egg. Put a portion on top of each chop and cook in a hot oven for 5 minutes.

Mix the batter ingredients together well. Remove dish from oven, pour batter round chops at once and return to the oven for about 20 minutes.

Decorate with parsley and serve at once with a green vegetable and sauté potatoes. *Serves 4.*

234 Lamb and leek casserole

You will need . . .

8 lamb cutlets
fat for frying
2 leeks, washed and sliced
1 onion, peeled and sliced
1 turnip, peeled and diced

Preparation time
10 minutes

225g/8 oz new carrots, scraped
600ml/1 pint stock or water
salt and pepper to taste
2 sprigs mint
100g/4 oz shelled or frozen peas

Cooking time
1 hour 35 minutes

Oven setting
180°C; 350°F; Gas Mark 4

Prepare and trim the cutlets, fry in fat for 5 minutes to brown. Drain, and place in a casserole.

Add leeks, turnip, onion and carrots to the casserole with the stock or water. Season with salt and pepper and add the mint. Cover the casserole and place in a moderate oven for about 1½ hours.

If fresh peas are used cook them separately and stir into the casserole just before serving. If frozen peas are used stir them into the casserole about 15 minutes before serving. *Serves 4.*

QUICK TIP

A Yorkshire pudding batter will rise better and become crisper if the batter is poured directly into very hot fat, and put straight into a hot oven without any delay. An extra egg or even an egg yolk makes it richer.

QUICK TIP

To give a glossy finish and good flavour to boiled potatoes add a little butter to them in the pan after draining. Gently shake. Empty into serving dish and sprinkle with a little chopped parsley.

235 Celebration pork

You will need ...

2 kg/4½ lb loin of pork with skin
melted lard
salt
8 eating apples
175g/6 oz granulated sugar
600ml/1 pint water
pink food colouring
few sprigs parsley

Preparation time
5 minutes

Cooking time
2 hours

Oven setting
180°C; 350°F; Gas Mark 4

Have the loin of pork chined and the skin scored. Put the joint in a roasting tin with the skin side upwards. Brush and sprinkle with salt (*see Quick Tip below*). Roast in a moderate oven for approximately 2 hours.

Meanwhile prepare the sugared apples for decoration. Peel and core the apples. Dissolve the sugar in the water over a gentle heat, then bring to boil. Add 1 teaspoon pink food colouring. Poach apples gently in the syrup until tender and well coloured (about 20 minutes). Remove on to a plate.

Boil syrup rapidly to reduce, and pour over the apples. Serve joint surrounded with sugared apples and decorate with parsley.
Serves 4-6.

236 Pork parcels

You will need ...

100g/4 oz long-grain rice
150g/5 oz frozen sweetcorn
150g/5 oz frozen peas
4 spring onions
salt and pepper to taste
4 pork chops
1 tablespoon soy sauce
4 tablespoons cider

Preparation time
20 minutes

Cooking time
40 minutes

Oven setting
180°C; 350°F; Gas Mark 4

Cook the rice, put into a basin. Meanwhile cook the sweetcorn and peas in boiling salted water for 2 minutes. Clean and chop the onions, add to the rice and mix well together. Season to taste.

Cut 4 large squares aluminium foil and put a chop on to each piece. Sprinkle well with soy sauce. Put one quarter of the mixture on top of each chop. Add a spoonful of cider.

Wrap into a parcel and place on a tin. Bake in a moderate oven for about 40 minutes. Serve direct from the foil on the serving plate.
Serves 4.

QUICK TIP

To ensure that the pork crackling is crisp, brush well with oil and sprinkle with salt before cooking. The skin can be scored in parallel lines 5-mm/¼-inch apart or in a diamond pattern.

QUICK TIP

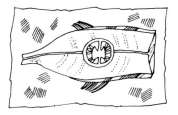

Aluminium cooking foil makes a completely airtight parcel, retaining all the moisture and delicate flavour of the food inside. Fold each join twice to make it air-tight. Use foil also for making lids for otherwise lidless containers.

237 Curried lamb

238 Oriental honeyed pork

You will need . . .
750g/1½ lb lamb, cooked
1 tablespoon oil
1 onion
1 apple
2 tablespoons coconut, sweetened
1 dessertspoon curry powder
1 tablespoon flour
225g/8 oz tomatoes
salt and pepper to taste
225g/8 oz rice

Preparation time
10 minutes

Cooking time
25 minutes

Peel onion and chop. Peel, core and chop apple. Skin, seed and chop tomatoes. Chop lamb in small dice and fry quickly in heated oil. Remove from pan. Fry onion and apple until softened; stir in curry powder and flour, mixing well. Cook for several minutes.

Meanwhile, pour 300ml/½ pint boiling water over coconut and stir well. Strain liquid onto onion and apple mixture gradually, stirring until blended. Return meat to pan with tomatoes and seasoning, cover and simmer for 25 minutes. Sprinkle the rice into a saucepan of fast boiling water – ½ teaspoon salt and 300ml/½ pint water to each 25g/1 oz of rice. After 12 minutes test a grain and when tender strain and put on a serving dish in the oven to dry out.

Serve curry on the rice on one dish or in individual portions. Fried poppadums or chapatties may be served as an accompaniment. *Serves 4.*

You will need . . .
350g/12 oz pork fillet
2 level dessertspoons seasoned cornflour
6 tablespoons corn oil
1 clove garlic, crushed (optional)
1 medium sweet green pepper
1 × 227g/8 oz can pineapple chunks
3 mushrooms, peeled and sliced
2 ripe tomatoes, quartered
For the sauce:
1 dessertspoon soy sauce
1 chicken stock cube
2 tablespoons honey

Preparation time
10 minutes

Cooking time
15 minutes

Cut the pork into 2.5-cm/1-inch cubes and toss in the seasoned cornflour. Remove stalk and seeds from pepper and chop. Drain pineapple cubes, reserving juice.

Heat the garlic (if used) in the oil, fry pork cubes briskly until brown on all sides. Lower heat, add chopped pepper and continue cooking over gentle heat for 10 minutes, adding pineapple chunks, mushrooms and tomatoes for last 4 minutes. Transfer to a warm serving dish.

Meanwhile, make sauce by dissolving chicken stock cube in 300ml/½ pint boiling water, mix with honey and soy sauce. Blend rest of cornflour with a little pineapple juice, add to mixture. Bring to the boil, cook for 3 minutes, stirring all the time. Pour over the meat in the serving dish. *Serves 4.*

QUICK TIP

Pour boiling water through the rice after cooking. If the grains have stuck together this will remove the remaining rice flour. Drain well and dry out in the oven. Lightly stir in a knob of butter to make the rice glisten.

QUICK TIP

To make seasoned flour: to 225g/8 oz plain flour, add 1 level tablespoon salt and ¼ level teaspoon pepper. Place in a screwtop jar, shake well. Use as required.

Spare rib
239 chops with almonds

You will need . . .

1 tablespoon mustard
1 tablespoon brown sugar
4 spare rib pork chops
25g/1 oz almonds, shredded
salt and pepper

Preparation time
minutes

350g/12 oz frozen chips
lard for frying

Cooking time
5 minutes

Mix the mustard and sugar together and rub over the chops. Grill on both sides until tender, about 12 minutes altogether. Sprinkle almonds over the chops and season with salt and pepper.

Return the chops to the grill to brown the almonds. Meanwhile, fry the frozen chips in the lard.

When cooked, let the chips drain on crumpled kitchen paper. Place the chops on a serving dish surrounded by the chips and serve with a green vegetable. *Serves 4.*

Braised
240 lamb with apricots

You will need . . .

1 shoulder of lamb, boned and rolled
2 large onions, peeled
25g/1 oz butter or margarine
2 large carrots, peeled
2 sticks celery, washed
1 chicken stock cube
1 × 65g/2¼ oz can tomato purée
12 dried apricots
1 heaped tablespoon flour
1 level teaspoon paprika
1 level teaspoon salt

Preparation time
10 minutes

Cooking time
1 hour 30 minutes

Ask the butcher to bone the joint, roll and tie with string. Mix salt, paprika and flour together, and dust the joint with it. Cube the onions, slice the carrots and celery in rings.

Melt the fat in a casserole. First brown the onions, celery and carrots and then the joint in it. Sprinkle in the rest of the seasoned flour, stir, add the tomato purée and apricots. Dissolve the stock cube in 300ml/½ pint boiling water. Pour over the casserole. Cover and simmer gently for 1½ hours.

Serve with fluffy boiled rice, well buttered (*see Quick Tip, recipe 237*). *Serves 4-6.*

QUICK TIP

When making your own potato chips fry briskly in deep fat until pale golden brown. Remove and drain on crumpled absorbent paper, fry again in very hot fat. Drain on fresh paper. This ensures that the chips are crisp and golden brown.

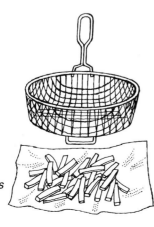

QUICK TIP

To transform boiled rice into Fried Rice: heat a tablespoon of cooking oil, stir in about 175g/6 oz cooked rice, breaking up with a fork. When hot stir in ½ teaspoon soy sauce, 2 chopped spring onions and 1 beaten egg. Cook, stirring, until egg is set.

Continental favourites

The recipes in this chapter are likely to appeal particularly to those housewives and members of their families who have enjoyed these delicious, refined and infinitely tasty dishes abroad or in one of the many foreign restaurants in England. But this does not mean that those who have not, as yet, had a chance to taste any of these tempting continental favourites in their original setting, should be timid and not dare to try them in the comfort of their own home! Soup, main courses, desserts and also snacks to serve in between meals . . . there will be little difficulty in finding the right dish to please all the family.

241 Osso buco (ITALY)

(illustrated on back cover)

You will need . . .
- 1kg/2 lb knuckle of veal cut into 5-cm/2-inch lengths
- 1 heaped tablespoon seasoned flour
- 3-4 tablespoons olive oil
- 1 clove garlic, peeled and crushed

Preparation time
10 minutes
- 1 onion, peeled and chopped
- 1 chicken stock cube
- 300ml/½ pint boiling water

Cooking time
1 hour 30 minutes
- 3 tablespoons tomato purée
- 1 tablespoon chopped parsley
- 225g/8 oz long grain rice

Toss the veal in the flour. Heat the oil in a saucepan and add the meat. Fry until brown, then add the garlic and the onion.

Dissolve the stock cube in the boiling water and add to the meat with the tomato purée. Cover the pan and simmer for 1½ hours.

Place in a serving dish and sprinkle with the parsley. Serve with saffron rice (*see Quick Tip, recipe 264*). *Serves 4.*

242 Moussaka (GREECE)

You will need . . .
- 3 tablespoons oil
- 1 small onion, finely chopped
- 450g/1 lb cooked lamb, diced or minced
- 1 × 65g/2¼ oz can tomato purée
- salt and pepper

Preparation time
25 minutes
- 225g/8 oz raw potatoes, sliced
- 1 large aubergine, sliced
- 1 clove garlic, crushed (optional)

Cooking time
15-20 minutes
- 225g/8 oz tomatoes, peeled and sliced
- 300ml/½ pint cheese sauce
- 50g/2 oz cheese, grated

Oven setting
180°C; 350°F; Gas Mark 4
- 1 egg yolk
- sprig of parsley

Heat a third of the oil in a frying pan. Add onion and allow to colour, then add the meat and shake over a brisk heat for a few minutes. Remove from heat. Add tomato purée and season well. Put in an ovenproof dish and keep warm. Heat the remaining oil in the frying pan; put in the potatoes and fry gently until brown. Then take out and arrange on top of the meat.

Add the aubergine to the frying pan and cook for 5-7 minutes. Then add the garlic, if used, and then sliced tomatoes. Continue cooking for a further five minutes and then pour over the potatoes. Meanwhile prepare the cheese sauce. Stir in the egg yolk (*see Quick Tip below*). Pour over the dish.

Sprinkle top with grated cheese and bake in a moderate oven for 15-20 minutes until well browned. Decorate with parsley. *Serves 4.*

QUICK TIP

To crush garlic: peel a clove of garlic and discard the skin. Slice thinly, then crush with the heel of a heavy knife. Use immediately as it does not keep. (You can also buy a useful gadget called a garlic press.)

QUICK TIP

To separate eggs: crack the shell in the middle against the edge of the basin. As the shell divides, let the white fall into the basin and cradle the yolk in one shell half.
Put yolk in fresh basin.

243 Frankfurter salad (GERMANY)

244 Crèmes au chocolat (FRANCE)

You will need . . .

450g/1 lb potatoes, peeled and diced
1 chicken stock cube
1 level tablespoon grated onion
1 heaped tablespoon chopped parsley and chives
150ml/¼ pint mayonnaise
4 pairs Frankfurter sausages
8 gherkins

Preparation time
10 minutes

Cooking time
5 minutes

Cook the diced potatoes for a few minutes, but do not allow to get mushy. Drain, using liquid to make up stock cube to 150ml/¼ pint stock. Shake potatoes once in the pan. Stir in the hot stock, grated onion, chopped herbs and finally the mayonnaise. Chill, if possible overnight.

Heat the Frankfurter sausages in plenty of boiling water (*see Quick Tip below*). Drain well.

Serve the potato salad in a mound with the hot sausages arranged on top. Decorate with the gherkins. *Serves 4.*

You will need . . .

3 eggs
100g/4 oz plain chocolate
75g/3 oz unsalted butter
75g/3 oz castor sugar
orange rind, grated
150ml/¼ pint double cream

Preparation time
15 minutes

Separate the eggs. Melt the chocolate, broken into small pieces, in a basin over a saucepan of boiling water (*see Quick Tip below*). Remove basin from heat, stir in the butter and sugar.

When well blended add the egg yolks, one at a time, beating well after each addition. Add the grated orange rind reserving a little for decoration. Whisk the egg whites until they form stiff peaks. Fold into the chocolate mixture and pour into little soufflé dishes. Chill, overnight if possible.

To serve, whip the cream until stiff and pipe or swirl on top of each dish. Sprinkle with grated orange rind. *Serves 4.*

QUICK TIP

Cook Frankfurter sausages by placing them in a saucepan of boiling water and fixing the lid on firmly. Remove from heat and leave for five minutes. Drain well, and the Frankfurters are ready to serve.

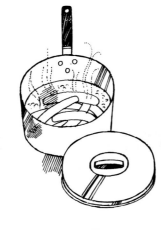

QUICK TIP

To melt chocolate: use plain chocolate. Cut into small lumps and put in a small basin over a pan of hot water. Allow to melt. Remove from heat. Stir gently until smooth. Do not overheat or chocolate will become oily.

245 Escalope milanese (ITALY)

246 Eggs florentine (ITALY)

You will need . . .

4 very thin slices veal or pork fillet
2 heaped tablespoons seasoned flour
1 egg, lightly beaten
toasted breadcrumbs for coating
1 heaped tablespoon grated onion

Preparation time
10 minutes

2 tablespoons olive oil or corn oil
1 × 65g/2¼ oz can tomato purée
salt and pepper to taste

Cooking time
15 minutes

1 level teaspoon sugar
oil for frying
1 chicken stock cube
225g/8 oz pasta shapes
1 level dessertspoon cornflour
25g/1 oz butter
25g/1 oz Parmesan cheese

If using pork fillet, which is more economical, split before banging flat (*see Quick Tip below*). Coat fillets in seasoned flour, dip in beaten egg, then coat in breadcrumbs.

Meanwhile make sauce. Toss grated onion in the hot oil for 1 minute, stir in tomato purée, salt, pepper and sugar. Dissolve the stock cube in 300ml/½ pint boiling water and add. Simmer for 10 minutes. Meanwhile fry the escalopes golden brown on both sides in a little more oil (about 6 minutes). Cook the pasta in boiling salted water and drain well. Thicken sauce with moistened cornflour.

Stir butter into the pasta to make it glisten. Turn on to serving dish, arrange escalopes on top and pour over the sauce. Sprinkle with Parmesan cheese. *Serves 4.*

You will need . . .

225g/8 oz spaghetti
1kg/2 lb fresh or 350g/12 oz frozen spinach
4 eggs
50g/2 oz butter

Preparation time
5 minutes

1 tablespoon cooking oil
good pinch nutmeg
salt and pepper

Cooking time
20 minutes

Cook the spaghetti in plenty of well salted boiling water until tender. Drain. Stir in 25g/1 oz butter. If using fresh spinach, wash well. Cook, drain and chop. Sprinkle with nutmeg and a little finely ground pepper.

Arrange the spaghetti on a hot serving dish and top with a layer of spinach.

Fry the eggs in the rest of the butter, adding the oil to prevent it from burning. Place the eggs on top of the spinach. Serve immediately. *Serves 4.*

QUICK TIP

A small thick slice of tender meat such as veal or pork fillet can be made much larger and thinner. Place between two sheets of greaseproof paper, or folds of a clean teatowel, and bang out with a wooden rolling pin or back of a large wooden spoon.

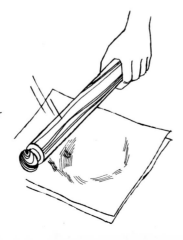

QUICK TIP

All pasta should be cooked in plenty of boiling salted water until just firm and tender. 1 tablespoon oil added to the water prevents pasta sticking together and also improves its flavour.

247 Shellfish vol au vent (FRANCE)

You will need . . .

450g/1 lb packet frozen puff pastry
1 × 70g/3 oz can lobster
25g/1 oz butter
25g/1 oz flour
1 chicken stock cube
150ml/¼ pint milk
2 tablespoons cream
1 teaspoon paprika

Preparation time
10 minutes

Cooking time
10 minutes

Oven setting
230°C; 450°F; Gas Mark 8

Roll out the pastry 5-mm/¼-inch thick. Cut 16 circles with a 7.5-cm/3-inch cutter. Half cut through surface of 8 'tops' with a small cutter just to show the shape of an inner circle. Arrange 8 'bases' on a *damped* baking sheet. Moisten surface lightly, place the 'tops' on these, pressing down very gently, prick the 'tops' (*see Quick Tip below*). Bake in a preheated very hot oven for 10 minutes or until golden brown. Remove lids and press in centres slightly.

Strain the lobster, reserving the liquor, and flake. Make sauce by blending butter and flour in a saucepan over medium heat. Stir in stock cube dissolved in lobster liquor made up to 300ml/½ pint with hot milk. Cook, stirring until smooth and thick, add cream and flaked lobster. Do not reboil.

Fill cases, sprinkle with paprika and replace lids at an angle. Serve hot. *Serves 4.*

248 Onion quiche (FRANCE)

You will need . . .

350g/12 oz shortcrust pastry
1 × 50g/1¾ oz can anchovy fillets
50g/2 oz melted bacon fat
450g/1 lb onions, peeled and sliced
salt and pepper to taste
2 eggs
50g/2 oz Gruyère cheese, grated

Preparation time
10 minutes

Cooking time
30 minutes

Oven setting
180°C; 350°F; Gas Mark 4

If using frozen pastry defrost until pliable enough to roll out. Line a fluted flan ring with pastry. Drain oil from anchovies. Heat the bacon fat, add the onions and seasoning. Cook gently, stirring occasionally, for half an hour in a covered pan. Cool. Meanwhile, line pastry case with greaseproof paper, weight with rice or baking beans and bake 'blind' for 10 minutes. Remove the paper and beans.

Beat the eggs lightly, add the onion mixture and cheese, stir well. Pour into the pastry case. Lay the anchovy fillets in a trellis pattern over the surface. Bake in a moderate oven for 20 minutes.

Serve as a snack, or as a main course, with, or followed by, a green salad. *Serves 4.*

QUICK TIP

Before putting the vol au vent cases in the oven, prick each 'top' four times at equal intervals with a skewer or knitting needle. This will help to ensure that the sides of the cases rise equally.

QUICK TIP

Peeling onions: put in cold water for half an hour before peeling and this will help to prevent irritation to the eyes. Alternatively, peel the onions under a running cold tap.

249 Bortsch (RUSSIA)

Bavarian
250 sauerkraut (GERMANY)

249 Bortsch

You will need . . .

1 large beetroot, uncooked
50g/2 oz butter
1 × 435g/16 oz can beef consommé
salt and pepper to taste
150ml/¼ pint soured cream
1 heaped dessertspoon chopped chives

Preparation time
5 minutes

Cooking time
40 minutes

Peel the beetroot and shred finely. Melt the butter in a saucepan and add the beetroot. Cook, covered, for about 20 minutes. Heat the consommé, diluted according to the directions on the can, in another pan, and add a little at a time to the beetroot. Cook until the beetroot is tender (about 20 minutes). Taste and correct seasoning.

Press through a sieve and reheat.

Add the soured cream (*see Quick Tip, recipe 263*) just before serving and sprinkle with chopped chives. *Serves 4.*

250 Bavarian sauerkraut

You will need . . .

1 cooking apple
1 large carrot
50g/2 oz butter
1 × 454g/1 lb can or jar sauerkraut
1 teaspoon caraway seeds (optional)
salt and pepper to taste
4 thick slices fat streaky bacon
4 Knackwurst or Frankfurt sausages

Preparation time
5 minutes

Cooking time
55 minutes

Oven setting
190°C; 375°F; Gas Mark 5

Peel, core and grate the apple. Peel and grate the carrot. Melt the butter. Put in an ovenproof casserole, stir in the sauerkraut, grated apple, carrot, caraway seeds if used, and seasoning. Lay the bacon slices on top and cover.

Bake in a moderately hot oven for 40 minutes. Remove lid, arrange Knackwurst or Frankfurt sausages on top and return to oven for another 15 minutes.

Serve from the casserole or turn on to a warm serving dish, arranging the sausages and bacon slices on the sauerkraut. *Serves 4.*

QUICK TIP

You can make a cold version of beetroot soup using 450g/1 lb cooked beetroot, skinned and diced, 2 cans beef consommé, 150ml/¼ pint soured cream or yogurt, 2 tablespoons lemon juice. Blend together and chill. Serve as above.

QUICK TIP

Sauerkraut can be served instead of a vegetable with any well seasoned continental sausage, veal, pork or bacon. To make the flavour richer, cook gently with a little stock or white wine. Cummin seeds can be added instead of caraway.

251 Spanish omelette (SPAIN)

You will need . . .

2 small tomatoes
1 small onion
1 tablespoon French beans, cooked
1 medium potato
25g/1 oz smoked garlic sausage
4 eggs
1 tablespoon peas, cooked
salt and pepper to taste
1 teaspoon olive oil

Preparation time
10 minutes

Cooking time
4 minutes

Peel and chop tomatoes removing seeds. Chop the onion and French beans, dice the potato and sausage. Beat the eggs lightly, add the vegetables, sausage, salt and pepper.

Melt the oil in an omelette pan, pour in the egg mixture and cook quickly for 3 minutes. Place for a further minute under a hot grill to brown.

Slide out without folding on to a hot plate. *Serves 2.*

252 Baked pears (FRANCE)

You will need . . .

8 ripe pears, cored from the base
6 tablespoons redcurrant jelly
1 tablespoon port or sweet sherry
pinch powdered cloves and cinnamon
1 tablespoon orange juice
2 tablespoons brown sugar
1 dessertspoon cornflour
8 cloves

Preparation time
15 minutes

Cooking time
12-15 minutes

Oven setting
180°C; 350°F; Gas Mark 4

Place pears in a lightly buttered ovenproof baking dish. Dissolve the redcurrant jelly, powdered cloves and brown sugar in the port or sherry and orange juice, making liquid up to 300ml/½ pint with water. Boil to form a light syrup.

Pour over the pears and bake in a moderate oven, for 12-15 minutes. Strain off syrup. Mix with blended cornflour and bring to boil. Cook until transparent stirring occasionally.

Pour over pears and allow to cool. Decorate with cloves. This can be served with whipped cream (*see Quick Tip below*). *Serves 4.*

QUICK TIP

The omelette can be varied by adding some prawns. Prepare these by pinching off head and stretching out tail end using the finger and thumb. Remove tail with a pinch and twist, and then the body shell. The roe too should be removed.

QUICK TIP

To whip cream: chill the bowl and the whisk. Whip the cream lightly and slowly away from heat. As soon as the whisk leaves a distinct trail, stop whisking, otherwise you will have butter.

253 Spicy red cabbage (POLAND)

You will need . . .

1 small red cabbage
225g/8 oz streaky bacon, rinded
50g/2 oz butter
2 large onions, peeled
4 dessert apples

Preparation time
15 minutes

salt and pepper to taste
2 tablespoons brown sugar
2 tablespoons vinegar

Cooking time
45 minutes

Slice cabbage finely, removing core and outside leaves. Fry the bacon until crisp in a little of the butter and remove to a warm plate. Add rest of butter to pan (reserving 15g/½ oz) and cook onions gently until pale golden. Core and slice the apples. (*see Quick Tip below*).

In a heavy saucepan place layers of cabbage, apple, onion and bacon, seasoning each layer with salt and pepper, a little sugar and vinegar. Pour over 1 teacup boiling water. Finish with a layer of sugar and a few knobs of butter.

Cover and simmer gently for about 45 minutes.   *Serves 4.*

254 Spaghetti bolognese (ITALY)

You will need . . .

350g/12 oz spaghetti
25g/1 oz Parmesan cheese
For the sauce:
1 onion
1 carrot

Preparation time
10 minutes

1 stick of celery
1 clove garlic (optional)
½ beef stock cube

Cooking time
40 minutes

1 tablespoon oil
50g/2 oz bacon, diced
225g/8 oz freshly minced beef
1 × 227g/8 oz can peeled tomatoes
1 × 65g/2¼ oz can tomato purée
1 bay leaf
salt, pepper and sugar to taste

Chop onion, carrot and celery finely. Crush garlic if used. Dissolve stock cube in 150ml/¼ pint boiling water. Melt the fat, fry vegetables, bacon and garlic gently until golden brown. Add mince, stir and cook until lightly browned. Add tomatoes and juice from the can, purée, bay leaf, stock, salt, pepper and a pinch of sugar. Cook gently for 30-40 minutes stirring occasionally.

Taste and correct seasoning if necessary. Meanwhile cook spaghetti (*see Quick Tip below*), drain and put on hot serving dish.

Pour the sauce into the centre. Sprinkle Parmesan cheese over the top.
Note: This dish looks more attractive served in individual portions, as the two shown in the photograph.   *Serves 4.*

QUICK TIP

When preparing apples for savoury dishes have a bowl of slightly salted water on the table. Put the apple slices in as they are prepared; drain well before use. This will prevent them from going brown.

QUICK TIP

To cook lengths of spaghetti: put one end of the bundle into boiling water and as it softens, coil round until the other end slips into the water without breaking. To save time use fancy shapes instead, such as shells or bows.

255 Sicilian orange dessert (ITALY)

You will need . . .

4 large oranges
175g/6 oz castor sugar
2 tablespoons Cointreau or Curaçao (optional)
300ml/½ pint water

Preparation time
15 minutes

Finely grate zest of two oranges (*see Quick Tip below*). Carefully peel all the oranges with a sharp knife removing the pith. Heat water slowly with sugar until completely dissolved and then boil gently for 5 minutes. Remove from heat and stir in the grated orange rind and liqueur, if used.

Arrange the oranges close together in a deep dish and pour the hot syrup over, then allow to cool.

Spoon the syrup over the tops of the oranges again when quite cold. Chill before serving. Serve cut across in slices. Spread slices on a plate and spoon syrup over them.   *Serves 4.*

256 Lamb pilaff (GREECE)

You will need . . .

1 small sweet red or green pepper
15g/½ oz cornflour
salt and pepper to taste
450g/1 lb stewing lamb, boned and diced
3 tablespoons olive oil or corn oil
3 onions, peeled and sliced
3 tomatoes, peeled and sliced
1 chicken stock cube
25g/1 oz seedless raisins
1 tablespoon lemon juice
175g/6 oz long grain rice

Preparation time
10 minutes

Cooking time
30-40 minutes

Oven setting
180°C; 350°F; Gas Mark 4

Remove stalk and seeds from pepper and chop finely. Season the cornflour and toss the diced lamb in it. Heat the oil and lightly brown the meat on all sides. Remove and keep warm.

Lightly fry the onions and chopped pepper in the remaining oil, add the tomatoes, stock cube, raisins, lemon juice and 450ml/¾ pint boiling water. Stir in the rice, transfer to an oven-proof casserole. Season to taste.

Place meat on top of the rice, cover and cook in a moderate oven for 30-40 minutes or until rice has absorbed all the liquid. Turn on to a warm plate and serve immediately.   *Serves 4.*

QUICK TIP

When grating the rind off an orange or lemon, hold the fruit and rub gently against the grater turning fruit round frequently. Take care not to grate off the pith as this will give a bitter taste.

QUICK TIP

To remove the rather dehydrated appearance of raisins, stone them (if not already stoned) and immerse in boiling water before use. This will make them swell out and appear plump. Treat prunes in the same way.

257 Trout with almonds (FRANCE)

You will need . . .

4 trout
1 tablespoon seasoned flour
75g/3 oz butter
75g/3 oz flaked almonds
1 tablespoon cooking oil

Preparation time
10 minutes

2 tablespoons lemon juice
few sprigs parsley

Cooking time
10 minutes

Toss the cleaned fish in seasoned flour. Melt 25g/1 oz butter in frying pan. Add the almonds, fry until lightly browned, then remove from pan and keep on one side.

Add remaining butter to pan with the oil. Fry the trout gently for about 10 minutes or until nicely browned, turning once during the cooking.

To serve, sprinkle with the browned almonds and lemon juice. Decorate with parsley. *Serves 4.*

QUICK TIP

To prevent butter from burning when used for frying fish, add 1 tablespoon of cooking oil. (A higher proportion of oil would alter the characteristic delicate flavour of butter.)

258 Sole Véronique (FRANCE)

You will need . . .

8 medium fillets sole
salt and pepper to taste
1 wine glass dry white wine
40g/1½ oz butter
25g/1 oz flour

Preparation time
10 minutes

150ml/¼ pint milk
100g/4 oz white grapes

Cooking time
10 minutes

Oven setting
190°C; 375°F; Gas Mark 5

Roll each fillet (*see Quick Tip, recipe 259*). Well butter a baking dish and arrange fillets in this. Sprinkle with salt and pepper and pour over the wine. Cook uncovered for about 10 minutes in a moderately hot oven. Lift the fish carefully on to a warm serving dish.

Meanwhile heat the butter, stir in the flour and a measured 300ml/½ pint of liquid made up of juices from the fish and milk. Bring to the boil and cook, stirring until smooth and thick. Taste and correct seasoning.

Pour over the fish and decorate with the grapes, seeded (*see Quick Tip below*) and halved. *Serves 4.*

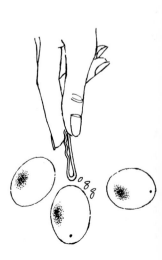

QUICK TIP

To seed grapes: sterilise a brand new hair grip by pouring boiling water over it. Push the loop end into the grape at the stalk end and pull out the seeds.

Fish in
259 spinach sauce (DENMARK)

You will need . . .

2 large plaice fillets
100g/4 oz fresh or frozen prawns
25g/1 oz butter
salt and pepper to taste
1 packet instant potato (for 4)
225g/8 oz fresh or 165g/5½ oz frozen spinach
25g/1 oz flour
150ml/¼ pint milk
2 tablespoons cream

Preparation time
15 minutes

Cooking time
10 minutes

Oven setting
190°C; 375°F; Gas Mark 5

Roll the fillets skin side inwards, and place on end close together in an ovenproof dish (*see Quick Tip below*). Fill centres with peeled prawns, reserving a few for decoration. Melt the butter, and pour half of it over them. Sprinkle well with salt and pepper. Cover with foil and bake in a moderately hot oven for 10 minutes. Place on a warm serving dish.

Meanwhile, make up the mashed potato and keep hot. Cook the spinach in as little water as possible; when tender, press through a sieve.

Blend the flour with the rest of the butter, stir in the milk, then the spinach purée. Season with salt and pepper. Cook, stirring, for 3 minutes, then withdraw from heat and add cream. Taste and correct seasoning. Pour over the plaice rolls. Top·each with a prawn and pipe or fork mashed potato round the sides of the serving dish.
Serves 4.

Normandy
260 apple flan (FRANCE)

You will need . . .

350g/12 oz rich short crust or flan pastry
600ml/1 pint thick apple purée, well sweetened
3 dessert apples, peeled, cored and sliced
juice of 2 lemons
2 tablespoons apricot jam
2 tablespoons water

Preparation time
5 minutes

Cooking time
35 minutes

Oven setting
190°C; 375°F; Gas Mark 5

Line a 23-cm/9-inch flan ring or tin with the pastry. Prick the base, and bake 'blind' for 5 minutes (*see method, recipe 248*).

Fill the flan case with the apple purée. Toss the sliced apples in half the lemon juice, and top the flan with concentric slices of apple. Bake in a moderate oven for 25-30 minutes. Remove and cool.

Heat the jam, water and rest of lemon juice until syrupy but do not allow to boil. Press through a sieve and spoon over the tart to glaze.
Serves 4-6.

QUICK TIP

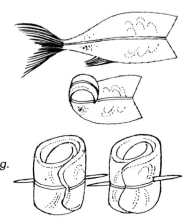

Remember always to roll tail end of fillet inside first and if necessary secure roll with a wooden cocktail stick, which can be removed when fish is cooked. For large fish, halve each double fillet before rolling.

QUICK TIP

To make a quick glaze: thicken sweetened fruit juice with arrowroot. Bring 300ml/ ½ pint juice to the boil, stir in 1 heaped teaspoon arrowroot mixed to a smooth paste with water. Cook, stirring until glaze clears.

261 Duckling à l'orange (FRANCE)

You will need . . .

1 oven-ready duckling (1.75-2.25kg/4-5 lb)
salt and pepper to taste
1 large onion, peeled
2 oranges
1 level tablespoon Bisto or gravy browning
1 tablespoon chopped parsley
1 small packet potato crisps
1 bunch watercress

Preparation time
5 minutes

Cooking time
1 hour 40 minutes

Oven setting
190°C; 375°F; Gas Mark 5

Sprinkle the duckling with salt and pepper. Cut the onion in half and put inside the bird. Use giblets to make stock while duckling is roasting. Place bird on a trivet in a roasting tin and roast in a preheated moderately hot oven for 20 minutes per pound plus 20 minutes over. Halfway through cooking time baste duckling and spoon out surplus fat from roasting tin.

Meanwhile, grate rind from one orange, peel and cut into slices. Squeeze juice from other orange. Place cooked duckling on a warm serving dish. Pour off rest of surplus fat. Blend Bisto with orange juice, stir into pan, add grated orange rind and sufficient stock from giblets to make a smooth pouring sauce.

Decorate duck with cutlet frills (*see Quick Tip below*), orange slices dipped in parsley, potato crisps and watercress.

Serves 4.

262 Red fruit compôte (DENMARK)

You will need . . .

1 × 425g/15 oz can stoned Morello cherries
1 × 385g/13½ oz can raspberries
1 heaped dessertspoon cornflour
40g/1½ oz flaked almonds
150ml/¼ pint double cream

Preparation time
15 minutes

Open the cans and drain the fruit into a fairly large saucepan. Make liquid up to 600ml/1 pint with water. Heat gently until boiling.

Blend the cornflour to a smooth paste with two tablespoons cold water, then stir with the fruit juice and simmer, stirring, until the mixture is thick, smooth and clear. Cool.

Put the drained fruit into a serving dish, pour over the sauce, stir gently, allow to cool. Sprinkle with the almonds. Serve with whipped cream.

Serves 4.

QUICK TIP

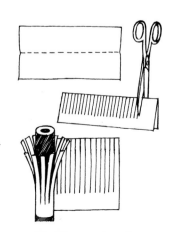

To make cutlet frills: cut strips of white paper 5 × 12.5 cm/2 × 5 inches. Fold each strip in half lengthways. Snip at 3-mm/⅛-inch intervals, making 4-cm/1½-inch incisions. Starting from the folded edge, wind each strip around a pencil. Slide off and secure.

QUICK TIP

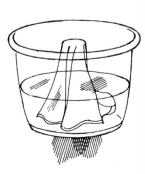

To keep cream without a refrigerator: stand the carton or bottle in a bowl of water and cover with a damp cloth. Leave the ends of the cloth in the water so it stays damp. Change the water twice a day.

263 Goulash (HUNGARY)

You will need . . .

50g/2 oz butter or margarine
225g/8 oz onions, peeled and sliced
450g/1 lb stewing veal, diced
1 level tablespoon paprika
225g/8 oz tomatoes, peeled and chopped
1 beef stock cube

Preparation time
5 minutes

1 × 65g/2½ oz can tomato purée
salt and pepper to taste

Cooking time
1 hour 45 minutes

450g/1 lb potatoes, peeled and sliced
100g/4 oz mushrooms
150ml/¼ pint soured cream

Heat the butter and fry the sliced onions and meat lightly in a strong saucepan. Stir in the paprika, then the tomatoes. Dissolve the stock cube and tomato purée in 450ml/¾ pint boiling water, add to the pan, season and simmer covered for about 1 hour.

Stir well, add the sliced potatoes and cook for a further 45 minutes. Add the mushrooms for the last 10 minutes only.

Serve in a heated casserole, top with warm soured cream, and sprinkle with a little more paprika.
Note: If the goulash is cooked in a flameproof casserole, this can be put on the table. *Serves 4.*

264 Andalusian chicken (SPAIN)

You will need . . .

275g/10 oz long grain rice
good pinch saffron
1 × 65g/2½ oz can pimentoes
450g/1 lb cooked chicken, chopped
150ml/¼ pint mayonnaise

Preparation time
15 minutes

salt and pepper to taste
6 small gherkins, chopped
few black and green olives
25g/1 oz flaked almonds

Cook rice in plenty of boiling salted water with the saffron until tender, about 12 minutes (*see Quick Tip below*). Strain, pour fresh boiling water through the rice to separate the grains. Cool.

Drain pimentoes, and cut into strips. Combine rice, chicken and mayonnaise. Season to taste.

Pile rice mixture on to a serving plate. Decorate with pimento strips, gherkins and olives. Sprinkle with almonds. *Serves 4.*

QUICK TIP

When using soured cream never allow dish to boil after adding the cream or it may curdle. To guard against this, heat the cream gently separately and then add to the dish.

QUICK TIP

To deepen the colour of saffron rice add a few drops of yellow food colouring to the water in which it is cooked. Do not omit the powdered saffron altogether or the rice will not have the characteristic delicate flavour.

Fancy cakes

There are occasions when cakes with a more 'professional' finish are needed: a party, perhaps, or a family celebration. By carefully following the recipes in this chapter, it is perfectly possible to produce really splendid, expensive looking cakes in your own kitchen.

The photographs illustrating this varied collection of large and small delicately decorated cakes speak for themselves.

The quick tips in this chapter will prove particularly useful: here, those 'tricks of the trade' which are such invaluable help in giving home-baking a professional air are explained in clear and concise terms. With these recipes, no one need find it beyond her to produce these high-class cakes.

265 Apricot baskets

(illustrated on back cover)

You will need . . .

Preparation time
20 minutes

Cooking time
15 minutes

Oven setting
190°C; 375°F; Gas Mark 5

75g/3 oz self-raising flour
pinch salt
50g/2 oz butter or margarine
50g/2 oz castor sugar
1 egg, lightly beaten
1 dessertspoon milk
few drops vanilla essence
1 × 213g/7½ oz can apricot halves
¼ packet lemon jelly
For the decoration:
150ml/¼ pint double cream
piece of angelica 12.5cm/5 inches long

Sieve flour and salt. Cream fat and sugar till light and fluffy. Beat in egg with a tablespoon of flour. Beat in milk, essence and more flour. Stir in the rest of the flour. Put mixture in 10 well greased bun tins and bake in a moderately hot oven for 15 minutes. Cool.

Drain the apricots, reserve the syrup, make up to 150ml/¼ pint with water, heat to dissolve jelly. Cool. Place half an apricot on each cake and coat with jelly. Allow to set.

Whip the cream and pipe small stars on each cake. Soak angelica in warm water until pliable. Cut narrow strips lengthwise, bend over and fix firmly into each cake.

QUICK TIP

Making a jelly glaze: make up a jelly in the appropriate flavour with half the quantity of water and spoon over when syrupy and almost set. If too liquid it will sink into the pastry or sponge and make it soggy.

266 Battenburg cake

You will need . . .

Preparation time
30 minutes

Cooking time
50 minutes

Oven setting
180°C; 350°F; Gas Mark 4

175g/6 oz butter
175g/6 oz castor sugar
3 eggs, lightly beaten
225g/8 oz self-raising flour, sieved
few drops vanilla essence
few drops raspberry essence
For the covering:
few drops vanilla essence
1 tablespoon seedless jam
1 × 250g/8 oz packet almond paste
glacé cherries and pineapple

Grease and line an 18-cm/7-inch square cake tin. Divide the tin by placing a piece of folded greaseproof paper down the centre. Make up the basic sponge mixture (*see method, recipe 267*). Divide the mixture, add vanilla essence to one half and raspberry to the other. Put each mixture into one half of the tin and bake in a moderate oven for about 50 minutes. Turn out and cool on a wire tray.

Trim the cakes and cut each into two even-sized lengths. Sandwich together with jam alternating the colours.

Soften the jam by gently warming and brush the long outside edges. Roll the almond paste into a rectangle large enough to cover the cake. Wrap paste round the cake and seal the join well. Criss-cross score the top and flute the edges, decorate with glacé cherries and pineapple.

QUICK TIP

To cut angelica: soak in hot water until pliable. Drain and dry well. Cut into narrow strips lengthwise and then diagonally across each strip to form diamonds. Alternatively cut each strip into small spikes.

267 Strawberry cream gâteau

You will need . . .

100g/4 oz self-raising flour
pinch salt
100g/4 oz butter or margarine
100g/4 oz castor sugar
2 eggs, lightly beaten

Preparation time
30 minutes

For the filling and decoration:
225g/8 oz strawberries
300ml/½ pint double cream

Cooking time
30 minutes

Oven setting
180°C; 350°F; Gas Mark 4

Sieve flour and salt together. Cream fat and sugar until light and fluffy. Beat in eggs, one at a time. Fold in dry ingredients with a metal spoon. Divide mixture equally between 2 well greased 15-18cm/6-7 inch sandwich tins. Bake in the centre of a moderate oven for 25-30 minutes. Turn out and cool on a wire tray.

Hull the strawberries, reserve half for decorating the top and roughly chop the rest. Whip the cream until it leaves a trail from the whisk.

Put the cakes together filling the centre with half of the cream and all of the chopped strawberries. Place the whole strawberries on top of the cake and, using a large star tube, swirl cream around the strawberries. As an alternative, when strawberries are not in season, use a tin of peaches, well drained.

QUICK TIP

To make cream go further: use equal quantities of single and double cream and whisk in a little castor sugar. Alternatively whip a small carton of double cream until thick and fold in two egg whites which have been stiffly beaten with a little castor sugar.

268 Congress tarts

You will need . . .

100g/4 oz plain flour
pinch salt
25g/1 oz lard
25g/1 oz margarine
cold water to mix

Preparation time
20 minutes

For the filling:
50g/2 oz butter or margarine
50g/2 oz castor sugar
1 egg, lightly beaten
25g/1 oz ground almonds
25g/1 oz self-raising flour, sieved
few drops almond essence
few drops vanilla essence
2 tablespoons jam

Cooking time
30 minutes

Oven setting
180°C; 350°F; Gas Mark 4

Sieve the flour and salt together. Add the fat cut into small pieces. Rub in with the fingertips until mixture resembles fine breadcrumbs. Add a little water and mix with a palette knife until mixture holds together but is not sticky. Knead well. Roll out thinly on a lightly floured board and cut into 7.5-cm/3-inch circles with a pastry cutter. Line two bun trays with the pastry.

Cream the butter and sugar together, add the egg and beat well. Add the remaining ingredients for the filling and mix to a soft consistency.

Put a little jam in each tart and a teaspoon of filling. Bake in a moderate oven for 30 minutes. Cool on a wire tray.

QUICK TIP

Adding a pastry decoration: roll out pastry trimmings, cut in narrow strips 5mm/¼-inch wide and 5cm/2-inches long. Lay two strips criss-cross on top of each tart before baking.

269 Marble cake

You will need . . .
225g/8 oz self-raising flour, sieved
175g/6 oz butter or margarine
175g/6 oz castor sugar
3 eggs, lightly beaten
few drops vanilla essence
few drops almond essence
green food colouring
pink food colouring

Preparation time
15 minutes

Cooking time
45 minutes

Oven setting
180°C; 350°F; Gas Mark 4

Cream together fat and sugar until light and fluffy. Gradually add the beaten eggs and fold in the flour. Divide the mixture into three. To one-third add a few drops almond essence and green colouring; mix thoroughly. To another third, add a few drops vanilla essence and pink colouring; mix thoroughly. Leave the remaining third untouched.

Drop the mixtures, in alternating spoonfuls, into a well greased fluted cake mould (savarin tin) and bake in the centre of a moderate oven for 40-50 minutes.

Turn out and cool on a wire tray.

QUICK TIP

To cream fat easily: remove from refrigerator or larder half an hour before use. If it is still too hard to cream, warm the mixing bowl with hot water and dry it before putting the fat in. Heating the fat itself causes it to become oily.

270 Peppermint cream cakes

You will need . . .
75g/3 oz self-raising flour
pinch salt
1 dessertspoon cocoa
100g/4 oz butter or margarine
100g/4 oz castor sugar
2 eggs, lightly beaten
For the icing:
225g/8 oz icing sugar
2 tablespoons water
2-3 drops green colouring
3 drops peppermint essence
For the decoration:
chocolate peppermints

Preparation time
20 minutes

Cooking time
10 minutes

Oven setting
200°C; 400°F; Gas Mark 6

Sieve flour and salt together. Cream fat and sugar until light and fluffy. Beat in eggs, one at a time. Fold in the dry ingredients with a metal spoon. Place in 18 well greased patty tins and bake in the centre of a moderately hot oven for ten minutes. Remove from tins and cool upright on a wire tray.

For the icing, sieve the sugar twice. Add the water very gradually and beat well after each addition. The icing should be stiff enough to coat the back of a wooden spoon. So as not to alter the consistency, the peppermint essence and green colouring should be added after 1 tablespoonful of water (*see Quick Tip below*).

Put a spoonful of icing on to each cake and spread over the top. Halve a chocolate peppermint cream and place one half upright in the centre.

QUICK TIP

Colouring and flavouring: to add food colouring and essence satisfactorily it is essential not to add too much. To ensure this, dip the end of a skewer into the bottle and then shake into the mixture drop by drop, stirring all the time.

271 Mandarin gâteau

You will need . . .

Preparation time
30 minutes

Cooking time
50 minutes

Oven setting
190°C; 375°F; Gas Mark 5

175g/6 oz butter or margarine
175g/6 oz castor sugar
3 eggs, lightly beaten
175g/6 oz self-raising flour, sieved
pinch salt
2 dessertspoons hot water
For the topping and decoration:
300ml/½ pint double cream or use ⅔
double cream mixed with ⅓ single
cream
1 dessertspoon castor sugar
40g/1½ oz finely grated plain block
chocolate
1 × 312g/11 oz can mandarin oranges

Grease and line a 20-cm/8-inch cake tin. Cream the fat and sugar together until light and fluffy. Add eggs one at a time, beating well. Sieve flour and salt together and fold in. Mix to a soft dropping consistency with a little warm water. Put into the tin evenly and bake in a moderately hot oven for 45-50 minutes. Turn out and cool on a wire tray.

Whip the cream until thick enough to stand in peaks, and sweeten to taste. Coat the side of the cake with a little of the cream and roll in the grated chocolate (*see Quick Tip below*). Place on a doily.

Drain the mandarin oranges reserving the juice. Prick the top of the cake with a skewer and sprinkle with the juice. Spread some of the cream over the top and decorate with the oranges. Pipe the remaining cream, using a large star tube, round the border and centre.

272 Genoese fancies

You will need . . .

Preparation time
30 minutes

Cooking time
30 minutes

Oven setting
190°C; 375°F; Gas Mark 5

75g/3 oz self-raising flour, sieved
75g/3 oz castor sugar
few drops vanilla essence
25g/1 oz butter
3 eggs
4 tablespoons apricot jam
2 tablespoons water
For the decoration:
225g/8 oz icing sugar
2 tablespoons water
1 teaspoon cocoa
pink food colouring
coloured cake decorations

Whisk the eggs and sugar together over a basin of hot water until the mixture leaves a trail from the whisk. Fold in the sieved flour and add vanilla essence. Slightly melt the butter and fold in gently. Pour mixture into a well greased Swiss roll tin 30 × 23 cm/12 × 9 inches, and bake in a moderately hot oven for 30 minutes. Turn out and cool on a wire tray.

Sieve the icing sugar well and divide into three. Sieve the cocoa into one and add the pink colouring to another. Add water to all three gradually and beat each to a coating consistency. Cut the cake into shapes with biscuit cutters or with a sharp knife. Heat the jam with the water for the glaze and sieve.

Brush each shape with glaze on a wire tray. Spoon the icing over each individually varying the colours (*see Quick Tip below*). Decorate as liked.

QUICK TIP

Coating cake sides: to coat the sides of a cake, place the decoration – chopped nuts, chocolate vermicelli, or grated chocolate – on a sheet of greaseproof paper. Holding the cake by the top and bottom, roll in the decoration until the sides are evenly coated.

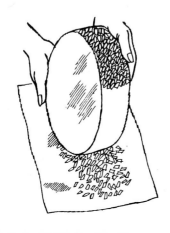

QUICK TIP

Coating small cakes: place cake shapes on a wire tray and brush each with apricot glaze to prevent lifting crumbs with the icing. Spoon icing over the cakes individually easing down the sides with a teaspoon. Put decoration in place before the icing has completely set.

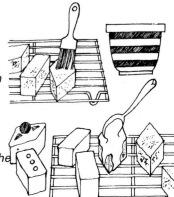

273 Chocolate butterflies

You will need . . .

50g/2 oz self-raising flour, sieved
pinch salt
1 dessertspoon cocoa
50g/2 oz butter or margarine
50g/2 oz castor sugar

Preparation time
20 minutes

1 egg, lightly beaten
1 tablespoon milk
few drops vanilla essence

Cooking time
20 minutes

For the filling:
40g/1½ oz butter or margarine
100g/4 oz icing sugar, sieved
2 teaspoons very hot milk

Oven setting
190°C; 375°F; Gas Mark 5

few drops vanilla essence

Cream fat until soft, add sugar, then beat until light and fluffy. Add egg with a tablespoon of flour, stir then beat. Beat in milk, essence and a little more flour. Add cocoa and stir in rest of flour. Half fill 10 baking cases or well greased bun tins and smooth the surface. Bake in a moderate oven for 15-20 minutes. Turn out and cool on a wire tray; if bun tins have been used, remove the cakes before cooling.

For the filling, cream fat until soft, add half the sugar and beat very thoroughly. Add the milk, the rest of the sugar and essence, beat until smooth.

When the cakes are cold, cut a round off the top of each. Put a spoonful of filling on each cake, or fill centre with piped rosettes. Cut tops in half and place on the filling, rounded edges outwards (*see Quick Tip below*).

274 Simnel cake

You will need . . .

175g/6 oz butter
175g/6 oz soft brown sugar
3 eggs, lightly beaten
225g/8 oz self-raising flour, sieved
½ teaspoon ground cinnamon
½ teaspoon ground nutmeg
100g/4 oz sultanas
350g/12 oz currants
50g/2 oz ground almonds

Preparation time
30 minutes

Cooking time
3-3½ hours

For the centre and decoration:
2 × 225g/8 oz packets almond paste
12 tiny Easter egg sweets

Oven setting
150°C; 300°F; Gas Mark 2

Cream the fat and sugar until light and fluffy. Beat in the eggs a little at a time. Fold in the dry ingredients and then stir in the sultanas, currants and ground almonds. Put half the mixture into a greased and lined 18-cm/7-inch cake tin (*see Quick Tip below*).

Roll out both packets of the almond paste thinly enough to cut circles round the cake tin; reserve the trimmings. Place one on top of the mixture in the tin. Cover with the remainder of the cake mixture and bake in a moderate oven for about 3-3½ hours. Turn out and cool on a wire tray, removing the paper.

Place the second circle of almond paste on the cake. Out of the trimmings make the 11 small balls for the top. Place around the edge of the cake. Little Easter egg sweets and fluffy chickens can be used as additional decoration.

QUICK TIP

To make butterfly wings: using a sharp knife cut a small round off the top of each cake and cut in half. Fill the centre. Place the two halves on the filling with the rounded edges upwards and at an angle, so as to give the appearance of wings.

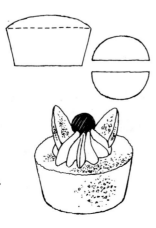

QUICK TIP

To line a cake tin: cut a circle of greaseproof paper to fit the base, and band 2.5 cm/1 inch longer than the circumference and 2.5 cm/1 inch wider than the depth of tin. Brush the tin with oil. Snip band at 1-cm/½-inch intervals, put inside the tin with the snipped edge at the base. Line the base.

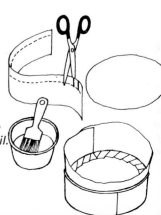

275 Madeleines

You will need . . .

100g/4 oz self-raising flour
pinch salt
100g/4 oz butter or margarine
100g/4 oz castor sugar
2 eggs, lightly beaten
For the decoration:
4 tablespoons apricot or raspberry jam
75g/3 oz desiccated coconut
glacé cherries
angelica

Preparation time
20 minutes

Cooking time
12 minutes

Oven setting
220°C; 425°F; Gas Mark 7

Sieve flour and salt together. Cream fat and sugar until light and fluffy, then beat in eggs one at a time. Fold in dry ingredients with a metal spoon and mix thoroughly. Half fill 18 well greased dariole tins. Bake in the centre of a hot oven for 12 minutes, or until firm and golden brown. Remove from tins and cool on a wire tray.

Heat the jam gently to soften and beat out any whole pieces of fruit. Insert a fork into the base of the cakes and spread the jam over the sides and top. Put the coconut on to a flat plate or a sheet of greaseproof paper. Roll the cakes in the coconut and press firmly on to the sides with a palette knife. Do not put too much coconut on the top of the cakes. Remove the fork.

Decorate each cake with a glacé cherry and two diamonds of angelica.

QUICK TIP

To brown coconut: put fine coconut on greaseproof paper on a baking sheet. Place in a cool oven and brown gently. Allow to cool. Store in an airtight jar and use for coating sides and tops of cakes.

276 Almond spring gâteau

You will need . . .

100g/4 oz self-raising flour
pinch salt
100g/4 oz butter or margarine
100g/4 oz castor sugar
2 eggs, lightly beaten
few drops vanilla essence
2 tablespoons apricot jam
For the decoration:
100g/4 oz butter
175-225g/6-8 oz icing sugar, sieved
few drops almond essence
few crystallised violets

Preparation time
15 minutes

Cooking time
15 minutes

Oven setting
190°C; 375°F; Gas Mark 5

Sieve flour and salt together. Cream fat and sugar until light and fluffy. Beat in eggs, one at a time. Fold in the dry ingredients and add the vanilla essence. Put into a well greased Swiss roll tin approximately 30 × 23 cm/12 × 9 inches. Bake in a moderately hot oven for 15 minutes. Turn out and cool on a wire tray and trim the edges whilst the cake is still warm.

Make the butter cream by beating the butter until soft and creamy, add the almond essence. Add the sieved icing sugar a little at a time beating well.

Place the cake on a flat surface and divide into three (*see Quick Tip below*). Soften the jam by gently warming and use to sandwich the cake together. Coat the cake with the butter cream, smoothing the sides and swirling decoratively on the top. Pipe shells along the top edge and decorate with crystallised violets.

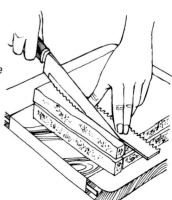

QUICK TIP

To make sure of a straight edge when trimming a cake place cake on a flat surface. Using a sharp, serrated-edge knife cut with one movement using a cake ruler as a guide.

277 Cherry nut gâteau

You will need . . .

Preparation time
20 minutes

Cooking time
20 minutes

Oven setting
190°C; 375°F; Gas Mark 5

100g/4 oz margarine
100g/4 oz castor sugar
1 dessertspoon honey
2 eggs
150g/5 oz self-raising flour, sieved
½ level teaspoon baking powder
few drops almond essence
3 tablespoons milk
For the decoration:
225g/8 oz icing sugar, sieved
2 tablespoons water
25g/1 oz butter
50g/2 oz icing sugar, sieved
green food colouring
8 walnut or almond halves
8 glacé cherries

Slice the fat and put into a slightly warm mixing bowl together with all the remaining ingredients. Beat with a wooden spoon until smooth. Spread into a well greased 18-cm/7-inch square tin and bake in a moderately hot oven for 18-20 minutes. Turn out and cool on a wire tray.

Add the water gradually to the 225g/8 oz icing sugar and beat well until of a coating consistency. Pour over the cake and smooth with a palette knife, moistened if necessary. At this stage the edges of the cake can be trimmed if the icing has trickled down.

Beat the butter until soft and creamy, add the icing sugar and green colouring. Beat well. Using a greaseproof piping bag, (*see Quick Tip below*), pipe the lines to form the 16 squares and decorate alternately with nuts and glacé cherries.

278 Iced coffee sponge

You will need . . .

Preparation time
20 minutes

Cooking time
25-30 minutes

Oven setting
180°C; 350°F; Gas Mark 4

100g/4 oz self-raising flour
pinch salt
100g/4 oz butter or margarine
100g/4 oz castor sugar
2 eggs, lightly beaten
1 tablespoon coffee essence
For the filling and decoration:
100g/4 oz butter
175-225g/6-8 oz icing sugar, sieved
3 teaspoons coffee essence
100g/4 oz flaked almonds, toasted
few chocolate buttons

Sieve flour and salt together. Cream fat and sugar until light and fluffy. Beat in eggs, one at a time. Fold in the dry ingredients and coffee essence; mix thoroughly. Divide mixture equally between 2 well greased 15-18-cm/6-7-inch sandwich tins. Bake in the centre of a moderate oven for 25-30 minutes. Turn out and cool on a wire tray.

Beat the butter until soft and creamy. Add the sieved icing sugar a little at a time beating well. Add coffee essence.

Put the cakes together filling the centre with a thin layer of butter cream. Coat the sides. Place the toasted almonds on a piece of greaseproof paper and coat the sides of the cake with them. Coat the top of the cake with the butter cream and mark prettily with a cake ruler (*see Quick Tip, recipe 280*). Decorate the top with chocolate buttons and almonds.

QUICK TIP

To make a piping bag: cut a 25cm/10-inch square of paper, fold it diagonally. Crease the centre of the fold and roll the two sharp points round and up to meet the right angle. Fold to secure the point. Cut off the end to take a small icing tube.

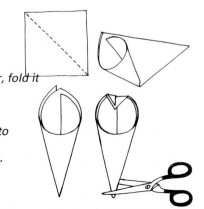

QUICK TIP

To blanch almonds: place whole almonds in a basin and pour boiling water over them. Leave for about five minutes. Drain. The skin will come off quite easily by pinching between the fingers and thumb.

279 Truffles

280 Lemon cream gâteau

You will need . . .

50g/2 oz butter
50g/2 oz castor sugar
few drops almond essence
75g/3 oz ground almonds
2 teaspoons cocoa, sieved

Preparation time
15 minutes

50g/2 oz cake crumbs, sieved
rum or sherry, or orange juice
For the coating:
chocolate vermicelli

Cream the fat and sugar until soft and fluffy. Add the almond essence, ground almonds, and cocoa. Beat thoroughly. Mix in sufficient cake crumbs to form a stiff paste. Add a few drops of rum, sherry or orange juice to flavour.

Knead well and roll into a sausage shape. Cut into equal sized pieces and roll each into a ball.

Roll each ball in chocolate vermicelli.

You will need . . .

100g/4 oz self-raising flour, sieved
pinch salt
100g/4 oz butter or margarine
100g/4 oz castor sugar
2 eggs, lightly beaten

Preparation time
30 minutes

Cooking time
30 minutes

Oven setting
180°C; 350°F; Gas Mark 4

1 lemon
For the filling:
100g/4 oz lemon curd
For the decoration:
100g/4 oz butter
175-225g/6-8 oz icing sugar, sieved
juice from the lemon
yellow cake decorations

Cream fat and sugar until light and fluffy. Beat in eggs, one at a time. Grate the lemon rind into the mixture and fold in the dry ingredients. Divide mixture equally between 2 well greased 15-18-cm/6-7 inch sandwich tins. Bake in the centre of a moderate oven for 25-30 minutes. Turn out and cool on a wire tray.

Beat the butter until soft and creamy. Add the sieved icing sugar a little at a time beating well after each addition. Add the juice from the lemon before all the sugar has been incorporated. Put the layers together filling the centre with the lemon curd. Coat the sides and top with butter cream, decorate with a cake ruler.

Stiffen the remainder of the cream with a little icing sugar and pipe rosettes, using an 8-star tube, around the top of the cake. Decorate with yellow cake decorations.

QUICK TIP

Using up cake crumbs: making truffles is an excellent method for using up the odd pieces trimmed from fancy cakes when making the layers even. Any flavour of cake can be used successfully. Crumble cake and store in an airtight jar until required.

QUICK TIP

Using a serrated ruler: hold the ruler lightly by both ends well clear of the cake and draw across the top towards you. For the sides, use a turntable, hold the ruler lightly against the side with one hand and turn the cake round gently.

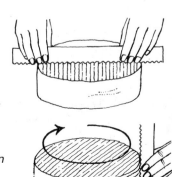

281 Iced gingerbread

282 Iced cup cakes

You will need . . .

	100g/4 oz margarine
	175g/6 oz black treacle
	50g/2 oz golden syrup
	150ml/¼ pint milk
	2 eggs
Preparation time	225g/8 oz plain flour
30 minutes	50g/2 oz castor sugar
	1 rounded teaspoon mixed spice
Cooking time	1 level teaspoon bicarbonate of soda
1¼-1½ hours	2 level teaspoons ground ginger
	For the icing:
Oven setting	225g/8 oz icing sugar
150°C; 300°F; Gas Mark 2	2 tablespoons water
	crystallised ginger slices

Melt margarine, treacle and syrup in a large saucepan. Add milk and allow mixture to cool. Beat eggs and add to mixture. Sieve dry ingredients together and add the liquid mixture gradually, blending in with a metal spoon. Pour into a greased and lined loaf tin. Bake in the centre of a cool oven for 1¼-1½ hours. Turn out, cool on a wire tray and remove the paper.

Sieve the icing sugar twice and add the water very gradually; beat well after each addition. The icing should be stiff enough to coat the back of a wooden spoon.

Pour the icing over the top of the cake and smooth with a palette knife. Decorate with crystallised ginger slices.

You will need . . .

	75g/3 oz self-raising flour
	75g/3 oz castor sugar
	few drops vanilla essence
	25g/1 oz butter
	3 eggs
Preparation time	*For the icing:*
30 minutes	225g/8 oz icing sugar
	2 tablespoons water
Cooking time	pink, green and yellow food colouring
10 minutes	*For the decoration:*
	glacé cherries
Oven setting	angelica
190°C; 375°F; Gas Mark 5	jellied lemon slices

Place 18 baking cases on a tray. Sieve the flour. Whisk the eggs and sugar together in a bowl over a basin of hot water, until the mixture leaves a trail from the whisk. Fold in the flour carefully with a metal spoon and add vanilla essence. Slightly melt the butter and fold in gently. Spoon mixture into the baking cases and bake in a moderately hot oven for 10 minutes. Cool.

For the icing, sieve the sugar well and divide into three. Add a little water very gradually to each, and tint pink, green and yellow. The icing should be stiff enough to stay in the centre of each cake.

Spoon on to the cakes (*see Quick Tip below*). Decorate the yellow iced cakes with a jellied lemon slice, the pink with a glacé cherry and the green with a diamond of angelica.

QUICK TIP

To measure golden syrup: because of its sticky consistency syrup can prove difficult to measure accurately. This can be overcome by covering the scale pan with flour. The syrup can then be tipped out quite easily.

QUICK TIP

To coat centres evenly: make glacé icing stiffer than for coating a whole cake. Drop a teaspoonful on to the centre of each. Hold cake in one hand and swirl icing round with the underside of the bowl of a teaspoon clockwise, turning the cake in the opposite direction at the same time.

283 Chocolate log

You will need . . .

3 large eggs
75g/3 oz castor sugar
75g/3 oz self-raising flour, sieved
25g/1 oz icing sugar
For the filling:
1 dessertspoon cocoa
150ml/¼ pint double cream

Preparation time
35 minutes

Cooking time
15 minutes

Oven setting
220°C; 425°F; Gas Mark 7

Whisk the eggs and sugar until thick, light and fluffy. Carefully fold in the sieved flour with a metal spoon. Pour into a greased and lined Swiss roll tin approximately 30 × 23cm/12 × 9 inches. Bake in a hot oven for 10-15 minutes. Remove the cake at once from the tin on to a piece of sugared greaseproof paper. Quickly trim the edge using a sharp knife. Then roll the sponge with the greaseproof paper (*see Quick Tip below*).

Dissolve the cocoa in a little water and whip into the cream until it leaves a trail from the whisk.

Gently unroll the sponge and spread evenly with a little of the cream. Re-roll, this time without the greaseproof paper and using a star tube, pipe the top and sides. Sprinkle with icing sugar through a fine sieve.

QUICK TIP

Rolling a Swiss roll: turn sponge on to a sheet of greaseproof paper dredged with castor sugar. Quickly trim edges. Starting at one end, roll up tightly so that the greaseproof is inter-rolled. When cool unroll. Spread the filling and re-roll.

284 Devil's food cake

You will need . . .

75g/3 oz self-raising flour
1 dessertspoon cocoa
pinch salt
100g/4 oz butter or margarine
100g/4 oz castor sugar
2 eggs, lightly beaten
few drops vanilla essence
For the marshmallow frosting:
100g/4 oz (25) marshmallows
2 tablespoons milk
2 egg whites
25g/1 oz castor sugar
For the decoration:
chocolate vermicelli

Preparation time
20 minutes

Cooking time
30 minutes

Oven setting
180°C; 350°F; Gas Mark 4

Sieve flour and salt together. Cream fat and sugar until light and fluffy. Beat in eggs, one at a time. Fold in the dry ingredients and vanilla essence using a skewer to measure (*see Quick Tip, recipe 270*). Divide mixture equally between 2 well greased 15-18-cm/6-7-inch sandwich tins. Bake in the centre of a moderate oven for 25-30 minutes. Turn out and cool on a wire tray.

Make the marshmallow frosting. Melt the marshmallows slowly in the milk, then leave to cool, stirring occasionally. Beat the egg whites and sugar until stiff and peaky, fold into the marshmallow. Leave to set a little.

Use to fill the centre of the cake and coat the top and sides. Sprinkle a little chocolate vermicelli on the top.

QUICK TIP

To test a sponge: press lightly with thumb on centre of cake. If ready, it will spring back immediately and the sides of the cake will have shrunk from the tin. Also, listen to the cake. If you can hear it gently sizzling it is not quite done.

285 Clock cake

You will need . . .

100g/4 oz butter or margarine
100g/4 oz castor sugar
2 eggs
75g/3 oz self-raising flour, sieved
1 tablespoon cocoa, sieved

Preparation time
40 minutes

For the filling:
50g/2 oz butter
100g/4 oz icing sugar, sieved

Cooking time
20 minutes

For the icing and decoration:
175g/6 oz icing sugar, sieved
1½ tablespoons water

Oven setting
200°C; 400°F; Gas Mark 6

pink or blue food colouring
chocolate buttons

Cream the butter and sugar until light and fluffy. Beat the eggs and add gradually, beating the mixture well. Fold in the dry ingredients mixing to a soft dropping consistency with a little warm water. Put the mixture into two well greased 18-cm/7-inch sandwich tins and bake in a moderately hot oven for 20 minutes. Turn out and cool on a wire tray.

Beat the butter until soft and creamy. Add the icing sugar a little at a time beating well. Fill the centre of the cake, reserving a little for the clock's hands.

Make the glacé icing which must be stiff enough to stay on the top of the cake without running down the side. Reserve a little for piping and colour as required. Arrange the twelve chocolate drops. Pipe the hands in the desired position, and the numbers on the drops, using a greaseproof piping bag.

QUICK TIP

Chocolate shapes: pencil any shapes required on greaseproof paper. Reverse paper and when melted chocolate is on point of setting, place a little on the shape with a teaspoon and run it out. Leave until cold. The shape can then be peeled off the paper.

286 Orange cream gâteau

You will need . . .

100g/4 oz self-raising flour, sieved
pinch salt
100g/4 oz butter or margarine
100g/4 oz castor sugar
2 eggs, lightly beaten
1 orange

Preparation time
20 minutes

For the butter cream:
100g/4 oz butter
175-225g/6-8 oz icing sugar, sieved
juice from the orange
jellied orange and lemon slices

Cooking time
30 minutes

Oven setting
180°C; 350°F; Gas Mark 4

Cream fat and sugar until light and fluffy. Beat in eggs, one at a time. Grate the rind from the orange, leaving pith intact, and fold in with the dry ingredients. Divide mixture equally between 2 well greased 15-18-cm/6-7-inch sandwich tins. Bake in the centre of a moderate oven for 25-30 minutes. Turn out and cool on a wire tray.

Beat the butter until soft and creamy. Add the sieved icing sugar a little at a time beating well after each addition. Add the juice from the orange before all the sugar has been incorporated.

Sandwich the cake together with the butter cream. Coat the sides and top swirling decoratively. Decorate with the orange and lemon slices.

QUICK TIP

Marking butter cream: simple effective decorations can be achieved by using the tip of a round-bladed table knife, fork or teaspoon, holding the end opposite to that being used to make the pattern.

287 Polka dot dandies

You will need . . .

100g/4 oz butter
100g/4 oz castor sugar
2 eggs
100g/4 oz self-raising flour, sieved
1 packet chocolate polka dots
2 teaspoons coffee essence
For the decoration:
50g/2 oz butter
75-100g/3-4 oz icing sugar, sieved
few drops coffee essence

Preparation time
20 minutes

Cooking time
20 minutes

Oven setting
180°C; 350°F; Gas Mark 4

Cream butter and sugar until light and fluffy. Lightly beat the eggs and add a little at a time beating well between each addition to prevent curdling. Add coffee essence and fold in the flour. Add the chocolate drops, reserving a few for decoration. Spoon mixture into paper cases, which should be lightly dusted with flour. Bake in a moderate oven for 20 minutes. Turn out and cool on a wire tray.

To make the butter cream, beat the butter until soft and creamy. Add the sieved icing sugar a little at a time beating well, then the coffee essence. Mix thoroughly.

Top each cake with a swirl of the cream and a group of 3 chocolate dots.

QUICK TIP

To be certain that cake tins have an equal amount of mixture, weigh tins when filled with the mixture and balance the quantity so that the same amount is in each, and both tins weigh the same.

288 Frosted walnut cake

You will need . . .

100g/4 oz self-raising flour, sieved
pinch salt
100g/4 oz butter or margarine
100g/4 oz castor sugar
2 eggs, lightly beaten
100g/4 oz walnuts, shelled
For the filling and covering:
450g/1 lb granulated sugar
150ml/¼ pint cold water
2 egg whites, stiffly whisked

Preparation time
30 minutes

Cooking time
30 minutes

Oven setting
180°C; 350°F; Gas Mark 4

Chop the walnuts reserving 7 halves for the top (*see Quick Tip below*). Make up the basic sponge mixture (*see method, recipe 267*) adding the chopped nuts with the flour. Divide mixture equally between 2 well greased 15-18-cm/6-7-inch sandwich tins. Bake in the centre of a moderate oven for 25-30 minutes. Turn out and cool on a wire tray.

Dissolve the sugar in the water, stirring continuously, and then allow to boil, without stirring. Keep the mixture boiling until a teaspoonful dropped into cold water forms a soft ball. Pour the syrup on to the stiffly whisked egg white. Whisk until mixture is thick and will coat the back of a wooden spoon. Quickly spread a layer in the centre of the cake and sandwich together. Pour the remaining icing over the top and sides swirling decoratively.

Decorate the top with the 7 walnut halves.

QUICK TIP

To chop: place nuts on a chopping board and use a sharp, pointed knife. Move the handle and blade up and down and work right to left across the board keeping the point of the knife down. Confine the chopping to the centre of the board.

Bacon and ham

The popularity of bacon and ham in British households is a fact that certainly nobody would dispute. Here are 24 recipes, each one exceptionally attractive, showing the many uses to which these familiar items on the menu can be put. They will provide a welcome change from the more conventional ways of preparing these cuts and, as will be discovered, they do not require a long time to prepare, or any specialised skill. You will find real pleasure in attempting one of the unusual dishes, such as an elaborate looking ham soufflé or liver and ham pâté, and you can be sure of success with our easy recipes.

289 Bacon in a pastry case

(illustrated on back cover)

You will need . . .	25g/1 oz butter
	1 onion, finely chopped
	100g/4 oz mushrooms, thinly sliced
	salt and pepper
	1 vacuum pack sweet cure bacon joint,
Preparation time	about 750g/1½ lb
30 minutes	1 egg yolk, beaten with 1 tablespoon
	water
Cooking time	*For the pastry:*
2 hours	350g/12 oz plain flour
	pinch salt
Oven setting	75g/3 oz lard
220°C; 425°F; Gas Mark 7	150ml/¼ pint water plus 2 tablespoons
160°C; 325°F; Gas Mark 3	frosted grapes for garnish

Melt butter and fry onion for 5 minutes. Add mushrooms. Fry for further 5 minutes. Season to taste.

Sieve flour and salt. Put lard and water into saucepan; bring to boil. Pour on to flour; mix with knife until it forms a ball. Roll pastry out to a circle reserving a little. Spread circle with onion mixture. Place bacon in centre. Brush edges with beaten egg; completely enclose joint. Seal edges well; place on baking tray. Decorate with pastry leaves and balls made from trimmings.

Brush with beaten egg. Bake in hot oven for 15 minutes. Lower heat; bake for 1¾ hours. If pastry becomes too brown cover with greaseproof paper. Serve with frosted grapes (*see Quick Tip below*). *Serves 4.*

QUICK TIP

For frosted grapes, brush small bunches of grapes with beaten egg white. Toss in castor sugar and leave to dry on greaseproof paper. Use to garnish bacon joint.

290 Ayrshire roll

You will need . . .	1.75kg/4 lb Ayrshire roll or piece of
	middle cut bacon
	25g/1 oz butter, melted
	For the stuffing:
Preparation time	25g/1 oz butter
20 minutes plus soaking	100g/4 oz mushrooms, finely chopped
time for bacon	75g/3 oz fresh white breadcrumbs
	1 egg, beaten
	2 tablespoons chopped parsley
Cooking time	salt and pepper
2 hours	225g/8 oz packet frozen Brussels sprouts

Oven setting
190°C; 375°F; Gas Mark 5

Soak gammon overnight in cold water. Wrap gammon round a jam jar and tie firmly. Place in a large saucepan with fresh cold water and simmer gently for 1 hour.

Remove, allow to cool slightly and remove skin. Melt butter and fry mushrooms gently for 5 minutes. Remove from heat and stir in remaining ingredients. Mix well. Remove jam jar and fill cavity of gammon with stuffing. Secure with fresh string if necessary. Make cuts about 5-mm/¼-inch apart over the fat for decoration.

Place gammon in a roasting tin, brush with melted butter and roast in a moderately hot oven for a further hour. Serve with Brussels sprouts. *Serves 8.*

QUICK TIP

If preferred, instead of making breadcrumbs, remove crusts from 75g/3 oz bread and soak in a beaten egg. When soft mash with a fork. Use in stuffings.

291 Huntingdon fidget pie

You will need . . .

450g/1 lb streaky bacon
225g/8 oz onions
450g/1 lb cooking apples
salt and pepper
150ml/¼ pint cider

Preparation time
15 minutes

For the pastry:
225g/8 oz plain flour
pinch salt
100g/4 oz butter
2 tablespoons water
For the glaze:
1 egg, beaten

Cooking time
50 minutes

Oven setting
220°C; 425°F; Gas Mark 7
180°C; 350°F; Gas Mark 4

Remove rind from bacon and dice, peel and chop onions. Core and chop apples. Mix well together and season. Put into 1.2-litre/2-pint pie dish and pour over the cider.

Sieve together flour and salt. Rub in butter until mixture resembles fine breadcrumbs. Mix with water to form a firm dough. Roll out and cover pie. Make four cuts out from the centre about 7.5-cm/3-inches long. Fold back the triangles of pastry to expose the filling. Roll out trimmings and cut out crescents, using a fluted cutter. Brush with beaten egg and place round edge of pastry.

Brush pie with egg and bake in a hot oven for 20 minutes, lower heat to moderate and bake for a further 30 minutes until pastry is crisp and golden. *Serves 4.*

QUICK TIP

Crisply fry bacon rinds, crush with a rolling pin, and use as a delicious and unusual seasoning for soups and stews.

292 Bacon-stuffed courgettes

You will need . . .

8 medium courgettes
25g/1 oz butter
1 large onion, chopped
450g/1 lb collar or forehock bacon, soaked
4 large tomatoes, peeled and chopped
½ teaspoon mixed herbs
salt and pepper

Preparation time
15 minutes

Cooking time
1 hour

Oven setting
180°C; 350°F; Gas Mark 4

Cut a wedge from each courgette.

Melt the butter and fry onion for 5 minutes. Finely chop or mince bacon, add to pan and cook for a further 10 minutes. Add tomatoes, herbs and seasoning and pile into courgettes. Put into an ovenproof dish.

Cover with foil and bake in a moderate oven for about 45 minutes, until cooked. *Serves 4.*

QUICK TIP

Vegetable marrow can be used when in season. Remove a slice from the top and scoop out the seeds. Fill with the stuffing, top with the lid, brush with melted butter and bake in a moderate oven, 180°C, 350°F, Gas Mark 4, for about 1 hour.

Sausages with 293 cheese and bacon

You will need . . .

450g/1 lb pork sausages
100g/4 oz Cheddar cheese
8 rashers back bacon
2 tablespoons apple chutney

Preparation time
5 minutes

Cooking time
20 minutes

Grill sausages slowly for 15 minutes. Make a slit halfway through each sausage, down the length.

Put slices of cheese in each slit. Remove rind from bacon and spread with chutney. Wrap round sausages, with the chutney inside. Secure with cocktail sticks.

Place under a hot grill for about 5 minutes until bacon is crisp and golden and cheese has melted.   *Serves 4.*

294 Glazed ham

You will need . . .

1 piece middle or corner gammon, about 1.75kg/4 lb
1.2 litres/2 pints water
1 large onion
1 bay leaf
6 peppercorns
For the glaze:
75g/3 oz soft brown sugar
2 teaspoons dry mustard
cloves

Preparation time
10 minutes plus soaking time for bacon

Cooking time
1¾ hours

Oven setting
220°C; 425°F; Gas Mark 7

Soak gammon overnight in cold water. Put into a saucepan with 1.2 litres/2 pints water, quartered onion, bay leaf and peppercorns. Cover and bring to the boil. Simmer for 1½ hours.

Peel off skin from gammon, mark fat into diamond shapes with a sharp knife and place in a roasting tin. Mix sugar and mustard together and press on to fat. Stick a clove in the centre of each diamond.

Place in a hot oven for about 15 minutes, until fat is crisp and golden. Serve with beans and carrots, if liked.   *Serves 8.*

QUICK TIP

Never prick sausages. Fry or grill slowly to prevent the skins from bursting, turning as often as is necessary to brown evenly.

QUICK TIP

Uncooked bacon joints need not be stored in the refrigerator. They should be wrapped in pieces of muslin and stored in a cool place.

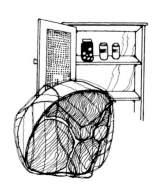

295 Somerset bacon chops

You will need . . .

5 boneless bacon chops
50g/2 oz butter
1 large onion
For the stuffing:
1 small onion, finely chopped
15g/½ oz butter
175g/6 oz cooking apples
75g/3 oz fresh white breadcrumbs
1 tablespoon sultanas
pepper
1 egg, blended

Preparation time
20 minutes

Cooking time
30 minutes

Oven setting
190°C; 375°F; Gas Mark 5

With a sharp knife, cut through bacon chops from the outside edge to within 2-cm/¾-inch of the inside edge, to form a 'pocket'.

Fry small onion in butter for 5 minutes. Peel, core and grate apples. Mix onion, apple, breadcrumbs, sultanas and pepper. Bind with blended egg. Use this mixture to stuff 'pockets' in chops. Place chops in roasting tin.

Spoon over 25g/1 oz melted butter and bake in a moderately hot oven for 30 minutes, basting from time to time, until chops are golden and tender. Cut onion into rings and fry in 25g/1 oz butter until golden. Garnish the chops with these.   *Serves 5.*

296 Hot bacon loaf

You will need . . .

40g/1½ oz butter
40g/1½ oz browned breadcrumbs
1 large onion, finely chopped
350g/12 oz cooked bacon, from a joint
½ teaspoon mixed dried herbs
½ teaspoon grated nutmeg
50g/2 oz fresh white breadcrumbs
1 egg, blended
150ml/¼ pint bacon stock
pepper
225g/8 oz frozen cut green beans

Preparation time
20 minutes

Cooking time
1 hour

Oven setting
180°C; 350°F; Gas Mark 4

Grease a 450g/1 lb loaf tin with 15g/½ oz butter and press 25g/1 oz browned breadcrumbs round the bottom and sides of the tin. Fry finely chopped onion in remaining butter. Mince bacon, add onion and remaining ingredients except beans. If bacon and stock are not very salty, it may be necessary to add a little salt as well.

Turn mixture into prepared tin. Cover with foil and bake in a moderate oven for 1 hour.

Turn out, sprinkle with remaining breadcrumbs and serve with cooked cut green beans.   *Serves 4.*

QUICK TIP

Try making this recipe with pork loin chops. It is equally delicious. Cut chops through to within 1-cm/½-inch of the bones to make the 'pocket' for the stuffing.

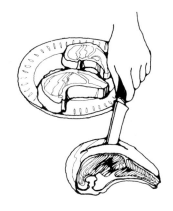

QUICK TIP

Cheap flank bacon gives a great deal of flavour to all kinds of casseroles. Cut it into cubes and add to the casserole with the other ingredients. It can be removed before serving, if preferred.

297 Liver and bacon pâté

298 Bacon jacket potatoes

You will need . . .

6 rashers streaky bacon
225g/8 oz pigs liver
225g/8 oz fat bacon
1 clove garlic
1 large onion

Preparation time
25 minutes

50g/2 oz butter
salt and pepper
3 bay leaves

Cooking time
1 hour

For the sauce:
150ml/¼ pint milk
2 blades mace

Oven setting
180°C; 350°F; Gas Mark 4

1 bay leaf
2-3 peppercorns
25g/1 oz butter
25g/1 oz flour

Remove rinds from streaky bacon and stretch on a board with the back of a knife. Lay rashers of bacon at the bottom and round the sides of a greased terrine or straight sided dish. Fry liver, de-rinded fat bacon, garlic and roughly chopped onion in butter for 10 minutes. Mince or put into a blender.

Put milk for sauce into a pan with mace, bay leaf and peppercorns. Bring very slowly to the boil, leave to stand for 10 minutes, then strain. Melt butter in pan, add flour and cook for 1 minute. Remove from heat and gradually stir in milk. Return to heat and bring to the boil, stirring all the time until sauce bubbles and thickens. Add to liver mixture and blend well. Season to taste.

Turn into prepared dish and top with bay leaves. Cover with foil and lid. Stand in a roasting tin of hot water and bake for 1 hour. Allow to become quite cold. Serve with toast. *Serves 8.*

You will need . . .

5 large potatoes
50g/2 oz butter
4 tablespoons milk
6 rashers streaky bacon
salt and pepper

Preparation time
15 minutes

100g/4 oz Cheddar cheese, grated

Cooking time
1½-2 hours

Oven setting
200°C; 400°F; Gas Mark 6

Prick potatoes with a fork. Bake in a moderately hot oven for 1½-2 hours until soft. Cut potatoes in half, scoop out soft insides and mash with butter and milk.

Grill bacon until crisp. Remove rinds and chop. Add to mashed potatoes and season well. Return to potato shells.

Sprinkle with grated cheese and grill until cheese is golden and bubbling. *Serves 5.*

QUICK TIP

Pâté is extremely useful for parties. For a quick cocktail snack, spread home-made or bought pâté on small savoury biscuits and top with chopped chives or paprika.

QUICK TIP

Blend cream cheese and chopped chives together, season well and serve in potatoes. Cut a cross in the top of each potato, squeeze base to open out the cut, and pile in the cheese mixture.

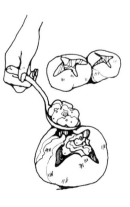

299 Ham bake

You will need . . .

75g/3 oz butter
50g/2 oz flour
150ml/¼ pint milk
100g/4 oz cooked ham, finely chopped
3 large eggs, separated
1 teaspoon dry mustard
salt and pepper

Preparation time
15 minutes

Cooking time
40 minutes

Oven setting
190°C; 375°F; Gas Mark 5

Melt butter in a pan, add flour and cook for a minute. Remove from heat and gradually stir in milk. Return to heat, bring to the boil, stirring all the time, making a thick sauce that leaves sides of pan. Remove from heat and blend in ham.

Stir in egg yolks, blended with mustard, salt and pepper. Carefully fold in stiffly whisked egg whites. Turn into a buttered 1.2-litre/2-pint soufflé dish. Run a teaspoon round the outside edge of the mixture, pushing it inwards to prevent the soufflé spilling over when baking.

Bake in a moderately hot oven for 40 minutes until golden and well risen.

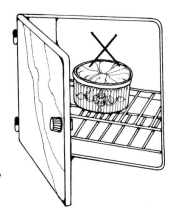

QUICK TIP

When making soufflés, never open the oven door while they are cooking as the draught of air may cause them to collapse. It is important always to use the size of soufflé dish given in the recipe.

300 Open bacon pie

You will need . . .

225g/8 oz self-raising flour
pinch salt
pinch cayenne pepper
25g/1 oz butter
75g/3 oz Cheddar cheese, grated
150ml/¼ pint milk and milk for glazing
For the topping:
8 rashers streaky bacon
25g/1 oz butter
1 large onion, chopped
350g/12 oz tomatoes, skinned and chopped
1 tablespoon chopped parsley
½ teaspoon sugar
salt and pepper
4 slices Cheddar cheese, from a wedge

Preparation time
20 minutes

Cooking time
30 minutes

Oven setting
220°C; 425°F; Gas Mark 7

Sieve together flour, salt and cayenne pepper. Rub in butter until mixture resembles fine breadcrumbs. Add cheese and bind with milk to form a soft dough. Roll out to an 33-cm/11-inch round on a floured baking sheet. Roll over 1-cm/½-inch of the dough, all the way round, to form an edge and prick the centre lightly with a fork. Brush with milk and bake in a hot oven for about 20 minutes until golden.

Remove rind from bacon rashers and chop 4. Fry in butter with onion for 5 minutes. Add tomatoes, parsley, sugar and seasoning. Cover and simmer for 5 minutes.

Place hot tomato mixture on scone dough. Top with bacon rashers in a radial pattern and place slices of cheese in between. Return to oven and bake for 10 minutes. Garnish with chicory spears, orange slices and parsley, if liked. *Serves 4-6.*

QUICK TIP

Bacon rashers should have the rinds snipped off. The rashers should then be placed in a cold frying pan, without fat, and fried slowly for 6-8 minutes.

301 Kentish bacon roly-poly

Bacon and
302 dumpling soup

You will need . . .

750g/1½ lb forehock bacon
1 small onion
1 tablespoon tomato ketchup
pinch dried sage
salt and pepper
225g/8 oz packet frozen mixed
vegetables
For the pastry:
225g/8 oz self-raising flour
pinch salt
225g/8 oz shredded suet
150ml/¼ pint water

Preparation time
15 minutes plus soaking
time for bacon

Cooking time
3 hours

Soak bacon in cold water for 6 hours or overnight. Place in a pan of fresh cold water with onion, bring to the boil and simmer gently for 25 minutes.

Remove rind from bacon. Cut meat from bone and chop finely or mince with cooked onion. Stir in ketchup, sage and the seasoning.

Sift together flour and salt. Add suet and mix to a soft dough with cold water. Roll out to an oblong. Spread bacon mixture to within 1-cm/½-inch of edges. Wet edges, roll up like a Swiss roll. Wrap in greased, greaseproof paper then foil, and steam for 2½ hours. Serve hot with cooked mixed vegetables.

Serves 4.

You will need . . .

2 onions
2 carrots
1 parsnip
1.2 litres/2 pints water
350g/12 oz collar or forehock bacon,
soaked for 4 hours
1 bay leaf
½ cabbage heart
salt and pepper
For the dumplings:
100g/4 oz self-raising flour
100g/4 oz pork sausage meat

Preparation time
15 minutes plus
soaking time

Cooking time
1 hour

Cut onions into rings and carrots and parsnip into strips. Put into cold water with bacon and bay leaf. Bring to boil and simmer for 40 minutes.

Remove bacon and cut into dice. Return to pan with finely shredded cabbage heart and bring back to the boil.

Sieve flour and mix with sausage meat. Form into 12 small balls. Place in boiling soup, cover and simmer for 15 minutes. Taste and season.

Serves 6.

QUICK TIP

Try using suet crust pastry, instead of short crust pastry as a topping for savoury pies.

QUICK TIP

Simmer bacon bones in stock or water with herbs and seasoning. This forms an excellent basis for many delicious soups.

303 Ham and melon balls

You will need . . .

1 medium-sized melon
175g/6 oz cooked ham, cut in two slices
pinch salt
pinch sugar
pinch pepper
¼ teaspoon French mustard
1 tablespoon vinegar
2 tablespoons oil
cucumber slices

Preparation time
15 minutes

Slice the top off the melon and scoop out the seeds. Scoop out the flesh from the melon using a ball cutter, or remove large pieces and cut into cubes.

Dice ham and mix with the melon balls. Mix seasonings with vinegar and add oil, mix well. Blend with melon balls and ham. Vandyke edge of melon shell with kitchen scissors. Return mixture to melon shell.

Chill until ready to serve. Garnish with slices of cucumber.
Serves 6.

304 Devilled ham rolls

You will need . . .

1 × 329g/11 oz can sweet corn
4 tablespoons French dressing
2 large potatoes, cooked
2 red-skinned eating apples
5-cm/2-inch piece cucumber
175g/6 oz cream cheese
2 teaspoons made mustard
3 tablespoons milk
salt and pepper
8 thin slices cooked ham
lemon juice
watercress

Preparation time
15 minutes

Drain sweet corn and mix with French dressing, place on serving dish.

Dice potatoes, one apple cored, but unpeeled and cucumber. Beat cream cheese, then beat in mustard and milk. Stir in potatoes, apple and cucumber. Season to taste with salt and pepper.

Divide potato mixture between slices of ham and roll up. Place on bed of sweet corn. Core other apple and cut into slices, sprinkle with lemon juice and use to garnish rolls together with watercress.
Serves 4.

QUICK TIP

To test if a melon is ripe, press gently with the thumb at both ends. If it gives slightly, the melon is ripe, if it remains firm it is not, and should be left for a few days before using.

QUICK TIP

An attractive variation of this recipe is ham cornets. Wrap the slices of ham round cream horn tins oiled on the outside. Secure with a cocktail stick if necessary, then remove tins and fill with potato mixture.

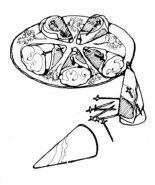

Gammon steaks
305 and pineapple

You will need . . .

4 gammon steaks, about 175g/6 oz each
50g/2 oz butter
1 × 227g/8 oz can pineapple rings
salt and pepper
few stuffed olives
parsley sprigs

Preparation time
5 minutes

Cooking time
15 minutes

Snip rind of gammon at 2.5-cm/1-inch intervals round each steak. Melt butter and add 2 tablespoons pineapple syrup from can.

Brush one side of steak with butter and syrup, season with salt and pepper and grill for 5 minutes. Turn, brush with remaining butter and syrup, season and grill for 5 minutes.

Make one cut in each pineapple ring and grill for 3-4 minutes until heated through. Place gammon steaks on serving dish and arrange pineapple rings interlocking with each other. Garnish with olives and parsley and serve with peas and chipped or mashed potatoes. *Serves 4.*

306 Ham-stuffed peaches

You will need . . .

1 × 411g/14½ oz can peach halves
100g/4 oz sliced, cooked ham
4 tablespoons mayonnaise
2 teaspoons chopped parsley
salt and pepper
lettuce
parsley sprigs

Preparation time
10 minutes

Strain juice from peaches and drain them on kitchen paper.

Mince ham finely and mix with mayonnaise and parsley. Season to taste with salt and pepper.

Pipe or spoon into stone cavity of fruit. Arrange on a bed of lettuce and garnish with parsley sprigs. *Serves 4.*

QUICK TIP

Add a small can pineapple juice and some ice cubes or balls to the syrup remaining from the can. This makes a pleasantly refreshing cool drink.

QUICK TIP

For a party, make a ham dip. Add 100g/4 oz minced ham and 1 teaspoon made mustard to 150ml/¼ pint thick mayonnaise. Season to taste and serve with crisps or savoury biscuits.

307 Stuffed chicken drumsticks

Chicken and 308 ham pancakes

You will need . . .

4 large chicken drumsticks
salt and pepper
4 canned pineapple spears or cubes
4 slices cooked ham
25g/1 oz butter
1 × 300g/10½ oz can condensed mushroom soup
225g/8 oz frozen peas
fried new potatoes
chopped chives

Preparation time
20 minutes

Cooking time
45 minutes

Oven setting
180°C; 350°F; Gas Mark 4

Remove bone from drumsticks (*see Quick Tip below*). Season with salt and pepper.

Place a pineapple spear on each slice of ham. Roll up and stuff chicken drumsticks with ham rolls. Secure openings with cocktail sticks. Fry in hot butter until golden.

Transfer to a casserole, pour over soup, cover and bake in a moderate oven for 45 minutes. Serve with cooked peas and fried new potatoes sprinkled with chives. *Serves 4.*

You will need . . .

For the pancakes:
100g/4 oz plain flour
pinch salt
1 egg
300ml/½ pint milk
1 tablespoon oil and oil for frying
For the filling:
40g/1½ oz butter
40g/1½ oz flour
450ml/¾ pint milk
175g/6 oz cooked ham
175g/6 oz cooked chicken
salt and pepper
tomato slices
parsley sprigs

Preparation time
15 minutes

Cooking time
15 minutes

Sieve together flour and salt. Add egg, then gradually add half the milk, beating well to a smooth batter. Stir in remaining milk and oil. Put a little oil into the frying pan and heat. Pour off surplus oil. Pour about 2 tablespoons of batter into pan and tilt so that the batter covers the base. Cook until underside is golden. Toss or turn pancake and fry until second side is cooked. Turn out of pan and keep hot (*see Quick Tip below*). Repeat with remaining batter to give 8 pancakes.

Melt butter in pan, add flour and cook for a minute. Remove from heat and gradually stir in milk. Return to heat and bring to the boil, stirring all the time until sauce bubbles and thickens. Add chopped ham and chicken and season well.

Divide filling between pancakes and roll up. Serve garnished with grilled tomato slices and parsley sprigs. *Serves 4.*

QUICK TIP

To bone out drumsticks, cut round at knuckle end with a sharp knife and pull meat away from bone. Pull meat inside out and pull out bone. Cut away from bone at joint.

QUICK TIP

To keep pancakes hot, place on a plate over a pan of hot water and cover with foil. If they are going to be allowed to get cold and reheated later, place a piece of greaseproof paper between each layer to prevent pancakes from sticking together.

309 Cornish ham pudding

You will need . . .

6 thin slices white bread
40g/1½ oz butter
3 thick slices cooked ham
3 tomatoes, thinly sliced
3 eggs
salt and pepper
600ml/1 pint milk

Preparation time
10 minutes

Cooking time
35-45 minutes

Oven setting
180°C; 350°F; Gas Mark 4

Remove crusts from bread and spread with butter. Place slices of ham on 3 slices of bread, top with tomato slices, reserving some for garnishing. Cover with remaining bread slices, buttered side up. Cut each sandwich into 4 triangles. Place in a shallow, buttered ovenproof dish.

Beat together eggs, salt and pepper and then blend in milk. Strain over bread and garnish with remaining tomato slices.

Bake in a moderate oven for 35-45 minutes or until 'custard' has set. *Serves 4.*

QUICK TIP

Beat eggs by stirring with a wooden spoon. This means that little air is incorporated and therefore a smoother custard results.

310 Wiltshire bacon cakes

You will need . . .

50g/2 oz streaky bacon
225g/8 oz self-raising flour
¼ teaspoon salt
25g/1 oz butter
75g/3 oz Cheddar cheese, grated
150ml/¼ pint milk
1 tablespoon tomato ketchup
dash Worcestershire sauce
milk for glazing
4 rashers streaky bacon
watercress

Preparation time
10 minutes

Cooking time
30 minutes

Oven setting
200°C; 400°F; Gas Mark 6

Remove rind from the bacon and grill until crisp. Cut into 1-cm/½-inch pieces.

Sieve together flour and salt. Rub in butter until mixture resembles fine breadcrumbs. Add three quarters of the grated cheese and all the bacon. Mix milk, tomato ketchup and Worcestershire sauce together and add to dry ingredients. Mix to a soft dough and roll out on a floured board to an 18-cm/7-inch circle, brush with milk and cut into 8 wedges. Arrange on a greased and floured baking tray in a circle, with the edges overlapping. Sprinkle with remaining cheese.

Bake in a moderately hot oven for 30 minutes. Remove rind from bacon rashers, cut in half and roll up. Place rolls on a skewer and grill until crisp. Place in centre of bacon cakes and garnish with watercress. *Serves 4.*

QUICK TIP

Brush day-old scones with a little milk and bake in a moderately hot oven 190°C, 375°F, Gas Mark 5, for 10 minutes to make them fresh again.

311 Cheesy leeks and ham

You will need . . .

8 medium-sized leeks
salt
8 thin slices ham
40g/1½ oz butter
40g/1½ oz flour
300ml/½ pint milk
175g/6 oz Cheddar cheese, grated
1 teaspoon made mustard
pepper

Preparation time
10 minutes

Cooking time
25 minutes

Remove outside leaves, roots and most of the green part of the leeks. Wash well in cold water to remove all the grit and dirt (see Quick Tip below). Cook in boiling, salted water until tender. Drain well, reserving 150ml/¼ pint of the stock. Wrap slices of ham round leeks and place in an ovenproof dish.

Melt butter, add flour and cook for a minute. Remove from heat and gradually stir in milk and leek stock. Return to heat and bring to boil, stirring all the time until sauce bubbles and thickens. Stir in 100g/4 oz of the cheese and the mustard, season to taste.

Pour over leeks, sprinkle over remaining cheese and grill until cheese is golden brown and bubbling. *Serves 4.*

312 Bacon burgers

You will need . . .

450g/1 lb collar bacon
1 small onion
1 cooking apple
pepper
25g/1 oz white breadcrumbs
1 egg, beaten
50g/2 oz lard
100g/4 oz mushrooms
4 tomatoes, halved

Preparation time
15 minutes plus soaking
time for bacon

Cooking time
20 minutes

Soak collar for 6 hours. Remove rind and mince with peeled onion and peeled cored apple.

Add pepper and breadcrumbs and bind with egg. Form into 4 cakes.

Melt lard and fry burgers for 10 minutes on each side, with mushrooms and tomatoes. *Serves 4.*

QUICK TIP

To clean leeks, insert knife about 5cm/2 inches from the base end of the leek and pull upwards. Open out and wash thoroughly under a cold tap.

QUICK TIP

Sweet-cure bacon joints need no soaking. Smoked joints must be soaked in cold water for at least 6 hours, preferably over-night, and unsmoked joints for at least 2 hours.

Cooking with cream

Cream has always been considered as the ingredient that gives a particularly luxurious touch to food, be it a sweet dish or cake, a beautifully smooth soup or a really extra-special main-course dish. The recipes in this chapter are not unduly expensive to prepare and each in its own category provides a true example of the rich and velvety taste that only real dairy cream can give.

To display the versatility of cream, a variety of dishes has been selected: some to be served as meal starters, some as main courses, various sweets and cakes and even superb creamy drinks.

313 Creamy drinks

(illustrated on frontispiece)

You will need . . .

GAELIC COFFEE:
4 tablespoons sugar
4 measures whisky
900ml/1½ pints hot strong black coffee
150ml/¼ pint double dairy cream

Preparation time
5 minutes each

CHOCOLATE FRAPPÉ:
8 tablespoons drinking chocolate
4 tablespoons boiling water
750ml/1¼ pints iced iced milk
65ml/⅛ pint double dairy cream
ICED COFFEE:
3 tablespoons coffee essence
750ml/1¼ pints milk
150ml/¼ pint single dairy cream
crumbled chocolate flake

GAELIC COFFEE: Put sugar into 4 warmed glasses. Pour over whisky then coffee and stir to dissolve sugar. Top with double dairy cream (*see Quick Tip below*). *Serves 4.*

CHOCOLATE FRAPPÉ: Dissolve chocolate in hot water and whisk into iced milk. Top with lightly whipped double dairy cream. *Serves 4.*

ICED COFFEE: Mix coffee essence with milk and single dairy cream, sprinkle over crumbled chocolate flake. *Serves 4.*

314 Coffee party soufflé

You will need . . .

1 oz gelatine
150ml/¼ pint water
3 tablespoons coffee essence
3 eggs, separated
50g/2 oz castor sugar

Preparation time
25 minutes

150ml/¼ pint double dairy cream, lightly whipped
For the decoration:
225g/8 oz plain chocolate finger biscuits
150ml/¼ pint double dairy cream, lightly whipped
hazelnuts or walnut halves

Put gelatine with water and coffee essence in a bowl and leave to soften for 5 minutes. Place over a pan of hot water until gelatine has dissolved.

Beat egg yolks and sugar in a basin over a pan of simmering water until thick and creamy. Remove and beat until cold and gradually beat in coffee and gelatine mixture. When thick, but not set, fold in the whipped cream. Beat egg whites until stiff and peaky and fold in.

Pour into a 15-cm/6-inch cake tin or mould and leave to set. Dip tin or mould into hot water for a couple of seconds and invert on to a serving dish. Trim chocolate fingers to the height of the soufflé and set them all the way round. Decorate top with piped whirls of cream and nuts. *Serves 6-8*

QUICK TIP

To make sure the double dairy cream floats on top of the Gaelic Coffee, pour it over the back of a spoon.

QUICK TIP

Whipped double dairy cream will go further if 1 tablespoon sifted icing sugar and 1 stiffly whisked egg white are folded into it.

315 Vanilla slices

You will need . . .

1 × 210g/7½ oz packet frozen puff pastry
75g/6 oz icing sugar, sieved
water to mix
red colouring
2 tablespoons jam
150ml/¼ pint double dairy cream, lightly whipped
few drops vanilla essence

Preparation time
25 minutes

Cooking time
12 minutes

Oven setting
220°C; 425°F; Gas Mark 7

Roll pastry out thinly and cut into 2 strips, 7.5 × 30cm/3 × 12-inches. Place on a damp baking tray and bake in a hot oven for 12 minutes or until well risen and cooked. Allow to cool.

Mix icing sugar with water to a coating consistency, and colour pale pink. Turn one pastry slice upside down and spoon over icing.

Spread remaining slice with jam. Spread cream, flavoured with vanilla essence, over jam. Top with iced slice. Cut into 8 slices.   *Serves 4.*

316 Chicken Simla

You will need . . .

4 roasting chicken joints
25g/1 oz flour
salt and pepper
2 tablespoons oil
50g/2 oz butter
1 chicken stock cube
300ml/½ pint hot water
2 tablespoons mild mustard
2 teaspoons Worcestershire sauce
150ml/¼ pint double dairy cream
For the garnish:
25g/1 oz flaked, toasted almonds
4 baked peeled tomatoes
watercress

Preparation time
10 minutes

Cooking time
1¼ hours

Oven setting
160°C; 325°F; Gas Mark 3

Toss chicken joints in flour, seasoned with salt and pepper. Heat oil and butter in a pan and fry joints on both sides for about 15 minutes until golden and tender. Arrange in a shallow, ovenproof dish.

Dissolve stock cube in hot water. Stir in mustard and Worcestershire sauce. Pour over chicken joints.

Cover and bake for 1 hour. Stir in cream and serve sprinkled with almonds. Garnish with baked tomatoes and watercress.   *Serves 4.*

QUICK TIP

When using frozen puff pastry, it is not necessary to leave the pastry to 'rest' before baking as you do with fresh pastry. This does not apply to ready-made pastry which is refrigerated but not frozen.

QUICK TIP

For a quick chicken vol-au-vent filling: Heat up a can of condensed mushroom soup with some diced, cooked chicken. Stir in 150ml/¼ pint dairy cream and spoon mixture into heated vol-au-vent cases.

317 Pork chops with cider

You will need . . .

4 pork loin chops
25g/1 oz butter
1 large onion, chopped
1 large cooking apple, peeled, cored and chopped

Preparation time
10 minutes

300ml/½ pint cider
salt and pepper
150ml/¼ pint double dairy cream

Cooking time
55 minutes

For the garnish:
parsley sprigs

Oven setting
180°C; 350°F; Gas Mark 4

Fry chops in butter on both sides for 5 minutes. Remove and place in a casserole.

Fry onion and apple together for 5 minutes and add to chops. Pour over cider and season with salt and pepper. Cover and bake in a moderate oven for 45 minutes or until the chops are tender.

Spoon over the cream and garnish with parsley sprigs.

QUICK TIP

Pork blends well with cider. Try making a stew with pork belly and cider, with a little dairy cream stirred in just before serving.

318 Chocolate cream gâteau

You will need . . .

4 eggs
100g/4 oz castor sugar
75g/3 oz self-raising flour
25g/1 oz cocoa
3 tablespoons oil

Preparation time
30 minutes

For the filling and topping:
300ml/½ pint double dairy cream
150ml/¼ pint single dairy cream
100g/4 oz castor sugar
½ teaspoon vanilla essence

Cooking time
45 minutes

For the decoration:
cherries (or other fruit)
pineapple pieces

Oven setting
180°C; 350°F; Gas Mark 4

Whisk eggs and sugar until thick and creamy and whisk leaves a trail when lifted out of the mixture. Fold in sieved flour and cocoa. Carefully fold in oil. Turn into a greased and lined 20-cm/8-inch cake tin. Bake in a moderate oven for about 45 minutes or until cake springs back when lightly touched with the tip of the finger. Turn out and cool on a rack.

Split cake into three. Lightly whip double and single cream until just thick. Beat in sugar and vanilla essence.

Spread some of the cream over bottom two rounds of cake and re-stack together. Spread cream over top, put remaining cream into a piping bag with a large star pipe. Pipe all over the sides. Decorate with cherries and pineapple pieces.

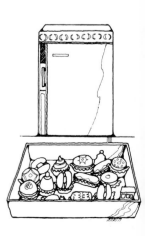

QUICK TIP

Dairy cream cakes should be stored in a box or cake tin and placed in the bottom of a refrigerator or cold larder.

319 Pork in mushroom sauce

You will need . . .

4 pieces pork fillet
25g/1 oz flour
salt and pepper
50g/2 oz butter
100g/4 oz button mushrooms, thinly sliced
1 × 411g/14 oz can carrots
150ml/¼ pint double dairy cream
1 tablespoon chopped chives

Preparation time
10 minutes

Cooking time
15 minutes

Beat out pork fillet until thin and coat in flour, seasoned with salt and pepper. Fry in butter for about 5 minutes on each side or until cooked. Place on serving dish and keep warm.

Add mushrooms to butter in pan and fry for 3-4 minutes or until cooked. Stir in any remaining flour and cook for a minute. Drain carrots and dice.

Remove from heat and stir in cream and a third of the carrots. Reheat very gently until piping hot. *Do not allow to boil.* Season to taste and pour over pork. Garnish with piles of remaining heated carrots, sprinkled with chives.   *Serves 4.*

QUICK TIP

For a quick snack, cook button mushrooms in butter add double dairy cream and heap on to toast.

Banana and 320 walnut cream

You will need . . .

4 large ripe bananas
1 tablespoon lemon juice
75g/3 oz sugar
50g/2 oz walnut halves
150ml/¼ pint single dairy cream
150ml/¼ pint double dairy cream
For the decoration:
1 large banana
1 tablespoon lemon juice
4 walnut halves

Preparation time
15 minutes

Mash 4 bananas with a fork and blend in lemon juice and sugar. Chop walnuts, reserving 4 for decoration, and add to bananas.

Lightly whip single and double dairy cream and fold into banana mixture.

Turn into glass dishes. Cut other banana into thin slices, sprinkle with lemon juice and arrange in circles on top of the banana mixture. Place a halved walnut in the centre. *Serves 4.*

QUICK TIP

For banana splits, split peeled bananas down the middle. Fill with ice cream, pipe whipped double dairy cream on top to seal in the ice cream.

321 Veal in tomato cream

You will need . . .
4 veal chops
1 tablespoon flour
salt and pepper
4 tablespoons corn oil
1 medium onion, peeled and chopped
1 × 65g/2¼ oz can tomato purée
1 level teaspoon sugar
1 chicken stock cube
150ml/¼ pint single dairy cream
For the garnish:
parsley sprigs

Preparation time
15 minutes

Cooking time
20 minutes

Turn the chops in flour seasoned with salt and pepper. Fry on both sides in the oil for a few minutes until brown. Remove chops from pan, reduce heat and add onion.

Cook gently until pale golden, sprinkle in remaining flour, stir, add tomato purée, sugar and stock cube made up with 175ml/6 fl oz boiling water. Return chops to pan, cover and simmer for 20 minutes or until chops are tender.

Place chops on hot serving dish, stir cream into sauce, reheat without boiling, pour round chops. Garnish with parsley. Serve with creamy mashed potato or buttered rice. *Serves 4.*

322 Gooseberry fool

You will need . . .
750g/1½ lb gooseberries
2 tablespoons water
100g/4 oz sugar
300ml/½ pint double dairy cream, lightly whipped

Preparation time
15 minutes

Cooking time
15 minutes

Top and tail gooseberries and wash. Place in a pan with water and put over a gentle heat, stirring frequently, until gooseberries are soft. Sieve or put into a blender, reserving a few for decoration, and stir in sugar. Allow to cool.

Fold in lightly whipped cream. Turn into serving dish.

Chill until ready to serve. Decorate with the remaining gooseberries. *Serves 4.*

QUICK TIP

Make a rich creamy gravy by adding 150ml/¼ pint real dairy cream to the meat juices in the baking tin then stir over a gentle heat for a few minutes.

QUICK TIP

A quicker way to top and tail gooseberries instead of using your fingers is to use a sharp pair of scissors.

323 Salmon mousse

You will need . . .

aspic jelly crystals
water
½ cucumber, thinly sliced
1 × 212g/7½ oz can salmon
150ml/¼ pint mayonnaise

Preparation time
40 minutes

150ml/¼ pint double dairy cream
2 egg whites
salt and pepper
For the garnish:
watercress
tomatoes

Make up 300ml/½ pint aspic jelly according to the instructions on the packet. Pour a little into the bottom of a 20-cm/8-inch ring mould. Allow to set. When set, arrange cucumber slices on top. Pour over a little more aspic jelly and leave to set.

Flake salmon and add to mayonnaise. Stir in cold aspic jelly. Lightly whip cream and fold into mixture when it is thick, but not set. Whisk egg whites stiffly and fold in. Season to taste. Turn mixture into prepared ring mould.

Leave until set. Quickly dip into a bowl of hot water and turn out on to serving plate. Garnish with watercress and tomato segments.   *Serves 4-6.*

QUICK TIP

When turning out a mould, always invert it on to a wet plate so that it can be easily moved if it is not in the centre.

324 Mocha éclairs

You will need . . .

150ml/¼ pint water
50g/2 oz butter
65g/2½ oz plain flour
pinch salt
2 eggs

Preparation time
20 minutes

For the filling and icing:
150ml/¼ pint double dairy cream
25-50g/1-2 oz castor sugar
few drops vanilla essence

Cooking time
25-35 minutes

50g/2 oz plain chocolate
2 tablespoons water

Oven setting
200°C; 400°F; Gas Mark 6

1 teaspoon instant coffee powder
150g/5 oz icing sugar, sieved

Put water and butter into a saucepan and bring slowly to the boil. Remove from heat and beat in flour, sieved with salt, to form a ball which leaves the sides of the pan clean. If necessary, return to a gentle heat. Allow mixture to cool to blood heat, then beat in eggs one at a time.

Put pastry into a piping bag with 1-cm/½-inch plain nozzle and pipe 14 7.5-cm/3-inch lengths on greased baking trays. Bake in a moderately hot oven for 25-35 minutes or until crisp and golden. Remove carefully from trays and cool on rack.

Lightly whip cream and add sugar and vanilla essence. Make a slit down the side of each éclair and fill with cream. Melt chocolate in a basin over a pan of hot water. Remove from heat and beat in water, then coffee powder and gradually beat in icing sugar. Spread on top of éclairs with a palette knife and allow to set.   *Makes 14.*

QUICK TIP

For a dessert, fill small choux pastry buns with spoonfuls of double dairy cream or ice cream, make a chocolate sauce and pour over buns.

325 Oeufs en cocottes

You will need . . .

100g/4 oz good liver sausage
6 eggs
150ml/¼ pint double dairy cream
salt and pepper
For the garnish:
paprika pepper

Preparation time
5 minutes

Cooking time
25 minutes

Oven setting
180°C; 350°F; Gas Mark 4

Lightly butter 6 ramekin dishes. Cut liver sausage into 6 slices and place in bottom of dishes. Stand in a roasting tin of hot water, cover completely with foil and place in a moderate oven for 10 minutes (*see Quick Tip below*).

Remove from oven and break an egg into each dish, top with a good tablespoon of cream and season with salt and pepper.

Bake, uncovered, for about 15 minutes or until egg whites are set and yolks are still soft. Garnish with paprika.   *Serves 6.*

QUICK TIP

If the individual dishes are heated before the eggs are added the whites will set quickly and will not become 'rubbery'.

326 Pineapple ginger cream

You will need . . .

1 × 423g/15 oz can pineapple cubes
150ml/¼ pint double dairy cream
2 pieces stem ginger, finely chopped
16 ginger biscuits
For the decoration:
slices of stem ginger

Preparation time
15 minutes
plus 12 hours chilling time

Drain pineapple cubes, reserving juice, and cut each cube in half.

Lightly whip cream and add pineapple and chopped ginger. Dip biscuits in pineapple juice and place round sides of 4 glass serving dishes. Spoon in pineapple and cream mixture.

Chill for 12 hours. Serve decorated with a slice of stem ginger in the centre of each serving dish.   *Serves 4.*

QUICK TIP

Mix chopped nuts of your choice with whipped double dairy cream to make a quick and delicious filling for sponge cakes.

327 Piquant herring salad

328 Orange boodle

You will need . . .

4 pickled herrings
1 small onion
1 eating apple
2 teaspoons lemon juice
150ml/¼ pint soured dairy cream or
double dairy cream and 1 teaspoon
lemon juice
salt and pepper
For the garnish:
1 small beetroot, peeled

Preparation time
15 minutes

Drain the herrings. Cut each herring in half lengthways and then cut each half into 4 strips.

Slice onion into fine rings. Cover with boiling water and drain after 1 minute. Core and slice apple and sprinkle slices with lemon juice. Reserve a few apple slices for garnish.

Blend herring, reserving a few pieces for garnish, onion rings, apple slices and cream. Season to taste with salt and pepper. Arrange on a serving dish and garnish with herring pieces and apple and beetroot slices. *Serves 4.*

You will need . . .

2 large oranges
25g/1 oz castor sugar
300ml/½ pint soured dairy cream or
double dairy cream and 2 teaspoons
lemon juice
12 sponge finger biscuits

Preparation time
10 minutes

Grate the rind of 1 orange into a bowl. Cut 4 thin slices of un-grated orange for decoration, then cut each orange in half and squeeze the juice. Stir orange rind and juice and sugar into soured cream.

Crumble 1 sponge finger into the bottom of each of 4 glasses and arrange 2 sponge fingers on the inside.

Pour in cream mixture and chill well. Decorate with halved slices of orange. *Serves 4.*

QUICK TIP

To pickle herrings, bone, clean and soak in brine for 2 hours. Pack into a wide-necked jar, pour over spiced vinegar and cover. Leave for at least 5-6 days.

QUICK TIP

Just before serving, lift the lids of mince pies and fruit tarts and put in a teaspoon of dairy cream. Cold apple turnovers can be split and filled with whipped double dairy cream.

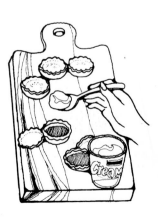

329 Toffee-topped peaches

You will need . . .
1 × 411g/14½ oz can peach halves
300ml/½ pint double dairy cream
175g/6 oz demerara sugar

Preparation time
10 minutes

Cooking time
5 minutes

Drain peaches and lay in the bottom of an ovenproof dish reserving one for decoration.

Lightly whip cream and spread over peaches. Chill.

Just before serving, sprinkle over sugar and grill until sugar melts. Cut remaining peach half in slices, place slices on top of sugar in a star pattern and serve immediately.   *Serves 6.*

QUICK TIP

Make a delicious topping for desserts by adding crushed meringue shells to whipped double dairy cream.

330 Boeuf stroganoff

You will need . . .
450g/1 lb fillet or good rump steak
3 medium-sized onions
50g/2 oz butter
1 green pepper
225g/8 oz button mushrooms
salt and pepper
150ml/¼ pint soured dairy cream or double dairy cream and 1 teaspoon lemon juice
For the garnish:
chopped parsley

Preparation time
10 minutes

Cooking time
15 minutes

Cut steak into strips 5cm/2-inches long, 5mm/¼-inch thick. Chop onions finely and fry in half the butter in a large deep frying pan until pale golden. Cut pepper into strips, discarding core and seeds. Thinly slice mushrooms. Add mushrooms and pepper to pan and cook for 5 minutes. Remove onions, mushrooms and pepper from pan.

Melt remaining butter and heat, then fry meat for about 4 minutes, turning so it becomes evenly cooked.

Return onions, mushrooms and peppers to pan season well, stir in soured cream and blend well. Heat until piping hot but *do not allow to boil.* Garnish with chopped parsley. *Serves 4.*

QUICK TIP

A tougher cut such as braising steak can be used if it is first cut into strips and marinated in lemon juice overnight to tenderise it.

331 Vichyssoise

You will need . . .

3 leeks
1 medium-sized onion
450g/1 lb potatoes
40g/1½ oz butter
900ml/1½ pints water

Preparation time
25 minutes

2 chicken stock cubes
salt and pepper
pinch grated nutmeg
300ml/½ pint single dairy cream

Cooking time
40 minutes

For the garnish:
chopped chives

Wash and chop leeks, chop onion and peel and slice potatoes. Melt butter, add leeks and onion, cover and cook for 10 minutes. Add water, stock cubes, potatoes, seasoning and nutmeg.

Bring to boil, lower heat and simmer gently for 30 minutes. Sieve soup or put into a blender. Stir in cream, reserving about 3 tablespoons.

Chill soup well. Just before serving, pour over remaining cream in a circle. Sprinkle with chopped chives.   *Serves 4-6.*

332 Raspberry ice cream

You will need . . .

450g/1 lb fresh or frozen raspberries
sieved icing sugar
2 eggs, separated
150ml/¼ pint double dairy cream, lightly whipped

Preparation time
20 minutes plus freezing

Sieve raspberries or put into a blender. Sweeten to taste with icing sugar.

Beat egg yolks and 25g/1 oz icing sugar until thick and creamy. Whisk egg whites until stiff and peaky and whisk in 25g/1 oz sieved icing sugar a little at a time. Gradually whisk in egg yolk mixture. Fold in raspberry purée and cream.

Turn into a freezing tray and freeze until firm. Serve in glasses with biscuits.   *Serves 4.*

QUICK TIP

Enrich a canned or packet soup, by adding a little dairy cream just before serving. It gives a touch of luxury and looks good too.

QUICK TIP

Great care should be taken when using an electric beater for whipping cream as it is very easy to over-whip and the cream will then turn buttery. Unless whipping a large quantity, it is safer to use a hand whisk.

333 Chicken in lemon sauce

You will need . . .

4 chicken breasts
salt and pepper
75g/3 oz butter
1 tablespoon sherry (optional)
1 teaspoon grated lemon rind
1 tablespoon lemon juice
150ml/¼ pint single dairy cream
75g/3 oz Lancashire cheese, crumbled
For the garnish:
pimento strips
parsley sprigs

Preparation time
20 minutes

Cooking time
15 minutes

Bone out chicken breasts (*see Quick Tip below*), and season with salt and pepper. Fry in 50g/2 oz of the butter for about 8 minutes until golden. Place in ovenproof serving dish and keep warm.

Add sherry and lemon rind and juice and cook for a minute, stirring. Slowly add the cream, stirring. Heat but *do not allow to boil*. Pour over chicken.

Dot chicken breasts with remaining butter, sprinkle with cheese and grill until golden. Garnish each chicken breast with a pimento cross and parsley sprigs. *Serves 4.*

334 Chocolate crunch pie

You will need . . .

For the biscuit crust:
100g/4 oz digestive biscuits
50g/2 oz butter
50g/2 oz soft brown sugar
For the filling and topping:
1 × 600ml/1 pint packet chocolate instant whip
450ml/¾ pint milk
150ml/¼ pint single dairy cream
150ml/¼ pint double dairy cream

Preparation time
10 minutes

Cooking time
5 minutes

Crush biscuits between two sheets of greaseproof paper with a rolling pin. Melt butter and stir in sugar and crushed biscuit. Press into a deep 20-cm/8-inch pie plate and chill.

Make up instant whip with milk and lightly whipped single cream following instructions on the packet. Turn into prepared biscuit crust flan and smooth over top.

Chill. Pipe lightly whipped double cream on top of the filling. *Serves 4.*

QUICK TIP

To bone out chicken breast, first cut off two wing joints. Using a small sharp knife, cut between the bone and the flesh of the breast. Scrape meat off the bone from remaining wing joint.

QUICK TIP

A spoonful of single dairy cream poured on top of milk puddings before you bake them will give them a delicious creamy skin.

335 Lamb chops with spinach

You will need . . .

1.5kg/3 lb spinach
salt and pepper
¼ teaspoon grated nutmeg
150ml/¼ pint double dairy cream
8 lamb chops

Preparation time
5 minutes

4 tomatoes, halved
50g/2 oz butter

Cooking time
0 minutes

Wash spinach in several changes of water. Discard any discoloured leaves and tough stalks. Put into a large pan without water and sprinkle in 1 teaspoon salt. Heat gently, pushing leaves down very well in the pan. When liquid is running from spinach, cover and bring to the boil. Simmer gently for about 10 minutes or until tender.

Sieve spinach or put into a blender. Season with salt and pepper and stir in nutmeg and cream. Reheat very gently, stirring. Turn on to serving dish. Meanwhile, cook chops.

Dot lamb chops and tomatoes with butter and season with salt and pepper. Grill chops for 10 minutes or until tender, turning once and grill tomatoes until soft. Arrange chops on the bed of spinach with the tomatoes.

Serves 4.

336 Creamy topped scallops

You will need . . .

8 scallops
1 small onion
300ml/½ pint white wine
25g/1 oz butter
25g/1 oz flour

Preparation time
15 minutes

150ml/¼ pint milk
salt and pepper
150ml/¼ pint double dairy cream
50g/2 oz Lancashire cheese, crumbled

Cooking time
15 minutes

Wash scallops thoroughly. Put scallops, onion and wine into a saucepan. Simmer until scallops become opaque, about 8 minutes. Remove scallops and onion with a draining spoon and chop. Reduce wine to 150ml/¼ pint.

Melt butter in a pan, stir in flour and cook for a minute. Remove from heat and gradually stir in milk and wine. Return to heat and bring to boil, stirring all the time until mixture bubbles and thickens. Stir in scallops and onion and season to taste. Turn into 4 small dishes.

Lightly whip cream and stir in cheese. Spread on top of scallop mixture. Put under a hot grill until golden and bubbling.

Serves 4.

QUICK TIP

Tie thick spinach stalks in bundles with string. Cook in boiling salted water for about 25 minutes or until tender. Serve with plenty of melted butter.

QUICK TIP

For a quick party dish, whip cream cheese with double dairy cream. Put into a piping bag and pipe swirls on the top of halved hard-boiled eggs.

Index

American measures are given by volume and weight; standard cups and spoons are used. The following lists give the capacity of the US standard measures and some commonly used ingredients in imperial measures with American equivalents.

US STANDARD MEASURING SPOONS AND CUPS

1 tablespoon = 3 teaspoons = ½ fluid ounce = 14.2 millilitres
2 tablespoons = 1 fluid ounce
4 tablespoons = ¼ cup
5 tablespoons = ⅓ cup
8 tablespoons = ½ cup
10 tablespoons = ⅔ cup (⅝ exactly)
12 tablespoons = ¾ cup
16 tablespoons = 1 cup = 8 fluid ounces = ½ US pint
32 tablespoons = 2 cups = 16 fluid ounces = 1 US pint

IMPERIAL	AMERICAN
1 teaspoon	1 teaspoon
1 tablespoon	1 tablespoon
1½ tablespoons	2 tablespoons
2 tablespoons	3 tablespoons
3 tablespoons	scant ¼ cup
4 tablespoons	5 tablespoons (⅓ cup)
5 tablespoons	6 tablespoons
5½ tablespoons	7 tablespoons
6 tablespoons (scant ¼ pint)	½ cup
¼ pint	⅔ cup
scant ½ pint	1 cup
½ pint (10 fluid ounces)	1¼ cups
¾ pint (15 fluid ounces)	scant 2 cups
generous ¾ pint (16 fluid ounces)	2 cups (1 pint)
1 pint (20 fluid ounces)	2½ cups
flour – plain or self-raising:	*flour – all purpose*
½ ounce	2 tablespoons
1 ounce	¼ cup
4 ounces	1 cup
cornflour:	*cornstarch:*
1 ounce	¼ cup
generous 2 ounces	½ cup
4½ ounces	1 cup
sugar – castor or granulated	*sugar – granulated*
1 ounce	2 tablespoons
4 ounces	½ cup
7½ ounces	1 cup
sifted icing sugar:	*sifted confectioners' sugar:*
1 ounce	¼ cup
4½ ounces	1 cup
sugar – soft brown:	*brown sugar – light and dark:*
1 ounce	2 tablespoons (firmly packed)
4 ounces	½ cup (firmly packed)
8 ounces	1 cup (firmly packed)
butter, margarine, cooking fat, lard, dripping:	*butter, margarine, shortening, lard, drippings:*
1 ounce	2 tablespoons
8 ounces	1 cup
grated cheese – Cheddar type, Parmesan:	*grated cheese – Cheddar type, Parmesan:*
1 ounce	¼ cup
4 ounces	1 cup

BRITISH	AMERICAN
EQUIPMENT AND TERMS	
Baked/unbaked pastry case	Baked/unbaked pie shell
Baking tin	Baking pan
Base	Bottom
Cocktail stick	Toothpick
Dough or mixture	Batter
Frying pan	Skillet
Greaseproof paper	Wax paper
Grill/Grilled	Broil/Broiled
Gut fish	Clean fish
Kitchen paper	Paper towels
Knock back dough	Punch down dough
Mixer/Liquidiser	Mixer/Blender
Muslin	Cheesecloth
Patty cases	Patty shells
Pipe, using a plain star tube in a piping bag	Pipe, using a fluted nozzle in a pastry bag
Pudding basin	Ovenproof bowl
Remove outer husk and silk	Husk corn
Stoned	Pitted
Top and tail gooseberries	Clean gooseberries
Whip/Whisk (eggs and cream)	Beat/Whip
Uppermost	Upward
INGREDIENTS	
Aubergine	Eggplant
Bacon rashers	Bacon slices
Bicarbonate of soda	Baking soda
Biscuits	Crackers
Biscuit mixture	Cookie dough
Black cherries	Bing cherries
Black olives	Ripe olives
Black pudding	Blood sausage
Boiling chicken	Stewing chicken
Broad beans	Fava or Lima beans
1 cabbage, lettuce	1 head cabbage, lettuce
Cake mixture	Cake batter
Capsicum	Red or green sweet pepper
Cauliflower sprigs/florets	Cauliflowerets
Celery stick	Celery stalk
Chicken/Beef stock cube	Bouillon cube
Chicory	Belgian endive
Chilli	Chili pepper
Cocoa powder	Unsweetened cocoa
Cooking apple	Baking apple
Cooking chocolate	Unsweetened cooking chocolate
Cornflour	Cornstarch
Courgettes	Zucchini
Crystallised fruits	Candied fruits
Crystallised ginger	Candied ginger
Curly endive	Chicory